French Fried

One man's move to France with too many animals and an identity thief

Chris Dolley

Book View Café

FRENCH FRIED

Copyright © 2010 by Chris Dolley

Published by Book View Café

Book View Café Publishing Cooperative
P.O. Box 1624
Cedar Crest, NM 87008-1624

www.bookviewcafe.com

ISBN 13: 978-1-61138-398-0

Cover art: The Swineherd by Paul Gauguin
Cover design by Chris Dolley and Pati Nagle

First printing, July 2014
First digital edition, July 2010

Contents

Books by Chris Dolley

Resonance

Shift

An Unsafe Pair of Hands

What Ho, Automata

Medium Dead

Magical Crimes

International Kittens of Mystery

How Possession Can Help You Lose Weight

The Move: Hell and Horseboxes

"Investment? What investment? You cancelled it in April."

It was now September. September 22nd 1995.

I froze. I'd only called Simon, our financial adviser, to ask a few routine questions. I hadn't expected this. He was talking about our investment bond – the bulk of the proceeds from our house sale, our life savings, the money that was going to fund our new life in France.

"No, I didn't," I replied, hoping that there'd been some kind of mistake.

I could hear a riffling of papers, pages being turned, a note of panic in Simon's voice.

"I ... er ... have the correspondence here. Yes ... April. You wanted the bond encashed and the money sent to your business account in Spain."

What business account in Spain? I didn't have any accounts in Spain. I didn't have any business accounts anywhere!

I couldn't believe it. This could *not* be happening. Not to me. Things like this happened to other people!

And then I thought about the chaos that marked our first seven months in France – the move from Hell, the neurotic car, the police roadblock, the fire, the ten foot long caterpillar, the day I accidentally signed for the local football team ... and realised ... I'm just the kind of person this does happen to.

It was a shock. That sudden shift in my internal picture. I was no longer the person who sat safe and warm watching events unfold upon the television screen. I was the person in front of the camera. The man standing in the doorway as the getaway car mounts the pavement. The man eating his sandwiches in the park when the sniper opens the attic window.

They're all me.

~

Seven months earlier...

It was the day before our move and doubt was sitting on my shoulder, whispering. Was moving to France a terrible mistake or just the result of unpardonable crimes in a previous life? Even the weather was against us. The latest forecast for Wednesday – the day of our ferry crossing – had the English Channel buried in isobars and lashed by gale force winds. What if the ferry was cancelled? The Channel Tunnel wasn't finished yet. We couldn't take a plane – unless British Airways considered two horses, one dog and three cats acceptable cabin luggage. And we'd have nowhere to stay either – the new owner would be moving into our farm tomorrow morning.

All we'd have were a single change of clothes and a collection of dog and cat bowls – our clothes and furniture having gone ahead of us. They were being loaded into the removal van today.

But moving to France had to be the right thing to do. We'd spent three years with more money going out than was coming in. Which gave rise to *The Plan* – sell our farm, free up the capital and move to rural France where we could buy a similar property for a third of the price and use the balance to live off of. Simple and brilliant. All problems solved and a better climate thrown in for good measure.

Even though it was a nightmare to organise.

We lived in Devon; the new house was in the foothills of the Pyrenees – an 800-mile drive and a six-hour ferry trip distant. We had a jeep and a thirty year-old tractor. Neither excelled at long journeys.

And then there were the animals. Two horses, three cats and an enormous puppy.

Even if we could fit the dog and cats into the Suzuki – which I doubted – could we all survive an eighteen-hour journey cooped up together and remain sane?

This thought fuelled a recurring nightmare – me behind the wheel of our jeep with my face being licked by the dog on my lap and a cat fight filling the rear-view mirror.

We had to find another way. Which led us to the horsebox. It was one of those rare moments in our move when everything suddenly came together. We knew we had to hire someone to transport the horses, could they take the dog and cats as well? They could? Excellent! Could they take us? Even better. And to prove there really was a deity they even reduced the price on the proviso that we doubled as grooms for the journey.

I didn't dream that night. A force field of contentment kept the demons at bay. I didn't have to drive; I didn't have to knock on hotel doors in the middle of the night covered in scratches and dog slobber. Bliss.

A word that could not be used to describe the weather. The storm hadn't arrived yet but the wind was picking up; playful gusts were turning meaner, clouds were looking busier. The one silver lining was that it hadn't started to rain yet. At least our possessions were being loaded into the back of the removal lorry in the dry.

We had thought our last day on the farm was going to be a quiet one – a day to say goodbye to our home of six years and walk the fields for the last time. But no, it's a day of constant interruption and visits – electric and water meters being read, removal men walking in and out, boxes being packed, furniture loaded, inventories filled in, telephone calls, vet inspections. The latter taking two whole hours as every whorl and marking of the horses had to be scrutinised and faithfully recorded on their travel documents.

Did I mention the cleaning?

We'd thought our house reasonably clean – for a farm – for a farm in a muddy winter overrun by cats and a dog with big feet. But, as soon as the rooms were cleared, bright islands appeared on our carpets where the furniture had been. Were the carpets really that colour when we bought them?

Which brings us to the dog, Gypsy, a four-month-old lurcher. For anyone unfamiliar with the breed, the lurcher is the one that fills the gap between the Irish Wolf Hound and the crocodile. She was immense. And her favourite game was dragging her favourite toy across the floor. Sad to say, her favourite toy was my leg. What can I say? I have highly desirable ankles.

Which can be a problem when you're rushing to clean a carpet ... and your dog decides it's playtime. Note to all husbands: being dragged across the floor by one's ankle is not a credible defence when your wife is under stress and expecting help with the carpet cleaning.

"Stop playing with the dog!" shouted Shelagh, trying to make herself heard over the sound of the vacuum cleaner. "You're supposed to be helping."

People who've never had their ankle between a canine's canines cannot appreciate the pain. It's a cross between having your funny bone tapped with a hammer and a tooth drilled. And it activates a nerve that has fast track access to the part of your brain (the Little-Girlie Thalamus) responsible for making your eyes water and raising your voice two whole octaves.

As I said, no defence.

Shelagh gave up Hoovering and resorted to bartering, trying to swap me for a biscuit – not the first time in our marriage she'd attempted this. Gypsy held out for two custard creams before unclamping her jaws. Which gave us time to lay a trail of biscuits leading to the lounge door, open the door, throw a biscuit through and ... goodbye hellhound. One point to the limping *Homo sapiens* team.

It took a lot of scrubbing but eventually the bright islands re-ceded and out came a passable example of the carpet we'd bought.

On to the next room.

This time we tricked Gypsy without having to resort to biscuits or displaying a provocative ankle. We opened the door, let her bound through, then slipped past her in the excitement, slamming the door shut behind us. An hour later, we'd shampooed, scrubbed and vacuumed the living room carpet back to acceptability.

Then I returned to the lounge to fetch Gypsy.

And stepped into an alternative universe – something that rarely happens in Devon. I was in the lounge. But the carpet wasn't the same freshly cleaned carpet I'd left an hour earlier. It was a different carpet. A much darker, dirtier carpet.

Teeth smiled at me from the centre of the room. Teeth pleased with themselves. Teeth wrapped around a small circle of carpet. My first thought was one of complete panic. Our dog had somehow managed to rip out a one-foot diameter circle of carpet which she was now devouring. My God, was anything safe!

But I couldn't see a hole in the carpet – one foot or any other diameter. I looked. I peered. Where the hell had it come from? And then came the realisation. Our log basket! We'd left it in the inglenook fireplace. Our wicker log basket with the one-foot diameter circle of carpet at the bottom to catch all the mess and bark and dirt and wet leaves and all manner of hideous things that clung to damp logs in the winter. Except now they were all clinging to our freshly cleaned carpet. Spread and ground-in from wall to wall. Gypsy was nothing if not thorough.

I screamed.

Twelve hours to go and I screamed.

Wednesday morning dawned to find us lying under a horse rug on our lounge floor. All our furniture was gone, a gale was rattling our windows and Gypsy's feet were digging into my back.

"Do you think Rhiannon will load OK?" asked Shelagh.

I'd almost forgotten about that.

Rhiannon, our six-year-old Arab mare, had a thing about horseboxes. Once inside the trailer, she was fine. Coming out, she was fine. But going in? She either dug in her heels and refused to move, or moved far too much, becoming the kind of wild horse that other wild horses couldn't drag anywhere near a trailer ramp.

We'd hired a horsebox a month earlier to wean her of her phobia and I'd almost been killed. Well, not exactly killed, but if you've ever been behind a horse when it suddenly leaps backwards and kicks out at you with both hooves flying either side of your ears, you get a distinct foretaste of the afterlife.

And we were going to have to try again in about an hour.

"At least we only have to do it once."

But how long would that take? Even with practice it still took anywhere from thirty minutes to an hour to load her. We'd warned the transporters but what if they didn't believe us? If the box was late or she took more than an hour to load we'd miss the ferry.

I went through the itinerary again. The horsebox was due to arrive at eight. So we had to be packed and ready by then, with the animals fed, watered, relieved and begged for their best behaviour – always a tricky negotiation.

And I had to ring Jan, my sister, to make sure she was still available to sign the house purchase agreement for us and collect the keys to the new house. And remind her that Pickfords said they'd have our belongings at the house about nine o'clock, Thursday, not to forget to unload the electric fencing first and we'd ring again when we had a firm time for our arrival.

It was fortuitous that my sister and brother-in-law had moved to France a month earlier. It meant they could sign the *Acte* for us and we could transport their animals – one of the horses and one of the cats were theirs.

Eight o'clock arrived with every animal present, correct and stuffed full of bribes.

But no horsebox.

By 8:25 we were in danger of wearing out the extraordinarily clean carpet between the window and the telephone. Is that a lorry? No it isn't. Was that the phone? No it's not.

Then we heard it.

A rumble down the drive and there was the lorry. At last!

Our joy lasted barely a minute. According to Sue, our driver, there might be a problem at Portsmouth. She was waiting for a phone call from the ferry company. In the meantime we'd have to wait.

We used the time to inspect the horsebox, which was much bigger than we'd expected – more like a removal lorry with extra doors. There was room for six horses inside. It even had a groom's compartment with a bed and a stove. And there was a pony already on board – a part-load on its way to Gaillac, two hours north-east of our destination. Which left plenty of room for us, the cats and our own luggage. This was another big advantage of travelling in the horsebox – plenty of space for any forgotten extras which had evaded the removal men – or had had to be rescued, like the Hoover for last-minute cleaning detail.

Then came the bad news. Portsmouth would not take the horses. It would be too rough to carry them. And all the Channel ports to the west were closing. Our only hope was Dover but that raised another problem – the new guidelines for the transportation of animals.

It would take six hours to drive to Dover and that would put the new journey time over the limit. Which meant putting the horses into lairage at Dover. Which meant a statutory eight hours rest before they could be loaded again.

Which meant we'd have to load Rhiannon twice.

"Oh," said Sue. "And maybe we'll have to stop at Bordeaux as well."

Three times.

The loading started well despite the wind whipping across the yard and rattling the metal cladding of our big barn. Jan's horse, Rain, went up the ramp at the second attempt and Sue closed the stall behind her. One horse loaded. One to go.

Shelagh clipped the lead rein onto Rhiannon's head-collar and walked her towards the ramp. Three strides later Rhiannon put on her stubborn face and dug in her front hooves. Shelagh turned her around and tried again. Same result.

We tried picking up Rhiannon's front feet and slowly walking her forwards. That worked for a while. We managed to place one hoof on the ramp but that was it. Rhiannon started sniffing the ramp suspiciously and snorting.

Then we tried apples. Letting her take a bite then drawing it away from her. We managed to get both front feet on the ramp – perhaps a push from behind might be enough to....

It wasn't. But it was enough to send her squirming backwards, off the ramp.

We tried another apple.

We tried Polo mints.

We tried a trail of Polo mints leading up the ramp into the box.

Nothing worked.

We walked her around for a while to steady her.

And then we tried speed. Perhaps if we approached at a fast walk, the momentum would carry Rhiannon up the ramp.

It carried her off the ramp even quicker, as she leaped sideways at the last minute.

Time ticked on. Rhiannon ditched her Miss Stubborn persona and alternated between Miss Spooked – the ears pricked, wild-eyed, 'what are you *doing* to me?' neurotic horse – and Miss Evil – the ears back, Second Horse of the Apocalypse who, having unseated War on the grounds that he was too much of a wimp, was eager for some serious retribution.

We tried to calm her down, keeping a close eye on the end that kicked as we walked her around the lawn a few times and plied her with mints and soothing words. Then back to the horsebox. We'd use lunge ropes this time.

We pushed. We pulled. We cajoled. At one stage we had all her feet on the ramp, but just when it looked like she was going in, she bounced back out. Apparently, the tread boards on the ramp were now the problem. Instead of picking her feet up and stepping over them – they were only half an inch proud of the ramp – she decided she had to drag her feet through them. And if they didn't move then neither was she.

More foot-lifting, horse-shuffling minutes ticked by. I'd given up worrying about ferries. I'd even started to look upon Gypsy in a more favourable light – puppies weren't that bad, really. Not compared to some animals.

And then it happened. Rhiannon trotted up the ramp, a couple of bounces, a head toss or two ... and disappeared inside. No back-breaking foot-lifting required. No pushing, shoving or mints with a hole. It was almost as though she'd said to herself – I'll give them forty minutes of hell first, just to show them who's boss.

The cats were next. They had their own deluxe travelling crates with separate areas for litter tray, food, water and sleeping. The only complication was the fact that we had to arrange them in a particular order. Our cat, Guinny, a five-year-old silver tabby, didn't like Minnie, the kitten. Put them within sight of each other and spit would fly all the way from Devon to Dover. Luckily we had plenty of room in the box with its feed passages and spare stalls.

Then came the blankets and rugs for the horses, the hay and the hay nets, the dog and cat food, their bowls and water containers.

And then our luggage – in by far the smallest bag – a change of clothing, some food, our money and all the papers we were going to need for the journey.

Finally, we collected Gypsy from the back garden, checked to make sure she hadn't uprooted any trees or buried a postman, and then we all climbed into the groom's compartment behind the cab.

We were ready. All packed and a whole new future ahead of us.

Then we remembered the Hoover.

And the log basket.

We said goodbye to the high banks and narrow lanes of Devon, to the white farmhouses and the slate and thatch. We passed through the chalk of Dorset and Wiltshire, across the lower reaches of Salisbury plain to the accompaniment of scudding clouds racing to beat us to Dover.

We were making good time – the one advantage of having a force eight gale at your back. We checked on the horses every half hour or so – walking back through the horsebox and checking their water and hay nets. And we talked to the two major feline powers, stressing the importance of maintaining the no-spit zone.

Most amazing of all was the behaviour of Gypsy. She was quiet, perfectly behaved, curled up on the floor or the bed, with lots of yawning and scratching but no barking, whining, biting or throwing herself through the hatchway at the driver's throat. Which was unexpected. And worrying – was she being too good? Was this a ploy to make her next descent into the diabolical even more terrifying?

As we approached Dover, Sue's mobile phone gave us the news that the ferry companies were predicting a window in the storm sometime during the night and could we be on stand-by. They didn't know when the window would come, not exactly, or how long it would last but it was probably going to be the only chance of getting the horses across before the week-end.

Which presented us with another problem – where would we stay the night? Sue had suggested a hotel and was ready to book us in. But Shelagh was worried they wouldn't take a dog and three cats. And would they have a night porter who could wake us up as soon as this window arrived? We couldn't afford to miss it.

Then Sue remembered the darts room at the lairage. It was a rest room provided for the grooms. A sofa, a few chairs, a dart-board – not exactly plush or indeed private – but it was warm and on-site. And if there weren't too many grooms staying over we might even be able to sleep.

The lairage was an impressive sight. A few miles outside Dover and room for about fifty horses. It was the equine equivalent of an airport hotel – close to the ferries and *the* stop over point for all the horses bound for the continent; the show jumpers, race horses, eventers ... and our two.

As we led the horses up the wide central aisle of one of the stable blocks we couldn't help but notice the change in Rhiannon. She'd seen the stallions. Which improved her mood considerably. The stubborn, I'm-not-moving-for-anything face, had been replaced by her look-at-me face. Complete with high tail carriage and flashy Arab trot, she pranced down the aisle, parading herself unashamedly before the gathered on-lookers.

It was now mid-afternoon and a lull in our journey. We'd seen to the horses, we'd checked on the cats. We'd walked Gypsy around the lairage a few times. Things were calm. Pulse rates were back below the critical level.

And the darts room wasn't too bad. It was small, just big enough for a sofa and a few chairs but it could have been a hell of a lot worse. There was even a bathroom next door with a shower.

By the evening there was still no sign of the promised window. If anything the wind was stronger. Sue suggested a meal at the nearby pub and we looked at Gypsy and then at each other and tried to forget the last time we'd taken one of our dogs to a pub for a quiet drink.

Zaphod had been our first dog – a whippet lurcher – and, generally, well-behaved. Except when provoked – usually by cats or loud noises or someone doing something unexpected, or wearing strange clothes, or looking at him funny, or walking within ten yards of a bone or anything else he claimed title to. In other words he was a normal, well-adjusted dog.

We took him into a pub in Hungerford – The Bear, I think it was – for a quiet drink and a ploughman's lunch. Something relaxing to complete a pleasant morning's drive.

I went to the bar, a fiver in my hand, pleasant thoughts wafting brain-side. And then all hell broke out behind me – overturned tables, spilt drinks, screams. And in the middle of it all – Zaphod – dragging Shelagh through a table. I turned, folded the fiver back into my pocket and slowly walked towards the exit. I have never seen these people before in my life – especially the little brown and white one with the terrier in its mouth.

Shelagh tells a different story. One with Zaphod as the innocent party. The two of them were merely walking towards an empty table when a small dog – the aforementioned terrier – who had been sitting under an adjoining table, loomed into view. I have never been too convinced about this part of the story – the thought of a very small terrier looming does not strike me as that credible. Zaphod, in a state of justifiable shock at the proximity of another dog and in fear of an imminent attack upon his mistress, naturally had no other recourse other than to leap under the table and attempt to eat the terrier. In the process he happened to drag Shelagh after him. She kept hold of the lead, which immediately went under the table; Shelagh's arm followed but her shoulders couldn't. So goodbye table and goodbye drinks. And hello adjoining table and adjoining table's former collection of drinks.

The staggering conclusion to this affair was that the owners of the terrier admitted full responsibility. I still can't understand why. The only explanation that stands even a modicum of scrutiny is that the terrier had a criminal record and the owners knew they couldn't afford another brush with the law.

Which, understandably, was why we weren't too keen on taking Gypsy to a pub. After all, what were the chances of finding another dog with form? Better to find an empty box, well away from any horses, and see if we could leave Gypsy there for a few hours.

Which is what we did. The grooms at the lairage said they didn't mind us using one of their boxes at the far end. And they didn't object to working to the accompaniment of a howling puppy.

We left before they could change their minds.

~

It was our last evening in an English pub. We had £10 left –
everything else was in Francs. We sat sipping our real ale and
draught cider surrounded by beams and antique brasses.

And watched the 9:25 weather forecast on TV. You could hardly
make out the English Channel beneath all the isobars. And it was
getting worse. The forecasts for Thursday and Friday were
horrendous.

Walking back to the lairage, we expected to hear a cacophony of
barks and screams but it was strangely quiet. Could everyone be
dead?

No. Gypsy was asleep in her stall, curled up in the straw and
looking angelic. And there was news about the window – it was
expected around eight o'clock the next morning. But only for a few
hours. And the vet inspection had been booked for 5:30.

What vet inspection?

We shouldn't have asked.

Apparently all our paperwork for the move was now obsolete. The
embarkation port had changed, as had the date. And our vet
inspection – which had to take place no more than twenty-four
hours before embarkation – had now lapsed. Which meant we had
to start again. Luckily the lairage was used to this and had all the
forms and their own vet on stand-by.

We performed our final check on the animals, cleaned out the
litter trays, changed the water, replenished the food, mucked out
Gypsy's box and said goodnight to the horses.

And then went to bed.

Or, at least, into the darts room. Which was starting to feel
distinctly cold. It was February, after all. Shelagh suggested we
fetch a horse blanket. We had a couple of spares.

The spares turned out to be two canvas New Zealand Rugs. The
canvas was cold to the touch and stiff rather than thick. I looked at
the padded, and very warm looking, quilted stable rugs both horses
were wearing. Couldn't we...

No we could not. As anyone who lives with a horse lover knows,
there are times – usually on a day with a 'Y' in it – when horse
welfare has to come first.

Back in the darts room – and clutching my cold, stiff, horsey
smelling blanket – I eyed the sofa. It wasn't big enough for two
people to sleep on. The only other place to sleep was the floor. So ...
we tossed for the sofa. I won. We argued. *You're the one who
wouldn't stay in a hotel. They wouldn't have taken Gypsy. We could
have left her here. Not for a whole night!* And so on.

Solely in the interests of equality I insisted that I had to take the
sofa. Anything less would have been an attack on the entire feminist
movement, which I just could not countenance.

Five minutes later Gypsy climbed on top of me and tried to get between me and the back of the sofa. Whether this was an attack by or against the feminist movement I was unsure. But she did manage to gain a foothold on the sofa.

For a while.

I threw her off, she jumped back, I threw her off again. But I was tiring and as I started to drift towards sleep, she wedged herself against the back of the sofa and started to use those long legs of hers to push and lever until I woke up at two o'clock and found myself on the floor. I hadn't even got a rug. Shelagh had one and Gypsy the other. A combined victory for the united feminists.

By 4:30 we were up and ready for whatever the day could chuck at us. I was cold, my back hurt, but I was alive. And by that time my threshold of expectation from life had sunk so low that being alive was about as good as it could get.

I took Gypsy out on the lead while Shelagh washed. It was still pitch black and a raw wind was searching out all the gaps in my clothing. Gypsy looked up at me and I agreed. We went back inside.

By the time the vet arrived we'd seen to the cats again and cleaned up the darts room. Sue was making coffee in the horsebox and all the yard lights were on and the lairage was awake.

The vet raced through the paperwork, documents stamped and signed in a few minutes. Then Sue called to us that we were booked on the 8:30 ferry, the window had arrived.

All we had to do now was load the horses.

And the less said about that the better. Suffice to say, Rain and the pony loaded like lambs and Rhiannon did not.

Customs was not what I'd expected. There were no spot checks on the animals, no one tried to match the horses against their Identikit pictures or check to see if we'd smuggled a few extra ones into the back. The documents were collected, stamped, handed back and we were waved through.

Once on the ferry, our next problem was what to do with Gypsy. Animals weren't allowed to wander the car decks and I assumed the same went for the passenger decks. Shelagh volunteered to stay in the cab with Gypsy as she didn't want any breakfast but she'd have to go to the bathroom first, so could I hang on with Gypsy for a few minutes? No problem. I wanted to check on the bow doors anyway.

The car deck soon emptied. Just a few stragglers remained from a coach party behind us. I watched in the mirror as they walked to the side luggage storage area ... and started taking their trousers off.

"Oh. My. God," I mouthed slowly as I sank lower in the cab, trying to drag Gypsy with me. Alone on a deserted car deck with a coachload of trouserless Scotsmen!

Why did I say Scotsmen? I thought for a while. Something subliminal? I craned a look back through the side mirror. Perhaps it was the large number of blue and white flags and 'SCOTLAND' written in giant letters all over the coach windows.

There were more of them now. All with blue jerseys and flapping kilts. Others were still changing.

That's when the penny slotted between the rugby posts – Scotland were playing France at the *Parc des Princes* on Saturday. This must have been the advance guard of fanatical supporters – sent on ahead to secure the bars.

And then we were alone again, not a kilt or a trouser in sight. Just acre after acre of cars and lorries.

It was desolate. There's something eerie about being alone in a giant car park – so many signs of life having once existed but nothing to prove it still did. Like the aftermath of some terrible disaster, only luggage and children's toys left to be seen. Like the *Marie Celeste*.

I shuddered. Best think of something else. Something to take my mind off the emptiness.

I looked in the mirror again. It was looking brighter outside. Turning into one of those bright showery days with strong winds and intermittent downpours. I could even see the famous white cliffs of Dover, with a decent pair of binoculars I'd have probably been able to see Vera Lynn[1] herself.

Why could I see the white cliffs of Dover?

I was in the car deck, looking through a side mirror. I shouldn't be able to see out. Should I?

Oh. My. God. The bow doors must be open!

My mind was awash with ferry disasters – all neatly numbered and arranged in order of death toll. And was that really the white cliffs of Dover or an incoming iceberg?

I pulled down the window and craned my head outside. A coach full of discarded trousers was all that stood between me and the English Channel.

What should I do?

And where was Shelagh? It must have been ten minutes since she set off for the bathroom.

Unless she couldn't get back. The entire crew and upper decks held hostage by terrorists.

It was going to be *Die Hard* all over again. One lone man against a boat load of crazed gunmen, his only advantage the fact that they didn't know he was on board. That and his trusty puppy. And, of course, his training, his years in the computer industry. Give him a week and he'd have a ferry booking system designed, coded and up and running.

He was also having trouble with reality.

It was being left alone – it gave the brain too much space to play in. Imagine anyone failing to close the bow doors after all the publicity there'd been since the last disaster.

I could.

But the terrorists had begun to fade – so some progress was being made.

There was only one thing for it. I had to get out and check the bow doors. Just to be on the safe side.

I walked past the coach and looked out.

They weren't there.

Largely because I was looking aft. Thank God, I said to myself as I looked down at the bobbing sea, a considerable distance below me. It would take a tidal wave to swamp this deck.

I scanned the horizon for tidal waves. It could happen. An unexpected earthquake in the vicinity of Dover, the cliffs fall into the sea, a huge body of water displaced and ... tsunami. We'd have bodies everywhere, cars, lorries and floating trousers...

I walked back to the horsebox. Too much space again.

Better to think things through logically. I was alone in the car deck when I should have been having breakfast. Therefore it was Shelagh's fault. This was a much more promising line of thought – righteous indignation. I had been deprived of food – I looked at my watch – for twenty minutes. Was not the European Court of Human Rights created for just such an occurrence?

Gypsy gave me a lick. She understood all about food deprivation.

By the time Shelagh returned, I was on my closing speech to the Convention at The Hague. They would show her no mercy.

Especially when they found out she'd stopped to have breakfast.

"You didn't want breakfast!"

"I know ... but Sue persuaded me. And it was free."

I met Sue just as she was coming out of the dining room. I was torn between the merits of extra sausages or fried bread when she stopped me.

"Oh, Chris, Shelagh forgot to pay me for her breakfast. It was £1.95."

I searched out the last of our English money and handed it over. There would be no breakfast for me that day. I turned and walked as far away from the smell of fried food as I could. Ending up at the bow, the bit with the doors.

I think they were closed.

France: More Hell, a Different Horsebox

We'd made it! Our spirits lifted with French soil all around us and the worst of the journey well and truly behind. From now on, it was all sight-seeing and watch that thermometer climb.

We filled up with diesel on the outskirts of Calais and then circled around for a while, trying to find the slip road onto the motorway. And there it was – the A26 – Paris and the South.

It was my job to navigate, so I started checking the road-signs. I'd just managed to translate one saying, 'Beware of Strong Cross Winds,' when a fierce gust of wind ripped the roof off our horsebox.

We stopped in bewilderment.

And looked back at a huge fragment of roof caught in the central reservation crash barrier, one hundred yards back down the motorway. A fragment the size of an average lounge carpet.

Which would have to be dragged off the motorway pretty damn quick before it caused an accident. Luckily, the motorway was practically deserted, but how long would that last?

And what about the horses?

Shelagh climbed back into the rear of the lorry, expecting the worst – Rhiannon, stretched horizontal by the wind, hanging onto the roof by her front hooves – but amazingly everything was calm. A few fragments of roof and skylight lay strewn around their feet, the inner skin of the roof was flapping and there was a lot more sky than there should have been, but otherwise it had been a remarkable escape.

Once outside, we could see that a complete section of the roof had ripped away and others were split or damaged. We could also see other fragments of roof further down the motorway.

So we ran after them, pulled two off the near lane and slid them down an embankment out of the way of the wind. Then we moved towards the main section which was kicking and bucking in the fierce cross wind but thankfully remained anchored in the central reservation barrier. We looked at it for a while, seeking inspiration. We had to pull it free but be very, very careful. The traffic was light but the danger of causing an accident was immense.

A gap in the traffic came, we ran out and grabbed an end of roof each and pulled as hard as we could. But just as we eased it free, a gust of wind wrenched it out of our hands and up it went. Flying like a kite, up and over the central reservation, the motorway and off towards Belgium.

Five minutes later we're all sitting in the horsebox in a state of shock. The roof has blown off our horsebox. We're sitting outside Calais in a convertible! The wind is blowing a gale. Rain is imminent. We are countless miles away from our destination.

We limped into the next service area, frightened to try any speed above a fast walk in case the rest of the roof tore away. We also closed the remaining skylight – the horses didn't need any extra ventilation at that point, and it was probably an open skylight that had allowed the wind to rip the roof off.

We found a screen of tall trees and parked to the leeward.

And then phoned England.

They didn't believe us.

It's often like that, I've found – purveyors of bad news met with incredulity. Of course your roof hasn't blown off, take another look.

So Sue's boss asked to speak to me. Though I couldn't think why – if he wanted someone practical to converse with, there were at last three better candidates in the back.

"Are you sure you can't put the roof back on?" he pressed.

"Not unless we go to Belgium first and pick up the remains."

There was a pause. Perhaps he was going to take me up on my suggestion.

"You'll have to come back to England then."

What! We'd sweated blood waiting for a window to appear in this storm, and as soon as we hit France, we have to turn round and start again? The weather forecast was horrendous. It might be Saturday, Sunday or Easter before we'd get another chance. And more lairage and forms to fill in and...

The dog and cats!

I could have kissed Gypsy. Thank God for quarantine. We couldn't go back or the dog and cats would be impounded for six months!

We were saved!

"Ah." He wasn't pleased, I could tell. "I'll ring back." The phone went dead and Gypsy got a hug.

But what could we do? We couldn't continue very far as we were. One more gust of wind and we'd be a hazard to every other road user.

The answer came very quickly. Sue's boss had arranged for another lorry to come out and meet us but it might take twelve hours or so to arrive. Which meant the horses would have broken their allotted number of hours in transit and...

"Lairage?"

"Yes, Lairage."

I should have known. But we were not sleeping in the darts room again.

We set off for Boulogne where the lairage was located. Leaving the motorway at the next exit and tracing a circuitous route through every back road and utilising every hillock and piece of shelter we could find. The sky above us was streaked with scudding clouds and getting darker by the minute.

The mobile phone rang again. We were booked into a hotel at Wimereux, just outside Boulogne.

"And they'll take the dog and cats?"

"Yes, no problem."

The fools! But thank God for the relaxed attitude of the French towards pets. We'd noticed this before on previous visits; how supermarket and restaurant doors would be opened for a lone dog to walk in and browse around. Unlike England, where lone dogs were seen as the biggest single threat to the nation's health; children's hands snatched away from them by anxious mothers, shopkeepers shooing them off doorsteps. But France was the country of *égalité* for all – even the hairy ones – and we were booked into a hotel!

But first, we had to find the lairage. We were told to look for a riding school on the cliff road between Boulogne and Wimereux. Which was just what we wanted – a nice exposed cliff road to drive up and down. We crawled even slower. We couldn't have been more exposed if we tried. Fate had opened a hurricane training academy out in the Atlantic and every gust of wind was lined up and racing down the channel straight towards us. The sea below was more white than blue and it was a long, open road to drive down.

And where was the riding school? We couldn't see any fields of horses or anything that looked like a stable block. We doubled back and tried again. Was that it? I noticed a small homemade road sign flapping in the wind up ahead.

We stopped. And squinted. Was that a picture of a horse? And did that say turn left up the track and then right after one hundred metres? I was convinced it did, but by then I'd perfected a method of translating every other word and filling in the rest with what I wanted to hear. It might not be accurate but it kept me happy.

And I must have been right for two turns and a hundred or so metres later we found the stables. Which couldn't have looked more unlike the lairage at Dover. While one had been purpose built and new, this one was old and still recognisable as a farm. And it had character. The old courtyard was surrounded by a brick-built farmhouse and outbuildings and beyond that were small paddocks and further buildings – all long and low with the familiar undulating roofline of age and bowed timbers.

And they were expecting us. We didn't have to explain our plight or throw ourselves upon their mercy in halting French. They knew our story and seemed unconcerned that we couldn't tell them exactly when we'd return – the fact that it might be in the middle of the night was dismissed with a Gallic shrug. *C'est la vie.* It certainly was.

The horses were a bit wary of the buildings at first. The entrance to the stables was low, narrow and dark. And only the Great Horse God knew what dwelt beyond.

But we pushed them through, the pony leading the way. And once inside they were out of the wind. And into another age. It looked superb – to lovers of the authentic – low beamed ceilings, uneven dirt floor, lots of wood and leather.

And the horses seemed to like it. Once their eyes had acclimatised to the darkness and they could verify the total dearth of demons dwelling in any of the shadows.

The rugs were next to be unloaded; along with hay nets and lunge ropes and reins and buckets. Horses never travel light.

And then off to the hotel. Following another set of directions – right at the first roundabout, then a left...

Wimereux was a traditional seaside resort – row upon row of small hotels stretched like a ribbon along the coast, all brightly painted in their summer colours, the bars and the pizzerias and the cafes now mostly deserted. And there, close to the promenade was our hotel. It really did exist.

We thanked Sue for all she'd done. The trip hadn't been easy for any of us and hers wasn't over yet – she had to drive the horsebox back to England. We made use of her mobile for one last call – Shelagh wanted to make sure we hadn't been abandoned and someone had noted down both the name of the hotel and its telephone number. Plus, was there an update on the relief horsebox? There wasn't, but not to worry, someone would contact us soon.

By this time we were a sorry sight. Stood on the pavement with assorted bags and animals, we looked like refugees from some Eastern European conflagration. Yugoslavia, most likely. Shelagh's often mistaken for a Slav. At least, when she worked in Germany, she was; her long dark hair and lack of German, being taken as proof positive of her Slavic roots. Whereas I had the dubious pleasure of once being mistaken for a Transylvanian. I was walking through the streets of York one night, in the days when I had a great profusion of long ginger hair and a big bushy beard, when I overheard a passer-by whisper to her friend, "and you said you never believed in werewolves?"

So, there we were, standing outside the hotel, a balding werewolf fallen upon hard times and forced to migrate west with Elvira, his gypsy violinist wife. Not to mention the Transylvanian menagerie of were-pets.

But we did have a hotel room. And a bath.

The room was even paid for. All part of the relocation service. The hotel rooms, the lairage fees – everything except for breakfast on the ferry – which I had still not forgiven Shelagh for. How these companies made any money during the winter I did not know. It must be a nightmare of cancelled ferries, diverted horseboxes, last-minute bookings and alterations. And Sue had been contracted to collect other horses after us for a return journey so presumably someone else would have to be diverted to fulfil that obligation.

All that was left before we said goodbye was one final walk round the interior of the horsebox to check we hadn't left anything behind – the odd horse or two that might have snuck back on. But no horses – just a Hoover.

We were still arguing over who should have left the vacuum cleaner at the stables when the receptionist arrived to book us in. We filled in the usual cards and presented our passports and did our best to make ourselves understood.

Which was difficult as neither of us was fluent. Shelagh had a grade 'E' French 'O' level, one step up from the failure grade of 'F', and I had a grade 'X'. Not many people have a grade 'X'. I'd secured mine by holidaying in the Lake District when I should have been attending the orals. Whether there are different grades for other holiday resorts, I don't know. But I'd like to think there were.

Anyway, most of our efforts were directed to making sure they understood we might not stay the night. But the receptionist didn't seem to mind how long we stayed for. After all, the room had been paid for. She was more interested in whether we'd be staying for dinner. I said yes, Shelagh said no.

Another argument ensued. Shelagh was adamant we couldn't leave Gypsy in the room by herself and equally that we couldn't inflict her on other guests. Why not? You know why not. No, I don't. Yes, you do.

The receptionist left to fetch the keys while Shelagh made up my mind. I looked longingly past the lobby into the dining room. People were eating. Normal people unshackled by animals. I was about to start drooling when our keys arrived. We were on the second floor.

I picked up the Hoover and had just started to mount the stairs when a woman burst out of the dining room and ran up to me.

"*Non! Non! Pas nécessaire*," cried the landlady, and various other words to the effect that the room was already clean.

I looked at the Hoover in my hand and the dog and the cats and the assorted luggage strewn over the lobby and tried to think of a short and concise way to explain everything. I couldn't. My schoolboy French had deserted me – probably for the Lake District.

"Er," I babbled. "Er ... *nous sommes Anglais.*"

"Ah," she replied and I could see a look of comprehension glide across her face. No other words were necessary. We were English. Everything was explained.

We smiled and started for the stairs again but Gypsy took one look at the polished wood and froze. Danger. No carpets. And look at those banisters, gaps where a puppy could be sucked through and eaten.

She looked up at Shelagh, appealing for help. Make the stairs go away.

We remonstrated with her. How could a dog with legs as long as hers have trouble walking up stairs? She whimpered a reply. Something about banisters. She'd never seen them before.

There was nothing else for it. I left the Hoover and the bags at the foot of the stairs and picked her up. She was a big dog. Already the size of an adult greyhound and growing heavier by the minute. Two flights of stairs later, we staggered into our room.

Thank God! I set Gypsy down on the floor and had a look around. The room was perfect – large and airy with an en suite bathroom. And a real bed – one where humans could lie in comfort. There was even a TV.

But we still had the bulk of our menagerie waiting downstairs in the lobby. So we turned to fetch them. And remembered Gypsy. Could she be trusted to stay by herself in a nice clean room? Shelagh and I exchanged knowing looks. No, she could not.

I grabbed the lead again and off we went. At the top of the stairs, Gypsy dug in her heels and slid to a halt. She was not going *down* the stairs either.

"Perhaps if we're firmer with her," Shelagh suggested, but with little conviction. I tried pulling on the lead, words of encouragement, scarcely veiled threats.

"Why don't we try picking up her feet and offering her polo mints?" I said, dripping sarcasm, before bending down once more to wrestle Gypsy into my arms and stagger downstairs. Approaching the lobby, I realised how stupid this situation was becoming. Why was I carrying Gypsy down the stairs when once at the bottom I would have to turn round and carry her back up again?

A similar thought was obviously passing through the assembled diners, who couldn't help notice a man carrying a very large black dog back down the stairs. Wasn't that the same man who just carried the big doggy up the stairs, mummy? Yes dear, the man with the Hoover.

~

Once installed in the room, it wasn't much better. Minnie, the kitten, started yowling and Guinny took exception. Even though we'd separated them from line of sight, Guinny could hear Minnie and that was more than enough provocation. She started making spitting noises. Which was viewed by Gypsy as an invitation to play. And bark. And worry my leg.

And they'd been so well-behaved in the horsebox! It was as though they'd waited until they'd got us alone.

I tried to quieten Gypsy, while Shelagh took Guinny off into the bathroom. Perhaps if we separated the cats for a while it might help. And besides, the cats' crates could do with a thorough clean and the bathroom was the only place we could safely let a cat out.

Quietening Gypsy was never easy. The easiest way was to let her do whatever she wanted. Which usually meant allowing myself to be chewed or dragged across the floor. Neither game was among my favourites.

I tried interesting her in some of her toys – her Womble, her chews and various rubber animals. She preferred my leg.

"Why don't you take Gypsy for a walk," a disembodied voice called out from the bathroom.

I could think of many reasons. But my ankles outvoted me. It might be safer outside.

I walked nonchalantly past the dining room carrying my dog. Trying to blend in with the background as much as possible and present Gypsy as more fashion accessory than pet.

I don't think it worked. I could still feel a large number of eyes lift from their dinner plates and bore into the back of my neck.

Outside, the wind had found an occasional shower and was in the process of throwing it against the Wimereux coastline. I turned to walk Gypsy towards the promenade and was immediately peppered with hail stones. I turned and looked longingly at the hotel door. Could I go back in? Which was worse – to be battered and soaked for twenty minutes or walk back past the dining room carrying a dog?

It was a close call.

But not that close.

We moved out of the worst of the storm and tried a side street. At least, with the buildings shielding us from the wind we could walk in some degree of comfort. Above us, the wind had sculpted an arch of hail and rain which whipped off the roofs to seaward and smashed against the upper storey of the houses across the road. Gypsy looked up in amazement. And then refused to lift her eyes from the pavement for the rest of the walk. There were some things a puppy should never have to see.

At the next road junction we hit the wall of rain and ice and fought our way through it as best we could. Then we staggered another block or two before turning round. We'd had enough.

I checked my watch as we slipped in through the hotel door. Three o'clock. Surely the dining room had to empty soon. I looked in vain for signs of another staircase or at least another passage. But there were none. From the lobby you either went up the stairs or left into the dining room.

I felt so self-conscious. Perhaps if I tried speed? Slipped from behind the reception desk and shot up the stairs before anyone had a chance to look up? Swift and silent. It could work.

We burst out of the lobby, a blur of anorak and black fur. I flew over the first step, the second, where's the third, trip, shit, grrrr, bark, bite.

The rest of the afternoon was taken up with dog-walking and worrying, sometimes both at the same time. Gypsy decided thirty minutes was tops when it came to lying quiet in a hotel room. And after that, the prospect of carrying her downstairs and being blown around Wimereux for twenty minutes became almost appealing.

But not for me. "I'm not taking her downstairs again."

"Why not?"

"I'm just not, that's all."

I wasn't going to say any more. I could still hear the waitress's voice. As I lay framed in the banisters, a dog fastened to my right ankle, an open-mouthed dining room silently waiting to see what we'd do next. "Anglais," she'd said, just the one word, mentioned in passing to one of the guests, as she flitted between the tables, collecting plates. But it was enough. Conversation resumed, glasses clinked and eyes left the stair-well. What kind of reputation do we English have in Europe?

So, Shelagh escorted Gypsy about town, while I phoned my sister to give her the news. She didn't believe it either but knew me better than to ask if I'd fixed the horsebox roof.

But we did have a house. The *Acte* had been signed, the furniture unloaded and the electric fence erected. I told her not to expect us until Friday or Saturday and to leave the front door key somewhere obvious in the outhouse.

And then I settled down to watch TV. I found all the English channels and was just starting to enjoy myself when Gypsy returned.

Which is when the real worrying started. Neither of us could remember seeing Gypsy relieve herself since we returned from the pub in Dover the night before. All the opportunities we'd given her since she'd spurned.

How long could a puppy remain bottled up? I didn't want to think any further than that. But more dog-walking seemed to be the preferable proposition. Especially now the dining room was empty.

I don't remember how many times we walked around Wimereux. Sometimes there were three of us, sometimes just Shelagh and Gypsy. We saw storms, we saw sunny periods, we saw everything except what we wanted to see.

She just wouldn't relieve herself while on the lead. That had to be it. We'd never had to leash her on the farm before because our fields were well-fenced and we'd never taken her for walks anywhere else. But could we unleash her here?

And expect to see her again?

Which would be worse – to tramp the wet and wind-lashed streets of Wimereux searching for a lost puppy or tied to a constipated one? We voted for the former, narrowly. Consequently, we staggered for interminable hours through the various shades of a force ten gale, humans and puppy eyeing each other in embarrassed silence.

As we approached the hotel for the seventh or eighth time, I looked through the spray and heaving sea towards our old home. To the place where thirty-two hours ago, we'd embarked on a thousand mile journey south. We were now 250 miles due east. At this rate we'd be in Poland by the week-end.

We pushed on towards the promenade, hoping to find a beach where we could let Gypsy off but either there wasn't a beach or the tide was in. And the promenade was covered in spray and breaking waves.

We returned to the hotel, wondering if we should try a laxative. Or would that present fate with too tempting a target? Just how quick can you run downstairs carrying an incontinent puppy?

Back in the room the phone rang. I'd reached such a low ebb by that time that I half-expected to hear that a freak tornado had whisked the new horsebox away to Cuba, but no, it was on its way and expected to arrive at the lairage between 1:00 am and 2:00 am. The driver would phone us at the hotel as soon as he arrived.

If we lasted that long.

But an unexpected chain of events was gathering in the ether. Minnie started mewling for no apparent reason, which set Guinny off, which in turn signalled to Gypsy that it was probably time to chew something human. I objected and in the ensuing excitement Gypsy's intestinal abstinence came to a sudden and, some might add, spectacular end in the bathroom shower tray.

I have never seen anyone so pleased to clean up after a dog before.

By nine o'clock that evening, life was becoming almost pleasant. We were warm, comfortable, bathed and dry. The animals were curled up and if not actually asleep, quiet.

I didn't even mind my second day of cheese sandwiches. Shelagh had packed half a loaf of them. Along with everything else we couldn't eat or pack into boxes during our last few days at the farm. Which gave us an assortment of chocolate bars, apples and cheesy biscuits. All thrown into a bag at the last minute. And somewhat beyond their best.

But I didn't mind. The prospect of eating in the hotel had lost much of its allure after the events of the day.

Then we had another phone call. Could we wait for the horsebox at the lairage? This was starting to take one of those worrying turns – what had happened to the original plan? I liked that one. We stayed in the warm, watching TV until someone came to fetch us.

But now, doubt was being cast. The horsebox was on the ferry – which was good news – but the driver's mobile phone didn't work outside the UK. Which was bad news. There was no way of contacting the driver. There were also doubts about what he'd been told to do. He might ring the hotel but then again he might not. And he might know where the hotel was and then again...

But, at least he knew where the lairage was – everyone agreed on that part of the story.

The confusion stemmed from the fact that Wendy, the woman who was organising our move, didn't actually own any transport – she hired the work out. And because the sub-contractor, Sue's boss, didn't have a spare horsebox to send out, he'd sub-contracted the work to someone else again. I think.

The result of which was that no one was quite sure who had said what to whom, when or how.

I still liked the original plan.

We lay there, heads awash with permutations – none of them good. Could we find our way back to the lairage? Would we want to? It must be two miles away. Did we really want to hang about all night on the top of a storm-battered cliff on the off chance we met a passing lorry? What if it didn't come? What if it went straight to the hotel?

But if we didn't?

We were in a small hotel in a town full of small hotels. Would the lorry driver know how to find it? Had anyone told him where we were? And what about the hotel switchboard – would it be closed when they rang? Was there even a night porter to answer the door?

I went downstairs.

There was a night porter – from what I could understand – who came on duty at ten. Perhaps. The receptionist might have said anything, I was now filling in entire sentences with what I wanted to hear. As for there being a night switchboard, my question was met with a lot of pointing at a telephone hanging on the wall. Which may, or may not, have been good news.

I went back to our room.

Had she been trying to tell me that the phone on the wall was a night phone? Or was she just pointing to the nearest telephone?

We tossed and turned through ten and eleven o'clock. By midnight I was hanging around the top of the stairs straining my ears for any sound of ringing. By one o'clock we were wrecked. Not another minute could we wait – even if it meant marching up and down the cliffs for the next three hours, we had to do something.

So we took Gypsy for a walk.

Retracing our steps as best we could, we headed out of Wimereux and up the hill towards the stables, our heads and bodies bent against the wind and the gradient. Never again. A silent vow was made that night that wherever the horses ended up at the end of this coming day they were never moving again. We'd buy the house next door.

At 1:45 we saw the headlights of a truck turning off the road up ahead. A turning that might be the one leading to the stables. Panicked into thinking the horsebox might drive on to the hotel if we didn't get to them in time, we ran. Usain Bolt could not have kept up with us that night. And if he had, Gypsy would have bitten him.

It was an anti-climax of a meeting. To this day I am absolutely astonished that we managed to arrive at the lairage within minutes of each other. But there was no fanfare or exchange of pennants. They'd been expecting to find us there, and we were too out of breath to disabuse them. And perhaps it was best not to ask what they'd have done if they hadn't found us at the lairage. I preferred not to know.

And, anyway, there was a more pressing problem. That of negotiating the two huge wooden gates that blocked the entrance to the stables. Were they locked?

I grasped a handle and prayed. They weren't locked. The huge doors swung and stuttered open. And then all hell, which had never been adequately shackled since the last time, was let loose again. Suddenly, dogs were everywhere. Assorted dogs barking, growling, jumping, running. Gypsy joined in, dragging Shelagh along on the leash. And then on came the farmhouse lights, then the courtyard's. So much for not disturbing anyone.

The farm dogs were gathered in, eventually, and the horsebox manoeuvred into the courtyard – it was even bigger than Sue's, more of a juggernaut than a horsebox. And then all the equipment and extraneous luggage were tracked down and taken on-board until all that remained was to load the horses.

Rain and the pony were a bit skittish to start with but after a few false starts bounced inside. Then came Rhiannon, snorting and prancing, the wind whipping her tail and mane, the courtyard alive with lights and shadows.

We knew she was going to be bad.

No one else did. The usual warning of, 'watch out, she kicks,' was met with the seasoned indifference of people who had spent a lifetime handling horses.

Five minutes later, seasoned professionals were running and ducking for their lives. Rhiannon had broken free of Shelagh's grasp after a spectacular bout of bucking and kicking. Which was, of course, too much for the farm dogs who immediately ended their short truce and raced after Rhiannon to join in the fun.

Pandemonium.

I think I counted five dogs and eleven humans that night. All running around a small courtyard in the middle of a stormy night on the cliffs. There might have been more, they made enough noise.

All we needed now was...

And there it was, right on cue, a clap of thunder, celestial applause.

Rhiannon was caught, escaped and caught again. Grooms and drivers and various family members of the lairage shouted encouragement, ran, fell down and threw themselves against walls. It was like Pamplona on a bad night.

And all around, the wind continued to blow and the rain to fall, the sky flashed and thunder rumbled.

It was a night to remember.

And then it was over. Rhiannon loaded.

As we left the lairage, I couldn't help but wonder at the forbearance of the people there. We had descended upon them in the middle of the night, chased them and their dogs around a courtyard for half an hour and still they waved us goodbye.

I wondered if they were used to it.

I hoped not.

All we had to do now was find our hotel. "What hotel?" said one of the drivers. There was silence for a while as the significance of his words percolated through our defensive shields. We had not wanted to know that.

I explained about the cats and the rest of our luggage. I thought it better to leave out the bit about the Hoover. There's only so much you can explain during moments of stress.

Back through the deserted streets of Wimereux we drove, eventually pulling up in the side street around the corner from the hotel. Nearly there, only one more hurdle to clear.

I slipped the key into the hotel door, turned it and ... nothing. The lock turned, but the door wouldn't move. It had been bolted from the inside. Or barricaded by frightened diners.

"I don't believe this!" I shouted, and started ringing bells and knocking on the door. No one answered.

A curtain twitched in the dining room and a face looked out. I pointed to the door and waved my hotel key. The face disappeared.

Perhaps they *were* barricaded in there?

We waited by the front door, trying to look as nonchalant as possible in case the drivers of the horsebox took fright and decided to abandon us. Nothing would have surprised me that night.

Then a door opened, not the one we'd been expecting but a door to the basement below the dining room. A head looked out and called to us.

We didn't need asking twice. We ran down the steps and burst inside. The night porter looked perplexed but we explained in a mixture of French, English and sign language that we were residents and needed to get to our room. And we were desperate, nothing short of physical force was going to stop us getting there.

Off we ran, through the bar, up the stairs, a right into the dining room, a left at the next set of stairs and then up again. We were not hanging around. And then back down with the cats. The night porter was just locking up when we burst into the downstairs bar.

"*Non, non!*" we implored and burst into another frenzied bout of attempted explanation. We're leaving, we need to get out. We were just coming back for our things.

He took a long look at the cats in their crates. And then unlocked the door. Probably a cat-lover, I thought as we staggered outside and deposited Guinny and Gally, her long-suffering brother, on the pavement outside.

The night porter was just attempting to lock the door for the second time when he saw us running back down the steps.

"There's more," we cried.

"*Mas,*" I added.

"Isn't that Spanish?" enquired Shelagh.

"*Encore?*" suggested the night porter.

I nodded, squeezing past him and then running for the stairs. A left, a right, a few straight aheads, we took them all. And with every step I thanked God we had the presence of mind to leave Gypsy in the horsebox.

I grabbed hold of Minnie, and Shelagh picked up a couple of bags and back we went again. Around and down and right and left. But this time the night porter looked worried as we staggered past him. He'd been thinking, and I couldn't fault his logic, that either we were the most daring team of catnappers Wimereux had ever seen, or we were guests leaving in the middle of night without paying.

He waved a piece of paper at us. It might have been a bill. It might have been the nearest he'd found to a white flag.

Words like *payer* and *chambre* were thrown about. I could understand that. "*Oui, tout est payé,*" I cried. Which I hoped meant everything had been paid for. And we gave him the number of the room and showed him the hotel key with the number on.

"*Bon,*" he smiled and looked immensely relieved.

We deposited our load with the rest of our windswept possessions on the pavement then ran back inside where we stopped him locking up for the third time and, with a cry of, "*encore,*" ran straight past him and through the bar.

We were slowing down by this point. Stairs and corridors were becoming a blur. But we couldn't afford to leave anything behind and so we made one last tour of the room, a final check of the bathroom and the cupboards and the drawers, and then we were away – the hotel room locked, and the last of our possessions secured in our grasp.

The night porter was waiting for us by the door, probably wondering if he was ever going to be able to close it again. As he caught sight of the Hoover, I could see words struggling to form in his throat. But he thought better of it. And, all things considered, I think that was the right decision.

We gave him the key and left.

France swept by in a blur. I had been looking forward to watching our progress through the countryside. To see the steep-pitched slate roofs flatten and turn terra-cotta pink. The black and white *colombage* buildings of the north turn to brick and then to stone – sometimes white, sometimes grey or yellow, sometimes hollowed out of cliffs like on the banks of the Loire. And then back to colombage again – this time unpainted with the wood sun-bleached grey.

But I couldn't keep my eyes open.

Paris passed by as a traffic jam. I think I heard someone say, "that's Paris," but it wasn't worth waking up for.

We made excellent progress. There were two drivers working in shifts – one driving while the other slept in a bed above the cab. And there were masses of food; bacon and bread and milk and coffee. And they liked Gypsy, who had switched back into paragon-mode, quietly sitting or curling up on the floor of the groom's compartment.

Night became day and north became south. We reached the outskirts of Bordeaux in the early afternoon. And the wind and rain melted into memory.

We had a choice approaching Agen – continue on the motorway or take the direct road through Auch. I suggested the Auch route because I knew it, but was outvoted in favour of the motorway. Which is another way of saying that what happened next was not my fault.

We only had fifteen miles to go. Spirits were high, the motorway was clear and it looked as though we were going to reach our new home in the light.

But then the motorway ended, became a dual carriageway and then an elongated car park. Roadworks! The new A64 Toulouse to Bayonne extension. Expected to finish at the end of '96. It was now February '95.

We watched the sun set and the skies darken. Occasionally edging a little further down the road but never very far. It took a very long time to reach our turn off.

And then we were flying again, along the D roads towards Aurignac, our nearest town.

Which is when the second mistake was made. Which although not directly my fault, I could have prevented, if I hadn't panicked.

I'd had the last few miles of our route meticulously planned. Our house was difficult to find, lying off a single track road, close to the middle of nowhere. So I'd photocopied a large-scale map of the area and traced a route.

But now I was having second thoughts. The horsebox was far larger than I'd expected and the route I'd planned followed a narrow road with some very tight turns. So I voiced my concern to the driver who had a quick look at his own map, and decided on a different route.

Which took us off my map. Our house was, of course, strategically placed on the edge of two large-scale maps. We'd bought both but packed the other on the idea that we wouldn't be coming from that direction. I could smell a disaster looming.

I navigated from memory. A four-month old memory that had never actually traced this particular route but sought to hunt down land-marks and trust heavily to luck.

Fate did not miss its chance.

I knew we had to look for a road parallel to the D81a but not the D81a itself, as it twisted and squeezed through the village so much that a small car had difficulty getting through. So we needed to take the next right. Which we did. Thirty yards later we're wedged on a bend. So we reversed out and tried the next right and found ourselves in a maze of unlit single track roads with high banks and hedges. Occasional lights appeared and disappeared as odd houses drifted by in the blackness. But no road-signs, no house names, no numbers and no signs of life.

All eyes turned upon me. Even Gypsy's. One of drivers tried to lighten the mood, telling us that this was nothing compared to that other trip they'd taken two years back. That one started with roads like this but then the trees closed in and grass started to appear in the middle of the road and...

"What like this?"

All eyes focussed on the growing band of grass running along the middle of the road and the trees closing in from both sides. The road was in imminent danger of disappearing into a thicket.

And then we saw a light up ahead on the right. A car headlight from a driveway. We stopped and I ran over to ask directions. There were two people trying to push a van that looked stuck in a muddy farm courtyard.

I tried my best French to ask the way to a small hamlet and back onto my map. They looked confused. I thought of another way. I knew it had a church. How about "Où est l'église?"

They talked amongst themselves for a while before saying something about down on the right.

It was then I realised they were talking to each other in English.

"You're English?"

I was amazed.

In the middle of nowhere and totally lost we'd found probably the only other English speakers for miles around.

But there was little time for small talk. There was some poor person in Gaillac who'd been waiting two days for their pony.

I memorised the directions and rushed back to the horsebox. All we had to do was follow the road we were on for a quarter of a mile, turn right at the main road and after a few hundred yards we'd see the church.

Brilliant!

We set off with renewed optimism. Until we found the candidates for main road. We had them narrowed down to two – one of them turned out to be a farm track, the other was narrower.

And we were wedged again. High banks of soil and stone all around us and no room to make a proper turn.

I have travelled past that junction many times since and every time I pass by, I marvel at the fact that anyone could turn a lorry that size in such a tight space. But they did. One driver at the wheel and the other outside shouting instructions. The giant horsebox moving a few degrees at a time, as it rolled backwards and forwards into the main road.

From there, we found the church and were back on my pre-planned route. A few minutes later we were pulling up outside our new home. It was nine o'clock, Friday evening. Sixty hours of hell were over.

We stepped out of the lorry into a mild star-lit night. No wind, no rain, no hint of sound. We'd arrived.

And the electric fence was up and working. The keys to the house were where they were supposed to be. It was as though a line had been written under the previous sixty hours – all torment wrapped up and safely buried in the past, a new life about to unfold.

How wrong can a person be?

The First Day, House Hunting and Toilets

I stood at the bedroom window the next morning, and looked out on a view that almost made the last three days bearable. Almost but not quite.

This was what we had come to France to see. A deep blue sky emerging from the twilight and there, framed between two hillocks, the Pyrenees. Mountains, sharp-edged against the early morning sky and looking magnificent. With the Pic du Midi in the centre, dark grey and flecked with white as the first rays of morning found the lying snow.

Breathtaking.

And in the foreground, bunches of mistletoe stood out like floating green islands against the bare trees – acacia and oak, maple and walnut. A striking blue cedar and a yellow-flowered forsythia added colour to the left, green fields and swathes of trees swept up to the skyline on the right. And over everything, hung the cold sharp breath of a winter morning.

I could have stayed there all day. But I was hungry. And getting cold.

I dressed quickly and went in search of the kitchen, stepping through the obstacle course of packing cases and assorted boxes, with one thought in mind.

Food.

Where was it?

We had intended to stop off at a supermarket on the way down and stock up with fresh food and essentials. That is before roofs started flying through the air and our leisurely journey through France became a mercy dash through Hell.

I found the remains of a digestive biscuit, the last survivor of our rations from the trip. I had envisaged our first breakfast in our new home as being something to remember – full of hot croissants and steaming coffee, a chocolate brioche or two, maybe a wedge of Brie. Instead, I was staring into a bagful of leftovers.

I tossed the bag aside. At least there was coffee.

I rummaged amongst the assorted boxes, thankful that we had labelled every one with a brief description of its contents. And there it was – coffee, both instant and ground. Things were looking up.

The percolator posed a more difficult problem. I knew I'd packed it at the bottom of one of the boxes marked, *Kitchen Materials*. But I couldn't remember if it was with the electricals or pots and pans. Or assorted tea towels and cutlery for that matter. Our system of packing had evolved radically when it came to the kitchen. Our first thought had been to pack by cupboard so we'd know exactly what each box contained. But the crockery weighed too much and the pots and pans didn't stack very well. So we started improvising and spreading the weight and filling gaps until we had an amalgam of kitchen goods.

Several minutes of hard rummaging later I found the percolator, pulled it out, unwrapped it and...

Plugs.

That was the other item on our list of things to buy on the way down. A French round-pin plug to fit onto our extension lead. It had seemed a brilliant plan, buy the one plug on the way down, fit it to a multi-socket extension lead and then we could use all our English square-pin electrical equipment from Day One without changing plugs.

But we didn't have that one plug so ... I sat the percolator down. It would have to be instant.

But not from a kettle – also electric.

I was not easily defeated. I'd made coffee from water boiled in saucepans before. As I leant over the sink and turned on the tap, I prayed that something would come out. I could look philosophically upon the lack of electricity, but the thought of being water-less, was not one that a veteran of a three-day mercy dash through Hell's maw should have to face.

Water gushed from the tap. Yay! The patron saint of house-movers had awoken from her slumbers.

Before promptly rolling over and closing her eyes again. We had no gas.

As Shelagh stepped through the kitchen door, she found her husband slumped over the kitchen table with a pan of water clutched in one hand and a jar of instant coffee in the other.

But we had the view. And the house.

And what a lot of house. An eight-bedroomed *maison de maître* set in seven acres of grounds, fields and woods. It even had a swimming pool ... of sorts. The sort without any water, and sides that cracked and bulged inwards at alarming angles. And there were two outbuildings, forming an L on the edge of the house. And an orchard with apples, pears, plum, cherries, figs and apricot. And it was all ours. For well under a third of the price of our three-bedroomed farm and forty acres of Devonshire mud.

But it had eight bedrooms. And there were only two of us, six if we counted all the animals.

"Eight bedrooms!" had been Shelagh's first reaction when I phoned her with the news of my purchase.

"It's a bargain," I replied. "Well within our budget."

"But eight bedrooms?"

Seeing as the bargain ploy wasn't going down too well, I tried a different tack.

"They'll come in handy."

"For what?"

"Well, a spare room for a start. And a study for the Great Novel." I could have added another room for the Great Novel's rejection slips but thought better of it. "And four of the bedrooms are in the attic, so why not look at it as a four-bedroomed house with a carpeted loft?" A touch of genius.

But house hunting is often like that. You start off with a tight list of what you want – the two-bedroom bungalow, the tiny stone cottage – refine it over a period of months, then let your husband loose in France while you look after the farm, and back he comes with the keys to an eight-bedroom mansion.

But it could have been worse. During my two-week house hunting expedition I discovered that the rural French builder had a flair for the unusual. And a hankering for an earlier time, when building was more art than science, before architects and building inspectors started framing laws to curb the creative householder. Like the man in Brittany who ran the mains water pipe through a working chimney.

"I think you might have to move the water pipe," the estate agent told me as we entered the lounge.

"Why?" I asked.

"It comes in through the chimney."

"Like Father Christmas?" I asked, wondering if perhaps it was there to provide water for the reindeer.

Unfortunately that didn't appear to be its purpose. The pipe entered the house through the back wall of the fireplace, hovered a few feet over the grate and then bent along the wall in search of a kitchen.

'Why?' is a question often asked in house hunting. Sometimes it actually precipitates an answer. This was not one of those times.

But we did have theories. A rudimentary hot water system? A useful pipe for hanging a cooking pot from? Favourite was the 'it was the closest point to the road – therefore less copper pipe to buy.'

Then there was the toilet in the Dordogne.

Now, I've seen toilets before – I'm a man of the world – and under the stairs has always been a popular space-saving location but ... at the foot of the stairs? With no privacy? Placed such that to climb the stairs one had to squeeze past the bowl?

I stood at the foot of the stairs, staring in amazement, and wondered – could the stairs have been a later addition? Maybe there was nowhere else to put the staircase when the upper floor was converted?

No. I looked; the plumbing appeared more recent than the staircase.

For days afterwards, I theorised and explored various possibilities for the unique placement of the toilet. It was like one of those mental agility tests starring dwarves in lifts. Could the owner have had one leg shorter than the other and needed the first step for balance?

Or perhaps it was a conversation piece. It certainly worked.

Then there was the log-burner in Gascony.

There's nothing intrinsically unsound about placing a fire in the centre of a room. It can look very stylish and certainly can be a good way to heat a large room. But ... something wasn't quite right about this installation. It was the flue. Which was where the problem started. Not, however, where it finished.

Most people installing a flue would take the pipe straight up from the fire and out through the roof. Very few would take the flue fifteen feet across the room at knee height until it reached a wall.

Even fewer would then knock a hole in that wall, take the flue through into the next room, angle it behind the sofa and around two more walls before sinking it into the chimney breast on the opposite wall. As I tracked the eight-inch diameter flue's progress through the house, I wondered if I was at the birth of an entirely new form of heating system – no radiators required, just one continuous flue.

I walked back and forth between the two rooms. One looked like a giant hand had pulled the log burner into the middle of the room, extruding the flue. The other looked like a neighbour had tapped into the chimneybreast while the owner had been out shopping.

Then came *The House,* an eight-bedroomed *maison de maître* with seven acres and views of the Pyrenees. Not that we wanted eight bedrooms, two was our target, but the asking price had been reduced so low that it was now one of the cheapest properties on my list, having come down to less than half of its original asking price.

So what was the catch?

I waited for the estate agent to mention the toilet at the bottom of the stairs and the missing roof but instead heard about banks and financial problems. The owner was desperate to sell to pay off his debts and had moved out of the house four years ago.

Aha. It had been empty for four years. Everything began to slip into place. The price, the need to sell, the image of encroaching rain forest smashing its way through the windows.

There was something about the speed in which the French countryside could reclaim properties, which bordered on the supernatural. From what I'd seen, I wouldn't risk leaving a house empty for the weekend. After four years, the lounge was probably thick forest.

When we arrived, I thought we'd come to the wrong house. It looked in too good a condition.

Aha, I thought, Indian burial ground.

It was the traditional *maison de maître* of the area with huge rooms, nine-foot high ceilings and stone walls of the thickness normally associated with small castles.

The hallway alone was three yards wide and big enough to garage a couple of small tractors. Apparently it was the local custom to design farmhouses that way to accommodate the trestle tables for the harvest festivities. When all the families who'd helped bring in the harvest would be wined and dined and stuffed with roast pig. Which sounded fun for everyone, except the pig.

As I walked around the first floor bedrooms I began to see a possible reason for the lack of sanitary facilities I'd encountered in earlier properties. They'd all been installed here. I had never seen so many toilets. And in so many unexpected places – like right next to the bed. In suite instead of en suite, I suppose.

Truly, here was a man who loved porcelain. Every bedroom had some. All had a sink, some had bidets, some had toilets, some had all three. None had partitions. Bidets and toilets stood side by side with beds and wardrobes. A 'proud to be porcelain' smile beaming out from their glazed countenances. When I entered the bathroom, I half expected to see a bed. All in all, I counted five toilets and four bidets in the house. I gave up on the sinks after the second recount. There were a lot.

When I rang Shelagh later that evening, I glossed over the excess of plumbing as best I could. The eight bedrooms hadn't gone down too well, so I thought the five toilets and four bidets were probably best left to another time.

But Shelagh wanted to know more.

"Did it have a second bathroom?"

"Er ... yes," I replied hesitantly. After all, it was the truth. It did have a second bathroom, in between the first and third.

"What about toilets. Did both bathrooms have one?"

Yes, again. As did the cupboard under the stairs and some of the bedrooms. But so what. We could open a showroom.

~

That morning – our first morning in our new residence and a so far breakfastless one – we sat down and made a list.

It was some list.

It was headed by a car. We had to have one. As we had to have logs, gas bottles, food, a cooker, plugs, telephone, money, a cheque book, hay, straw, fence posts and undoubtedly a thousand and one other things that temporarily eluded us.

But we lived in the middle of nowhere with not a shop in sight. Or a bus stop or a telephone kiosk or a man who knew semaphore. After all, this was what we had wanted – to be away from it all. What we hadn't envisaged was the sheer desperation of our trip down. All thoughts of plugs, food and stopping to phone ahead had been pushed aside, locked away by the certain knowledge that any attempt to deviate from our course would have resulted in unimaginable disaster. Any supermarket we stopped at would undoubtedly have been struck by a meteorite within seconds of us pulling up outside.

But today was another day. Paranoia was living somewhere in Northern France and we needed to find a phone.

So we grabbed a map and took Gypsy for a walk.

Which went down very well with Gypsy, who was enjoying her new life. After all, she'd had breakfast. Like the cats, she didn't need her food heated and we had plenty of tins and no problem locating the tin opener. I think the cats had packed a spare one just in case.

We left the cats unpacking – there's something about large boxes full of screwed up paper that cats find irresistible. They'd be busy for hours.

We thought we'd try Tuco first as it was the nearest village. Well, perhaps not quite a village. With three houses, a church and a road sign, it was large enough to rate a mention on our map but that was about it.

Walking down the winding country lane it was difficult to believe that this was winter. The mid-Februarys that we remembered were the coldest part of the year – with howling gales and biting winds vying with snow and drizzle and thick grey blankets of cloud that could hang around for weeks.

But here, the sky was clear, there wasn't a breath of wind and the sun had real strength to it. Even this early in the morning you could feel its warmth on your skin. Which made the transition between light and shade the more noticeable. Step into the shadow of the trees and it felt cold – you could feel the frost beneath your feet, hear the crackle on the tarmac. Step into the sun and it felt like spring, the grass was green and the road was dry.

We ambled along the curving lane as it wound down the little valley. A steep-sided wood rose up on our left, another almost as steep on our right. Ahead of us, we could make out the steeple of the tiny village church and beyond that another tree-lined hill marked the far side of the main valley. It was a beautiful spot. Rolling hills and valleys, tiny villages, forests and fields. Just what we wanted.

A few minutes more and our little valley widened out into the larger valley in which Tuco stood. We could see for miles. Tiny white spots of habitation dotted the far hills. Patches of green marked out the growing crops against the predominant browns of wood, ploughed fields and scrub.

It was idyllic.

Until the advance guard of the Tuco dogs spotted Gypsy.

We dragged her past the first barrage of woofs straight into the teeth of the main contingent. Four dogs of various size and pedigree held us at bay while a large black dog harried us from behind. Gypsy was not a happy dog. It was probably the first time she'd seen other dogs since leaving her mother. And these were growling at her in French.

Then a farmhouse door opened, and out shot a small dark-haired woman alternating shouts and smiles as she tried to chastise her dogs and welcome us at the same time. The dogs ran back inside the yard and lay down, yawning and looking the other way as though whatever had just happened had had nothing to do with them.

Gypsy took this as an opportunity to shout abuse at them from behind our legs – amazing how brave a puppy can be after the danger has passed.

Another figure appeared from a barn, a curly-haired man in his late thirties, wiping his hands on his overalls as he walked up to meet us. There was the usual hand shaking and then...

It was our first introduction to the local dialect. I had expected it to be a variation on the French we'd heard on the language tapes and schools' programmes. But not this much of a variation. It was unintelligible.

I'd been reasonably confident of my French up until that point. I'd coped with estate agents who couldn't speak English, I'd survived restaurants and hotels. I could usually make myself understood – eventually. And I could normally pick up the gist of what was being said to me – if it was repeated slowly and often enough.

But this was beyond me. It sounded more like Spanish. Perhaps we'd been learning the wrong language. And as my entire knowledge of Spanish was limited to beer, squid and airport, my conversation would be less than inspiring.

The best way to describe the dialect is to imagine French being spoken at speed by a Spaniard who has taken out all the words and linked them together with that rolling Spanish 'r' sound, to form one long unintelligible word. And as my normal method of translation depended on recognising one or two keywords in a sentence and then gradually working out the others from the context, I was stumped. There wasn't room for even the smallest keyword to breathe – everything was so well wrapped up in 'r's.

And if anything the man was worse. He was a lisping version of his mother, adding a liberal sprinkling of Spanish 'th' sounds.

But this was the *campagne*. What did we expect? If we'd been a French couple knocking on a Devon farmhouse we'd have probably been as lost, meeting a stream of broad Devonian.

I began to suspect that we might not be listening to French or Spanish at all, but one of those ancient Pyrenean languages I'd read about – Occitan, Catalan or some such mixture of old French and Spanish.

But then I started to grasp the odd word – as the woman slowed her speech down and unrolled the occasional 'r'.

Her name was Claudine and Roger was her son. Not the most earth-shattering of revelations, but after ten minutes of total confusion, it was as precious to us as the Rosetta stone. We were beginning to understand.

We then embarked on an attempt to ask them if they could tell us where the nearest telephone was. An ambitious enterprise but we were desperate.

After a considerable effort and many blank looks we succeeded.

"*Là*," said Claudine, pointing over our shoulders.

We turned as one and looked at the very distinctive glass booth with the word *téléphone* prominently displayed. It was ten feet away. Ah, that telephone kiosk. I declined to ask if there was one closer. *Nous sommes Anglais*, after all.

But we had found a telephone, and from that moment, time shifted into overdrive. I rang up Jan, arranged to borrow her car, fixed a time for the kitten to be picked up, the horse transported, everything. I declined to give too many details about our journey down, as no one could possibly carry enough change in their pocket to do the story justice over a pay phone.

"I will tell you later," I concluded.

The day continued at the same pace. We stocked up with plugs and fresh food, a couple of 13kg bottles of Butagaz. We priced cookers and telephones and collected free papers for their car adverts.

Which was our next priority – we had to have a car of our own.

Cars, *Cartes* and *Campagne*

I thought buying a car would be easy, so I drove off to buy a car while Shelagh carried on with the unpacking and plug changing.

I found three local car dealers all relatively close to each other and toured the rows of second-hand cars. Most were outside of our budget. But that was what I'd expected. We'd set our sights on something cheap and basic – we didn't expect to do much driving and just wanted something that transported us from A to B and didn't cost too much to run.

By the third garage, I was wondering if I was going to have to increase our 20,000 Fr budget. Then I saw the old Citroen DS. I'd had one as a child – as a toy, that is – and had always been fascinated by its strange aerodynamic shape. It had been so unlike all the other cars of its time.

I walked over and had a closer look at it. It still exuded a plush elegance, but this model must have been well over twenty-five years old. I thought about it, weighing up all the pros and cons. The 4,000 Franc price tag was the biggest pro. Explaining to Shelagh why I'd bought a vintage saloon, was the lead-weighted con.

She had said, "I don't mind what it's like, as long as it's not red." But had she really meant it? If I returned home with a silver antique, would its colour be enough?

"You bought *what*?" was the reply my mind encountered the most as I played through the various scenarios. After the eight bedrooms and the five toilets, I didn't think I could quite carry off the vintage Citroen as well. No matter how cheap.

So I reluctantly said goodbye to a childhood memory and strolled on to the next row of cars. More Citroens. But still within budget and far more modern. This was more hopeful. Except for the one very noticeable drawback – they were all red.

I replayed another set of scenarios. "You bought *what*?" was still very much in evidence, but less so if I played the 'it was either this or the vintage saloon' card.

And we had to have a car. Even a red one.

But there was another problem – the one which looked the best deal did not have local number plates. Which meant I'd have to change them. In France, number plates were issued by *département*. This one had a sixty-five number – Haute Pyrenees. I'd need a thirty-one – Haute Garonne. According to my *Living in*

France bible, that would mean an extra trip to the *Préfecture* and a new number plate to buy and register. Would it be expensive?

No, said the garage. Neither would it be a problem, they did it all the time, and if we wanted they'd do all the paperwork for us – the *carte grise*, the number plates, the lot. We wouldn't have to set one English foot inside the *Préfecture*. Which sounded brilliant. And a useful card to add to 'it was either this or the vintage saloon.'

The next day, we returned complete with 15,000 francs in cash and all the papers we possessed – passports, birth and marriage certificates, the lot. We'd heard about French bureaucracy and came prepared.

It went very well, we were succeeding in making ourselves understood, we had all the documents they asked for. And we had cash – which seemed to please them the most.

Then they produced the car's papers. The *contrôle technique* (certificate of roadworthiness), the old *carte grise* (log book) and the bill of sale. Everything was there – except a current tax disc. But that wouldn't be a problem, they told us. All they needed was a passport from us and they'd handle the rest. They'd go to the *Sous-Préfecture* at St. Gaudens, have the number plates changed, the car re-registered and taxed by next week.

Next week? What would we do for transport in the meantime?

No problem, they said – I liked this garage – you can drive it away now. They even had a special form for just such an occasion. I looked at the form. I'd never heard of it. Could my *Living in France* bible be out of date?

I tried to ask for more details, but the more they explained, the more it seemed akin to a Monopoly 'Get out of jail free' card. Had I heard it correctly? If stopped by the police, show them this paper – it grants you fourteen days to obtain the correct documents. Excellent! I'll take two.

So we drove away in our new car. Well, I drove and Shelagh returned Jan's car. And as I pulled away from the garage, I couldn't help thinking how easy it had been. I'd read so many horror stories about buying cars in France – the interminable hours spent queuing for the right papers only to be sent somewhere else. Hadn't they heard of the 'Get out of jail free' card? Perhaps I should pen a letter to *French Property News*.

Little did I know what the future had in store.

But I should have.

The first inkling trickled forth two hours later when we stopped at a small garage for petrol. It wasn't self-service but I had all my, 'fill it up,' and, 'a hundred francs worth, please,' phrases memorised and to hand, and was feeling confident. That is until I tried to unlock the petrol cap. The key I'd been given didn't fit. I tried the other keys – the ignition, the boot key. Nothing. The petrol cap wasn't moving.

If ever someone looked as though they'd just pulled into a garage in a stolen car, it was me.

And then my French deserted me. I could almost hear the, 'we're off!' as all the verbs and nouns ran for cover. Shelagh took one look at the situation and wound up her window. She was a hitch-hiker and had never seen me before in her life.

I was alone on the forecourt with a confused petrol pump attendant and a non-functioning key.

"Er ... *nous sommes Anglais,*" I ventured after a while, added a few shrugs, opened my mouth again in case a stray noun or two had stayed behind. Then I pointed to the road. *"Je suis* er ... off."

Then I left. Swiftly. Another garage added to the list of places I could never return to.

The next problem was could we reach the car dealer before we ran out of petrol? Naturally this was but a smokescreen. The real question we should have been asking ourselves was 'would the garage close for a half day five minutes after we'd bought the car?'

The answer was, of course, yes.

We left the deserted showroom and drove home with eyes fixed firmly on the petrol gauge. It was on red but what did that mean? A gallon? Two? And how accurate would the gauge be?

The next day we returned to the garage. The car, however, had other ideas. Perhaps it was colder than I thought or I pushed the choke in too quickly, but whatever the reason the engine kept cutting out.

I dreaded the possibility that we were running out of petrol. The gauge was on red but not by much. Surely there was enough to get us to the garage?

After a while the car started to behave itself. Perhaps it was just the cold after all. Shelagh wondered if we should mention it to the garage but neither of us had the words and we didn't want to confuse the situation further. We needed a key to the petrol tank. The rest could wait.

At the garage we quickly went into our prepared speech. Petrol cap had turned into quite a mouthful. According to our dictionary it was a *bouchon de réservoir d'essence.*

"*Je ne peux pas ouvrir le bouchon de réservoir d'essence. Le clé ne pas fonctionner.*" It was probably my largest speech ever in a foreign language and delivered without a pause for breath. The sales manager looked baffled. Whether by my accent or the fact that the petrol cap wouldn't open, I wasn't sure. I thrust my sheet of paper at him and pointed to my lines, adding a few key-turning finger twists to augment the words.

He still looked baffled.

"How is it possible?" he asked in French to no one in particular, as he stared at our key ring.

I could have told him. I expect one of my ancestors chartered the *Marie Celeste*.

A collection of different keys were collected from drawers and hooks and we joined the deputation marching out to our car. One by one each key was tried, accompanied by mumbled French words of astonishment as each key failed.

And then one key succeeded and smiles replaced the mumbles. The keys were switched, we filled up with petrol and for a short period all was well with the world.

That is until the next day when the car died.

We had barely left home when the engine started cutting out. I played with the choke and managed to revive it a few times but it seemed to be getting worse. We had been gradually acclimatising to the car's quirks, we recognised that if the engine revs dropped appreciably any time in the first five minutes of a journey, the engine would cut out. But then it had been a simple matter of pulling the choke out and restarting the engine. It worked every time. Until now.

And we were in the middle of nowhere.

Well, not exactly the middle of nowhere, as that's where our house was. More accurately, we were halfway from the middle of nowhere – a far worse place.

"I knew we should have told the garage yesterday," said Shelagh.

You can always count on your passenger for helpful advice at times of stress.

"I thought we agreed not to mention it to them."

"*You* agreed."

"And what would we have said? It took us half an hour and a dictionary to come up with the petrol cap key doesn't work."

I thought my logic was unassailable but the conversation deteriorated from that point into a series of, "who bought the stupid car?", "I never wanted to come to France," and "I told you not to buy a red one." No wall of logic could withstand that kind of assault.

I tried the engine again. Nothing. I pushed the choke in, I pulled the choke out. Nothing.

I looked at the scenery. Hoping to find an unexpected garage hiding behind the wall of greenery that spread from horizon to horizon.

"Lovely view," I said before I could stop myself.

"Try the engine again," came the terse reply.

Nothing happened.

We were stuck in the depths of rural France and ... I could see large buzzards circling above our car.

After another round of helpful suggestions from my passenger, I countered with a "You try!"

"All right, I will."

We exchanged seats. I cast a nervous eye skyward as I walked around to the passenger side. I was sure there were only three buzzards the last time I'd counted.

Shelagh tried the same variations of turns, clicks, pulls and pushes. Was that a hint of life? The engine turned. We were saved! A frustrated squawk came from above. It would have to be mouse for dinner again.

We made it as far as the next junction before the car stalled once more. But we were making progress. We were nearly three quarters from the middle of nowhere.

Fifteen minutes later and several stop-starts, we limped into Tournas. It was only a small village but it was like Rome to us. Civilisation! It had a shop. It had people. It had a phone box.

We parked. The car was good at that.

And it was then that a possible answer to our car's performance presented itself. An answer that had been waiting for all the panic to die down. Perhaps we'd flooded the engine? Which would explain why it suddenly stopped working with the choke out. And why it suddenly started again after a pause.

It didn't explain everything. It didn't explain the engine's predilection for cutting out whenever the revs dropped. But it did explain our inability to restart it.

Perhaps there was something wrong with the idle speed that caused the car to stall? Perhaps it was time to take it back to the garage?

We decided to postpone our trip to the supermarket and return home for the dictionary. But first we'd stock up with food at the village shop. Just in case the car broke down again and we needed to feed the buzzards.

From that point the car behaved itself perfectly. I am convinced it heard us mention the word 'garage'. The word 'vet' has a similar effect on dogs. One mention and all symptoms of illness miraculously disappear. What me? Sick? Never!

Stocked up with a new page of hastily scribbled phrases pertaining to idle speeds, chokes and errant engines, we returned to the garage.

I had my phrase, "I bought a Citroen Ax here on Tuesday," handy in case they wondered who I was. But it wasn't necessary. They remembered. And, *pas de problème,* they'd have a mechanic check our engine for us.

Which was when we noticed that our car bonnet didn't have an arm to prop it open. The mechanic was totally confused. He looked all over. I felt like turning out my pockets to prove I hadn't taken it. In the end he grabbed a piece of wood to prop the hood up.

I was told to sit inside and depress the accelerator every now and then, so the mechanic could hear the engine turning over. He made some adjustments, listened some more, adjusted some more and then with a, "*bon,*" that was it. Car fixed. We could say goodbye to the garage.

That is until a week later when we returned for the car documents. They were desolated. "*Je suis désolée,*" the manager repeated. A computer error – what else – had prevented them from getting a particular form from the Haute Pyrenees *Préfecture*. Apparently they needed a *Certificat de Situation* to prove the car had no outstanding hire purchase agreements. I'd never heard of that one. Luckily we still had seven days on our 'Get out of jail free' card.

We agreed to return in a couple of days time. And again a few days after that. More computer errors, more reassurances. On the last day of our 'Get out of jail free' card, we pulled up at the garage in a desperate frame of mind. No broken computers or papers in the post were going to deflect us.

"*Pas de problème,*" said the manager and handed us another 'Get out of jail free' card. He'd copied the details across from the old one, except that he'd advanced the date of purchase by two weeks.

Ah. This did not look exactly legal. I'd had my doubts about the old 'Get out of jail free' card, but at least the information it carried had been accurate.

"Don't worry," we were assured. Another few days and he'd have all the car's papers. It was easy, he added. They did it all the time.

Two days later, I'm flagged down at a police roadblock. No tax disc, no documents and a forged 'Get out of jail free' card.

I had been on my way to Samatan market. A trip I didn't have to make but one I'd thought would be fun. Our neighbour, Claudine, had recommended it – it's good to have someone else to blame. She'd said it was the largest local market by far and something not to be missed. It was held every Monday and attracted huge crowds.

No one said anything about police roadblocks.

It had all started when we dropped in at Claudine's for hay and straw … and came home with four pints of milk. Nothing to do with our inability to speak French this time but the unfailing generosity of our neighbours.

We arrived at dusk to a deserted farmyard. Deserted, that is, except for four lounging dogs lying by the gate. Eventually, the smallest and most alert of the four guard dogs noticed our intrusion and raised the alarm. The largest dog, the redoubtable *gardien de vache,* opened a solitary eye, cast an appraising look in our direction, sniffed and went back to sleep. Not worth the bother.

Claudine appeared in the doorway of an old stone building at the side of the yard and beckoned us in. We'd arrived in the middle of milking.

As we stepped through into the light we wondered what we'd find. French farmers were generally vilified, depending on which section of the English press you read, as either inefficient and subsidy-ridden or barbaric animal torturers who loved nothing better than to import cuddly English calves and lock them up in veal crates. As usual, the truth was somewhat different.

There were twenty cows of assorted breeds, colours and ages. Including three very young calves, who, far from being housed in veal crates, were still suckling from their mothers.

This was not modern industrial farming. No gleaming stainless steel vat or state-of-the-art milking parlour. No vast homogenous herd, economies of scale or labour-saving devices. This was a small family farm as small family farms used to be. When all animals had names and labour was long, hard and mostly manual. The only hint of technology I could see was a small portable milking cluster which Roger was carrying from cow to cow.

Steam rose from the backs of the cattle as we took out our script and launched into our prepared speech. Did they have any hay or straw that we could buy?

Claudine shook her head and then burst into a stream of tightly packed and indecipherable French.

It was the longest 'no' I'd ever heard.

Or was it a 'yes'?

Gradually the odd word untangled itself from amongst the 'r's. They couldn't sell us any hay or straw because we were *voisins* – neighbours. They'd *give* us a couple of bales instead.

We tried to press money on them. More head shaking, more 'r's, lots of *voisins*. This was the *campagne,* a land where neighbours helped each other out.

And did we want any milk?

Before we could answer, Roger came out from behind a cow with the milking cluster and Claudine was off looking for something to put the milk in.

Did we want any cows?

I looked at Shelagh, had I heard that correctly? Had Roger offered us a cow? Were we about to walk back up the hill carrying a bucket of milk and leading a cow? Would it be bad manners to decline a *voisin's* gift? Or were we supposed to offer something in exchange? Gypsy, for instance.

I was just warming to the idea of an animal exchange, when Claudine launched into a glowing account of Samatan market. You could buy anything there. If we wanted to have cattle, that would be the place to go.

Aha, now, I understood.

By this time our French conversational skills were pretty much exhausted. We managed a few more sentences about cows and weather but that was about it. To me, conversing in French is very much like holding your breath – after a minute, I'm spent and speechless. Words and phrases were flying over my head as Roger and Claudine chattered on about this and that. I looked at Shelagh, she looked at me. What were they saying? Claudine and Roger tempted us with a few more sentences but even after three repeats I was still lost.

A silence descended.

An awkward silence that I felt compelled to fill.

Always a big mistake.

I thought I'd try and work horses into the conversation – find a common subject we could talk about. I wondered if they'd ever used horses on their farm.

"No, never," they said.

I should have quit at that point. I'd asked a question and received an answer I understood. My daily quota had been filled. But my interest had been piqued. What had they used on the farm before the advent of the tractor? Oxen? I'd seen a picture showing a working oxen team pulling a plough in the Central Massif as late as 1970. Had they used oxen here?

The conversation went downhill from that point. What was the French for ox? Guidebooks won't tell you. They don't cover rural small talk. Plenty of phrases for 'Where is the station?' and 'Can you tell me where the toilets are?' but 'Where are the oxen?' – don't even bother to look.

I tried *grande vache,* rationalising that a big cow was worth a shot.

It wasn't.

Shelagh's eyes had rolled into the top of her head and she was slowly, sidling away from the conversation. Claudine and Roger were transfixed. Big cow? What was that about the big cow?

I pressed on, if I couldn't find the words, I'd mime them. I fastened my wrists to the top of my head. But before I could stop myself my fingers splayed and my hands started waggling. My horns had evolved into antlers.

And immediately frightened off the few French nouns that I had left.

And in between the waggling, came the babbling.

I tried to say, 'In England, before tractors, we used to have oxen.' It came out more like, 'In England, all tractors are preceded by giant elk.'

If not a man with a red flag.

It was time to go.

Shelagh grabbed hold of my left antler and tugged me towards the door.

As I stood at the roadblock, blowing into a little plastic bag, I couldn't help but reflect on how sporting the police were being. Breathalysing motorists at 10:00 am on a market day was not going to provide a rich catch of drunks. Whereas, if they'd waited a few hours until after *déjeuner* and the mix of market day enthusiasm and cheap wine had reached its peak ... well, they would have filled the cells.

Which, on reflection, was probably why they timed their roadblock earlier. A police station crammed to the ceilings with drunken farmers and a car park full of abandoned tractors was not something to be solicited lightly.

The bag blown up and the crystals scrutinised, I was taken inside for processing. The roadblock being outside the police station, I didn't have far to walk. And then came the interrogation.

Where was my identification?

"Er ... *à la maison*?"

Much shaking of heads. All French citizens were obliged to carry identification at all times. Even when drunk in charge of a tractor.

Where were the car's papers?

"Er ..." Now that was a long story, crammed full of nouns, verbs and several adjectives – all of which had fled the scene the moment the first gendarme's hand had alighted on my shoulder.

I pulled out my 'Get out jail free' card and slid it over the counter, adding a nervous smile and a telepathic onslaught. 'This card is not forged. This man is not the man you are looking for. Let him go.'

I'd seen Star Wars.

The police sergeant hadn't. More shakes of the head. And a tch tch.

The Force was strong with this one.

Then he hit me with a question I wasn't expecting.

What was my father's date of birth?

"*Pardon*?"

He repeated the question. I was thrown. It was thirty-five years since my father's death. I'd been five at the time. I had no idea what day he'd been born.

I shrugged. He looked dumbfounded and glanced at his colleagues. They shrugged. I shrugged. We looked like a room full of marionettes on elastic strings.

And then he asked me another question.

What was my mother's date of birth?

I couldn't believe this. I was without a dictionary, I had no script and I was being asked to recite all my family birthdays! Surely this was against the Geneva Convention?

Never cease to be amazed by French bureaucracy. It took half an hour to be processed. I filled up a whole page in their ledger. Most of it with birthdays.

And I had to return to my nearest police station – Aurignac – within three days, complete with passport, birth certificate, *carte grise* and tax disc.

And I had to tell Shelagh.

In all my years of driving in England I had never been stopped or breathalysed. One month in France and all that had changed.

Although, on further recollection, it wasn't exactly my first encounter with a French roadblock. That honour having come a few months earlier. But then I hadn't been the driver.

I was with Peter, a South African chef cum estate agent. A rather novel combination but indicative of the frequent plight of the newly-arrived in France – the need to augment one's living with a second job. Which meant he occasionally showed people around houses in between cooking meals at his restaurant.

And on this occasion he was having some difficulty locating the property I'd asked to view. We'd toured a particular area for a growing amount of time without success when we turned a corner and ... there it was.

A roadblock.

Two police cars blocked a junction between two single-track roads in the middle of nowhere. The obvious place for a roadblock.

We stopped and out came the documents and back came the questions – what are you doing here and why? They were very inquisitive. And they were armed.

But very helpful. They asked to see the picture of the house we were looking for and peered at it a few times, took it over to the officers in the other police car, conferred, brought it back. Shrugged.

And then out of nowhere appeared an ancient cyclist. A gaunt old man in a beret struggling with heavy pedals and weaving from side to side as he crawled along the road on his vintage bicycle.

Within a flash, a policeman was out into the middle of the road, arm upraised and hand resting on his gun. I wasn't sure if the cyclist would be able to stop – he didn't look very safe as it was without the additional pressure of a police roadblock and an emergency stop. I saw the ditch on the side of the road beckon for a good few moments as in panic he threw in a few extra wide swerves.

But he stopped, after a fashion, standing astride the cross bar looking less than comfortable and distinctly shaky. I wondered why he'd been stopped. Surely they weren't going to breathalyse him or search his bike?

They didn't. Instead, they showed him the picture of our house.

The next we knew, we had a smiling policeman waving us on and telling us to follow the cyclist – he knew the house and would take us to it.

I wondered if anyone had given him the opportunity to refuse.

We followed the cyclist for some time, omitting the more eccentric swerves but otherwise exactly matching his snail-like lead. And it was during that epic slow-motion pursuit that we decided that whatever house he led us to, we'd agree it was definitely the one in the picture and thank him profusely for all his trouble.

Eventually he pulled his machine to a stuttering halt and pointed down a hill towards a farmhouse obscured by trees. We quickly agreed that that was undoubtedly the place and thanked him for all his help.

Amazingly it *was* the right house, but after a few minutes inspection I could see it wasn't the place for us – there was too much work to do for the price and the location wasn't ideal.

So, slightly disheartened, we climbed back into the car and headed off for the next property. Hopefully without finding any more police roadblocks.

But we were lost and the roads were winding this way and that and so narrow that they all looked the same. And, as tends to be the case in the France, all were completely un-signposted.

It's one of those unwritten laws – that when you're lost, places you're trying to find never appear and those you're trying to avoid keep coming back.

We saw the police cars first, then the cyclist.

We were back.

As we passed the cyclist I could see the worried onset of a bout of deja vu form upon his weather-beaten face. Did we have any more houses for him to find? Would he ever see his own home again?

And then we were stopped and the smiling face of the law leaned into our car. Had we found the house? Yes? Were we going to buy it?

I wondered why he had his hand on his gun as he asked me? Perhaps I *should* buy it. Perhaps I should buy it *now*. How much cash did I have with me? There's nothing like an armed police roadblock to bring out the paranoid in the law-abiding.

Peter smiled and said his clients were considering it and could he tell us the way to Tarbes. I think I heard a groan from the cyclist. Tarbes was over twenty miles away, he'd never be able to make it.

The *gendarme* was only too pleased to give us directions. He waved and pointed over various fields and clumps of trees and sprinkled his speech with plenty of rights and lefts. I didn't have a clue what he said but Peter seemed to be nodding in all the right places.

With a wave and chorus of farewells we eventually left the roadblock. I think we could have held out for a police escort.

Shelagh did not take my news lightly about being stopped on the way to Samatan market. She wasn't sure whether to blame me, the garage or the fact that the car was red.

The debate continued into the car as we headed back to the garage armed with my police summons.

"Ah," said the manager as we told him what had happened. Apparently, the car's documents weren't quite ready yet. I waited to hear 'computer error' or 'the wrong kind of leaves on the line outside Clapham Junction', but neither excuses were forthcoming. Instead, it was the wife's fault – far more plausible – she was supposed to have taken the forms in that morning but had forgotten.

I waited to hear *pas de problème* and was not disappointed. He would take the documents in himself.

"And when would they be ready?"

"*Demain.*"

"Morning?"

A shrug. "*Après-midi.*"

We'd be back.

The next day came and the afternoon saw us on familiar territory – in the manager's office at the garage.

"*Une problème,*" he said. I didn't like the way he said that. What had happened to *pas de problème*? It had a much better ring to it. More lyrical. More comforting.

The *Sous-Préfecture* had refused to process our documents, he explained.

"What! Why?"

Because we didn't have a *carte de séjour*.

This was not what my copy of *Living in France* told me. It clearly stated that you needed either a passport <u>or</u> a *carte de séjour*. Not both. Something was wrong.

"How do we get a *carte de séjour*?"

He shrugged.

But the police...

He shrugged again and pushed our pile of documents –

Shelagh's passport, the *contrôle technique*, the old *carte grise* and the bill of sale – across the desk towards us.

It was now our problem. And far from *pas*.

As the days progressed I began to think that perhaps *pas de problème* was best translated as the father of all problems. If not a mother as well.

First we decided to confront the *Sous-Préfecture*. Surely there had been some kind of mistake. Perhaps, they didn't like a third party trying to register a car with someone else's passport?

Our trip to the *Sous-Préfecture* underwrote everything ever said about French bureaucracy.

It started well. We'd tracked down the *Sous-Préfecture* with the aid of the Tourist Information Centre. It was open and we even found a small building with *Carte Grise* written on the door.

But then we opened that door.

The place was packed. A room full of people clutching handfuls of documents and cheque books. But where was the queue? It looked more like a melee.

And, of course, there was only one person on duty and he wasn't in a good mood.

Minutes passed. We stood at the back of the nearest thing resembling a queue and waited. Somehow the wedge of people ahead of us didn't diminish. Instead they seemed to rearrange themselves. People would reach the counter, chat a while then move towards the back. No one seemed to want to leave. And then other people would walk straight in, force their way to the front and somehow be served immediately. It was chaotic. But no one seemed to mind. It was as though everyone knew the system except us.

Eventually we began to discern a pattern to the behaviour. People were being processed in several stages. One to hand over their documents, and another to receive and pay for the newly printed *carte grise*. I didn't know how the man kept track of who he was serving. To confuse matters more some of the customers appeared to be dealers registering large numbers of cars who flitted in and out of the office and appeared to have their own fast-track queuing system.

We attached ourselves to the back of someone who looked as though they knew what they were doing and inched forward behind them. Very slowly.

As the counter approached we went over and over our prepared phrases. I felt like I was reciting a mantra. *Nous voudrons une carte grise, nous voudrons une carte grise*. But wasn't that superfluous? We were in the *Carte Grise* office, what else would we be asking for?

After a hasty script conference we decided to stick with the original opening line. And out it came, on cue and perfectly enunciated. I handed over the documents, he took them, ticked them with his pencil, clipped the corner off the old *carte grise* and said:

"*Carte de séjour?*"

"*Non. Passeport,*" I said pointing to the passport I'd slid towards him.

"*Non. Carte de séjour,*" he said, pushing my passport back.

I tried to reason with him. After all, the only reason for the *carte de séjour* was proof of identity. If I'd been French he'd have asked to see my identity card. And what better proof of identity was there than a passport?

"*Non. Carte de séjour.*"

We showed him our birth and marriage certificates. We pleaded, we babbled, we mentioned the *gendarmes*.

"*Non!*"

We left. It was Wednesday morning. I had to have a *carte grise* and a valid tax disc at Aurignac police station by Thursday. God knows what they'd do to me if I didn't produce them on time.

Driving home we began to put the matter into perspective. If they wanted a *carte de séjour* we'd have to get one. After all, we'd need them soon. We'd read that you could only live in France for ninety days without one. But we'd planned on waiting for a month or two as tax residency was determined from the date of application for a residency card and I wanted to push that date as far back as possible to make sure all the house sale proceeds were dealt with under the British tax system.

But given the choice between that and the *gendarmes*...

Back home, I dusted off the notes I'd made on *cartes de séjour*. I'd culled the facts from several sources and all seemed to be slightly different – the confusion being caused by recent European Community moves to give equal rights to all member citizens. Some argued this included the right of abode – in which case the *carte de séjour* was unnecessary. Others argued it didn't and warned of deportation unless the card was held.

No one said you couldn't buy a car without one.

We read further and collected together all the supporting documents we'd need – birth certificates, marriage certificate, passports. The only things we didn't have were passport size photographs.

So off we went, carefully avoiding all police cars and roadblocks, on our search for a photo booth. Unfortunately, we found one of those booths with the built in blink detector – Shelagh always finds them. They're designed to catch you in mid-blink or, failing that, to install such fear of being caught in mid-blink that your face takes on a fixed wild-eyed stare. It worked – out came eight perfect pictures of a demented half-lidded psychotic and her husband, Mungo – just the kind of couple you'd want to grant residency to.

We toyed with having them redone. But did we have the time? Not really. So off we rushed to the *Mairie* at Cassagne.

Which was closed.

Opening hours were 9:00 am to 11:00 am. This was late afternoon.

The next morning we descended upon the *Mairie*. We were desperate and only a few hours away from being criminalised. Our only hope was a *carte de séjour*. Could we have one?

"*Oui.*"

"How long will it take?"

"Three months."

I waited to wake up. I sat back and mentally nudged myself a few times. Come on, snap out of it. This had to be one of those frustration dreams where nothing went right and every attempt at escape was thwarted in helpless slow-motion.

It wasn't.

I was wide awake and staring across a desk at a wiry little man I'd dreamt was the Mayor of Cassagne.

He still was.

I wondered if Spain took political refugees. It was only fifty minutes away. Would driving without a current tax disc be considered political?

We threw ourselves upon the mercy of the Mayor. Told him about the roadblock, the garage, the problem with the documents, the Giant Elk. I didn't need to consult a script, I knew all the words off by heart. I'd rehearsed them so often, going over and over them in my mind. I'd even stop passers-by in my dreams and rant at them about cars and missing tax discs.

The Mayor was brilliant. He picked up the phone and with a, 'This is the Mayor of Cassagne speaking,' proceeded to intervene on our behalf with the *Sous-Préfecture*.

But the *Sous-Préfecture* refused to budge. Rules are rules and they had a lot of them.

The mayor offered to vouch for our identity. They refused. He suggested another type of residency permit. They refused. He hung up.

But he wasn't beaten. Next in line for 'This is the Mayor of Cassagne speaking' were the *gendarmes* at Aurignac.

We listened avidly, trying to cull sense from the few words we understood. Was he plea bargaining? Or was that something about the weather?

He replaced the receiver. We waited, hearts thumping, what was he going to say?

"*Bon*," he smiled.

And that was enough.

If we took all the papers we had to Aurignac that morning, they'd wait for the rest.

Which was a considerable relief. And in the meantime, we'd begin the process of applying for our *cartes de séjour*.

Which turned out a lot easier than my notes suggested.

"Don't you want to see our marriage certificate?" I enquired.

"*Non, pas nécessaire*," he said and told us that, although *gendarmes* were naturally inquisitive and would want to see the marriage certificate and anything else they could lay their hands on, Mayors weren't.

I liked the Mayor.

We completed our applications in triplicate, had our passports and birth certificates photocopied, handed over our embarrassing photographs of Mr. and Mrs. Mungo and left.

Outside, we breathed the fresh air of freedom. Things were indeed looking up.

We found the *gendarmerie* on the outskirts of Aurignac. It was a small single storey building, so small it didn't even rate a car park. But there was a lay-by outside – just large enough to take three cars – and we parked in the middle.

As we walked inside the station, I couldn't help but notice a board full of wanted posters running along one of the walls. I had to have a look and ... phew, mine wasn't there – though I think we'd all used the same photo booth.

Out came my prepared speech. Not quite the one I'd wanted to give – I thought '*Nous sommes* banged to rights' was an excellent opening line. But I'd been out-voted by Shelagh and the cats – the iniquities of living in a one paw, one vote democracy.

Still, we presented our documents and they ticked them off their list. They saw our passports, driving licenses, marriage and birth certificates. They thumbed through our car's papers, glanced momentarily at the 'Get out of jail free card' ... and then asked, "what is your father's date of birth?"

There is something obsessive about this interest in birthdays. I read somewhere that the Mormons have a similar obsession – some enormous database of family trees they hold in Salt Lake City – something about needing to trace everyone's ancestry back to the original Osmonds.

Maybe the *gendarmes* had a similar fixation. Certainly, I now know where to go if I ever forget a birthday.

Besides dates of birth, they were particularly interested in what we intended to do in France. We weren't retired, we weren't working. What were we doing?

We did our best to explain in halting French but nothing we said seemed to be understandable. Guide-books again – plenty of entries for 'I am a postman' or 'my husband is a doctor' but nothing under 'well, we kind of gave up working to live self-sufficiently, grow our own food and write science fiction.'

But *gendarmes* are persistent and need to know.

"*La Chasse?*" he suggested.

Yes, we agreed – very swiftly – *La Chasse*. That's exactly why we came to France. For the hunting. Well, why not?

He sounded envious. A faraway look formed in his eyes. I could see him thinking about such a life. Days of endless hunting. A man and his dog. Utopia.

"*Bon,*" he concluded with a start. And then dropped his bombshell. He'd see us again when we produced the *vignette* – the tax disc. In the meantime, the car would have to remain off the road. It took several repetitions and a few words written down and looked up in the dictionary but eventually we understood.

Aha. We can't drive the car until we have a tax disc. The car parked outside the *gendarmerie*. Our only means of transport.

It was a five mile walk home.

Or at least it would have been a five mile walk, but we were hardened criminals by then.

"Why did you have to park right in front of the *gendarmerie* door?" hissed Shelagh as we walked outside. It's one of the many lines of small print in the marriage contract – the partner is always the one at fault. Shelagh tells me it's somewhere after 'in sickness and in health.'

We casually walked past the car. How visible was it from the *gendarmerie* window? It was about thirty yards away and there was a slight hedge. And no one was looking out the window. And the alternative was a five mile walk. Perhaps if we gave it a few minutes, wandered into Aurignac for a window shop and waited for the *gendarmes* to change shift?

Five minutes later we were speeding along back roads, feeling as guilty as any hot-wirer in a stolen car.

An hour later I was on the phone to my sister.

"Can we borrow your car again."

"What happened to your own?"

"Don't ask."

A week later we received a call from the Mayor. There was a problem. Apparently the *Préfecture* at Toulouse had returned our application forms. They wanted more information. How did we intend to support ourselves? Did we have health cover?

This did not seem to accord with the European ideal of equal rights for all member citizens.

We rifled our document case. Would they accept the E111 health form as proof of health cover? And as for supporting ourselves, would they need an attestation in French from an accountant? Or would they accept a photocopy of a building society pass-book?

We took what we had. The mayor liked our freshly issued and stamped E111 forms. And he took a photocopy of our pass-books. Everything was bundled up and re-submitted to Toulouse. Leaving us to do what we had most practice at – wait and hope.

Time dragged as only time can. The car continued to sit outside our house. We'd see it through the window, we'd see it every time we opened the door. It was like having a Christmas present you couldn't open until Easter. Look but don't drive.

So we had to borrow a car once a week, which wasn't ideal for anyone. Jan lived ten miles away, ten miles of winding country lanes and we seemed to spend more time ferrying the car back and forth between the two properties than actually using it.

It was ridiculous. The *vignette* only cost 100 francs. I had the money. I wanted to pay. But no one would accept the money!

Then I had an idea.

If it was only the *vignette* that was preventing us from using the car, could we buy one without re-registering the car?

It was worth a try.

Off we went to the *Carte Grise* office. We joined the same melee of people, waited the same amount of time. But came up with a new question.

No more *nous voudrons une carte grise*, this time we wanted a *vignette*.

"*Non.*"

"*Pourquoi?*"

We couldn't catch what he said but it didn't sound good. Our script for alternative replies wasn't very helpful either as we'd gambled everything on a successful response to the opening line.

I tried handing him the money but he pushed it back – probably thought I was trying to bribe him.

"What are we supposed to do?" I asked, more in frustration than expecting an answer.

"Go to Tarbes," he said. At least, I think it was Tarbes. Whether that was helpful advice or a well-known Pyrenean insult I couldn't tell.

I thought it best to leave. I didn't like the way Shelagh was clenching her fists. We already had one felon in the family and I didn't think a brawl in the *Sous-Préfecture* would help our application for residency.

But had we found a solution to our immediate problem? Was it possible that the *Sous-Préfecture* at St. Gaudens couldn't issue us with a *vignette* because the car was still registered in the *Haute Pyrénées*? And did that mean that the *Préfecture* at Tarbes, the capital of the *Haute Pyrénées*, would be able to sell us one?

And what was worse, it was all beginning to make sense. I was becoming attuned to the local bureaucracy.

We debated the pros and cons of going to Tarbes most of that evening. Perhaps we were becoming defeatist but I couldn't see any outcome other than failure. We would ask for a tax disc, they would ask for a *carte grise*, we would show them our cancelled one with the corner clipped off and they'd show us the door.

That was one of the better scenarios. Others had us being arrested for trying to tax a stolen car – why have you got someone else's *carte grise*, where is your *carte de séjour*, what is your father's date of birth?

And to make matters worse, the next day we met another English couple and *cartes de séjour* casually cropped in conversation, as they frequently do amongst the newly arrived. And we found to our horror that they'd been one day away from being deported. They'd lobbied the *Mairie,* the *Sous-Préfecture* and the *Préfecture*. It was only a last-minute trip to Toulouse and an insistence on seeing the person in charge that resulted in their *cartes de séjour* being issued and their deportation order rescinded.

This was not news we wanted to hear. They'd been law-abiding citizens, I was Mungo, the man with the forged 'Get out of jail free' card.

What had started out as a simple matter of buying a second-hand car was rapidly advancing towards deportation and the loss of our home.

March disappeared into history and we met April, car-less and potentially stateless. Surely something had to happen soon? How long did Toulouse need?

On the Fourteenth of April we received a letter.

I hardly dared open it. I could see it was from the *Mairie*. I slowly began to peel back the flap of the envelope, until I found a patch so firmly glued that it refused to budge, so I ripped the envelope to shreds in a passable imitation of a shark at the height of a feeding frenzy.

I was desperate. We both were. We read the letter, our hearts beating wildly.

There was something waiting for us at the *Mairie*. We read it again, comparing our translations. It had to be the *cartes*, didn't it?

Back on the phone again.

"Jan, we need a car. The *Mairie* closes in less than an hour. But don't worry it'll be the last time we ever have to borrow a car."

I could feel Nemesis shuffling on my shoulder the moment the words passed my lips. Didn't I know better by now? Had tempting fate become an obsession?

We arrived at the *Mairie* with minutes to spare. I was already calculating how long it would take to drive to St. Gaudens, park and then walk to the *Sous-Préfecture* and could we do that before the *Carte Grise* office closed for lunch?

There were two blue A5 cards on the Mayor's desk. Was that them?

Not exactly ... they were *récépissés*.

What the hell was a *récépissé*?

Apparently it was an interim *carte de séjour* valid for three months and issued as a receipt to acknowledge the fact that a *carte* had been applied for and would be issued in due course. I was on the verge of asking why they didn't just issue the *cartes de séjour* if they'd accepted the fact that they were going to, when I realised that I was dealing with a bureaucracy. Why issue one card when you could issue two with different names?

But they did look official. They had our photographs on them. And the stamp of the *Préfecture* at Toulouse. Would that be enough for the *Sous-Préfecture* to accept them?

The Mayor rang and asked.

"This is the Mayor of Cassagne speaking," he began. We waited. The *bon* took a while but there it was. They would.

Back inside the car again, out the village, through the countryside, into the suburbs, the car-park, the *Sous-Préfecture*, the *Carte Grise* office.

"We have our *récépissés*. Give us our *vignettes*!"

"*Non.*"

"What!?"

Apparently our *Certificat de Situation* – a certificate to prove there were no outstanding loans against the car – had lapsed. It was only valid for a month following the date of issue.

"But you saw it when it was valid," I shouted.

I showed him the tick he'd made in pencil on the form.

He wasn't interested.

There was so much more I wanted to say but couldn't. It wasn't so much that my French had deserted me but all the verbs were having to be restrained by the nouns. They wanted blood.

How could our car's situation have changed in the last month? It hadn't moved. We couldn't drive it. We couldn't tax it. We couldn't register it. And we had all the documents. So how the hell could anyone secure a hire purchase loan against it?

I think the *Carte Grise* man was starting to weaken at this point. Perhaps he took pity on our plight. Perhaps he was fed up with seeing us. Perhaps he saw the look in Mrs. Mungo's half-lidded eye.

He stepped over to the back of the office and pulled an application form from a tray on the shelf. It was a request for a new *Certificat de Situation* and he filled it in for us. He even wrote down the address of the *Préfecture* in Tarbes for the application to be sent.

We returned home in a subdued mood. The optimism of the early morning replaced by a quiet determination.

We posted the application and waited. It was Easter week-end. The *Préfecture* probably took three weeks off to paint eggs.

But on the Tuesday, the glorious eighteenth of April, the new certificate arrived. What a surprise, there were still no outstanding hire purchase agreements on our car.

Back to the *Sous-Préfecture*. We had our *récépissés*, we had our passports, the old *carte grise*, the bill of sale, the *contrôle technique*, two *Certificats de Situation* and a sawn-off shotgun.

Well ... strike the last item. We didn't actually have a sawn-off shotgun but I think he could tell that we were just the kind of people who would the next time.

He took all our documents, ticked them again, and ... gave us a new *carte grise*.

"*Et la vignette?*" I ventured, determined that we were not leaving until we had everything.

"*Non.*"

What! This was not happening. Not again. The nouns were wavering, reinforcements from the adverbs and pronouns department were drafted in to keep the verbs from shredding the *Carte Grise* man where he stood.

"*Pas ici,*" he continued very quickly as Mrs. Mungo advanced upon him. And then he started pointing and saying something about the *Centre des Impôts*.

Ah, I've heard of that, the tax office.

As we left, I began to experience a worrying thought that perhaps we'd been enquiring at the wrong office all the time. That perhaps if we'd known that *vignettes* were issued at the *Centre des Impôts* we could have gone there earlier.

It was not a pleasant thought.

Luckily it wasn't an accurate one either. The first thing the woman at the *Centre des Impôts* did was to ask for our *carte grise*. I doubted if she'd have looked very favourably upon a cancelled one from a different department.

A few seconds later back came a shiny tax disc. We were legal. We could drive our car.

Well, almost. We had to buy new number plates and change the insurance to reflect the new plates. But that was hardly a Herculean task.

It was something of an anti-climax after that. After months of frustration and hitting brick walls at great speed, suddenly everything was easy. We showed our *carte grise* at the auto-shop and there were no supplementary questions or requests for extra papers or birthdays. We didn't need a script or a phone call from the Mayor. It was: thank you very much, and back five minutes later with a pair of yellow and white plates.

A similar story at the insurer's. A quick update of the file and out came a new green disc from the printer.

It's amazing how easy life is when you have the right papers.

And how impossible when you don't.

Logs, Language, Fires and Flues

Although the days were warm that first February, the nights were not. By six o'clock all warmth had disappeared with the sun and a star-lit cold descended upon us.

It wasn't a freezing cold – we weren't in any danger of hypothermia. But it was persistent and always a few degrees below anything approaching comfort level. Spending the evening wrapped in blankets watching your breath steam was not conducive to a happy frame of mind.

We hadn't noticed it the first night. Not that we were in much condition to notice anything that night. We found the door, we found the bed. What else was there?

But as the temperature plummeted on the second night we quickly pencilled in the word 'Logs' at the top of our list for things to buy the next day.

We decided Claudine was the best person to ask about logs. She had to know the name of the local supplier. After much discussion, some of which I actually understood, we left Claudine's with a name and directions. Two sets of directions, it later transpired.

I'd walked away from Claudine's basking in our improving ability to converse in French.

"Do you realise we actually understood a whole sentence of Claudine's directions," I'd boasted.

"Up until the right turn," Shelagh replied. "I didn't quite catch the last bit."

"What right turn?"

I stopped. There hadn't been a right turn. "*Tout droit* means straight ahead not turn right."

"She never said *tout droit*."

"Yes, she did."

"No, she didn't."

We walked up the hill, the sound of our footsteps drowned out by a series of 'dids' and 'didn'ts.'

But we did agree on the name she'd given us – George – he was our man. He had plenty of logs and he lived at the second house on the left, straight on at the crossroads at the top of the hill. Or possibly the farm by the cross after the right turn. Or...

"Why didn't you say something if you didn't understand what Claudine was saying?" I remonstrated.

"Because I thought you understood what she was saying."

"And I thought you understood. You were nodding."

"I always nod, it's the only way to make them stop."

Which was true. A well-timed nod and a '*oui*' was often the only way to extricate yourself from the conversational equivalent of Groundhog Day.

We continued our walk up the hill, resolving to try my route first.

Now, locating houses in the depths of rural France is not easy – no road names, no numbers. And some houses, like George's, didn't even have names. How any mail ever gets delivered in the *campagne* is a constant source of wonder. And a tribute to the rural postman, whose job it was to know everyone's name and where they were hiding.

If ever there was a cue for a passing postman, this was it. I scanned the horizon. No postmen ... just fields and trees and a rising chain of mountains.

We walked straight on at the crossroads, past the ruin on the corner and the five goats cudding on the porch. Which introduced another problem. Were ruins counted as houses? Were we looking for the second inhabited building on the left or the second clump of stones?

Yet another problem for people like ourselves untrained in the postal arts – the ubiquitous ruin. A century and more of rural depopulation had left the countryside strewn with abandoned properties. And you couldn't always tell which were which. We'd strolled into farmyards before, convinced they were derelict, only to be greeted by an elderly couple and their entire extended family.

We passed another ruin, its sun-drenched stone walls gleaming golden in the morning sun, and marvelled. An abandoned building in a town is an eyesore – smeared in graffiti and stuffed full of detritus. But out here they weathered into rocky outcrops – the perfect prop for cascading vegetation and the local wildlife – and they looked so natural. The dry stone construction helped – even the inhabited buildings hardly had any mortar between the stone – giving the ruins a natural cairn-like feel as though they'd been part of the landscape for millennia.

We trudged on, over a rise, watching the Pyrenees slowly fill the sky from east to west. We could see the foothills now in the near distance, rounded green mounds of forest undulating before the sharp grey peaks of the mountains proper. We could see for miles. We could see everything ... except George's house.

Or was that it? Over to the left there was a collection of buildings – or upmarket ruins – nestling at the bottom of a long farm track.

As we approached, we were heartened to see a long stack of logs at the side of the track. French log stacks are often the neatest part of a French farm. I never cease to be amazed by their perfection. All the logs appear uniform and straight, usually two metres long and stacked in alternating layers lengthways and crosswise. Often these stacks stretch for thirty of forty yards, forming a six-foot high wall of wood.

Where do they find all these straight-branched trees? In England, most of our logs had been gnarled and L-shaped.

I was still pondering the arcane secrets of French tree sculpting, when we rounded the last log and found ourselves in a small U-shaped courtyard. Usually, when you walk up to a property, you have a pretty good idea where the house is. Not with this property. Three buildings stared back at us, three battered stone buildings with red canal-tiled roofs. All had a single door and a few irregular windows. Some of the windows had shutters, some had cracked or broken panes of glass. None of the buildings looked inhabited but they didn't look like outbuildings either. And there *was* a mail box in the yard.

I looked at Shelagh. She looked at me. Do we knock on all three doors? Could the doors stand up to a knock?

I surveyed the three candidates again. And noticed only one of the buildings had a chimney. Miss Marple would have been proud.

I walked over to the door and knocked. And waited. A cat appeared from nowhere and started rubbing against my legs. At least someone was home.

And then the door opened and out came the tallest pair of trousers I'd ever seen – they ended just below the owner's armpit. And housed a very gaunt old man who peered at us from beneath his beret.

"George?" I asked.

"George?" he replied, cupping a hand behind his ear.

"George?" I continued, louder this time.

"George?" he shouted.

This had all the hallmarks of a very long conversation.

"Claudine," I said, thinking I'd try another tack and pointed back towards Tuco.

"Claudine?" he echoed, craning a neck outside the door and following my finger toward the horizon.

"Claudine," I confirmed.

"Claudine?" He repeated, turning to Shelagh, who was already backing away and glancing longingly towards the track.

I knew we should have stopped off on the way up and composed a script. I was stuck on the cast list and failing badly.

"*Avez-vous bois de chauffage*?" asked Shelagh in a moment of inspiration. I was about to return to another chorus of 'George?'

"*Bois de chauffage*?" he repeated, making me consider the

possibility that somewhere in those giant trousers lurked a giant parrot.

"*Oui, bois de chauffage,*" said Shelagh, nodding. Had she caught it too? Was there some kind of parrot flu going around.

I stabbed a finger at the huge stack of logs along his drive. "*Avez-vous bois de chauffage à vendre?*" Surely, he had to understand now.

"*Non.*"

The parrot flu fever had broken. He didn't have any logs for sale. Was he even George?

I tried to ask and explain that Claudine had sent us but I could feel a giant elk impersonation coming on. We said goodbye and left. And as for going back to the crossroads to try the other direction – no – I wasn't going anywhere near another George until I had a script in one hand and a large dictionary in the other. If not a can of parrot repellent.

Back home, we had just about given up on the idea of obtaining logs locally when a car pulled up – a battered Citroen 2CV with an equally battered occupant. A stocky man in his early forties climbed out, his face tanned and weather-beaten but with lines that suggested a face that knew how to smile. And huge hands that suggested a life of hard manual labour.

We exchanged a few words which neither of us understood and shook hands. Then we smiled, attempted a few more sentences and decided to fall back on the hand shaking.

He didn't use as many 'r's as Claudine or repeat everything we said like 'He who might have been George.' He even spoke slowly but...

We still couldn't understand a word he said. The cigarette fixed between his lips didn't help. He sounded like a Gallic version of Marlon Brando, with smiles and a wheezy laugh punctuating the mumbled dialogue.

But had I heard the word *bois*?

I seized upon it. "*Bois de chauffage?*"

"*Oui,*" he nodded. And added several other words which trailed off in a haze of cigarette smoke.

After several abortive attempts to re-direct the conversation back to logs, I resorted to sign language – giant elk or no giant elk, I was desperate. I hoped I conveyed the fact that we needed logs for our fire. I may have ordered a dozen wildebeest.

As he drove away, I wondered if we'd ever see him again. I think he said something about returning but whether it was today, tomorrow or sometime next week, I hadn't a clue. I hoped it wouldn't be long, the thought of another fireless night was not a pleasant one.

An hour later he returned. This time, he had company. It looked like he'd brought his father. We exchanged *bonjours* and shook hands and then I launched into my prepared script.

I'd spent the last hour reading through all the adverts for firewood in the local paper and translating them with the help of our dictionary. I'd learnt that logs were ordered not by the ton but by the *stère* – a cubic metre. I'd also noted down a number of likely woods and the going rate. It seemed that most of the wood for sale locally was oak, chestnut or acacia. I had them all jotted down and my ears trained to listen out for them.

I opened with a request for a *stère* of logs. The father replied with a yes. This was a good start. I then asked the price – 250 francs. What type of wood was it? Oak. Could they deliver it? Yes.

This was brilliant. This was what it was supposed to be like. I was having a conversation in French!

It was then that the 'father' turned to his 'son' and said, "I don't know what the bloody hell I'm doing here. He speaks French."

"You're English?" I said, amazed.

"Welsh," came the reply with a speed that conveyed the almost certain probability that I'd just delivered a terrible insult.

But I was impressed. Not only had our log man called round to see if we needed anything but he'd returned within the hour with an interpreter. And he could supply fence posts as well.

This was a man we could do business with.

We ordered three *stère* of logs and fifty fence posts. Which would be delivered the next day. In the meantime, we had to keep warm. We were not going to spend another night wrapped in blankets.

So we scavenged the outbuildings for wood. We combed copses and dragged the underbrush, staggering back to the house with long branches of rotting wood over our shoulders. If it looked flammable we took it. Nothing was going to stop us from having a fire.

A few hours later we all gathered around the lounge fireplace, Gypsy and the two cats vying for the position nearest the fire.

The kindling caught, the flames rose. And then ... out came the smoke and there went the animals. Three worried faces stared back at us from the safety of the hallway.

We quickly closed the fire doors. Our fire was supposed to have two glass doors but one had been broken and replaced with what looked like two scraps of aluminium welded together. It wouldn't win any prizes for style but at least it kept the smoke in.

We returned to our settees and waited for the heat to hit us.

And waited.

Nothing.

So we opened the fire doors to load more wood and a wall of smoke shot out and enveloped the mantelpiece.

Arrggh! We rushed to the windows, flung them open to clear the air, and then tried again.

Same result.

Perhaps if we kept the windows ajar? Sometimes it helps the fire to draw.

It helped the smoke.

This was ridiculous. We couldn't get at the fire without filling the room with smoke.

And the grate was far too small. We couldn't stack the fire, throw in a match and then close the doors for the night. There was barely enough room for a ten minute blaze.

But, strangely enough, it did keep us warm that night – in a lateral fashion. The continual getting up, opening windows, closing windows, fanning the air with the door and fighting Gypsy off as she fastened her teeth around our ankles kept us remarkably active.

Perhaps that was how this fire worked – by providing aerobic exercise for the owners. And I could see exactly what had happened to the missing glass door. I felt like kicking the other one in myself.

The next day we decided to take a longer look at the fire. After all, we'd had years of experience with log burning stoves and coal fires. Surely saving this fire could not be beyond us?

It was what the French call an *insert*, a metal firebox inserted into an existing chimney. As 90% of all heat from an open fire disappears up the chimney, the idea of the *insert* is to trap some of that heat and channel it back into the room. Most inserts have a heat exchanging mechanism above the firebox to strip the heat and feed it back into the living accommodation.

All very logical.

Except that this one seemed to have a smoke exchanger – it took clean air from the lounge and exchanged it for smoke and toxic fumes.

And I couldn't see how the air was supposed to feed the fire. Most log-burners I'd seen had an adjustable vent at the front designed to feed air into the seat of the fire. It was placed just above the ash layer. After a few days the ash layer would build up and start to block the holes and you'd know it was time to clean out the fire. Nice and simple.

But this *insert* had no vents. With the fire doors shut the only way I could see air entering was from beneath – through the ash layer. Which didn't make sense. Wood ash was very fine – not the best medium to percolate air through.

And why was the grate so small? It was a sizeable firebox but only the back half was used. The front half was a hinged metal lid which tipped up to reveal a box underneath – presumably an ash box for cleaning. But why have an ash box twice the size of the grate?

And how were you supposed to empty the ash box? Through the hinged lid at the front of the fire? One scoop at a time?

We checked the ornamental fire surround again and found one of the bricks was loose. Removing it provided a channel for the ash box to slide out. And with the brick and the ash box removed, air could reach underneath the fire. Was this the beginning of a discovery?

Not quite. Air still had to percolate up through a layer of ash – and what was the point of having an ash box if the fire only worked when it wasn't in place?

Unless the airflow was regulated by the ash box? Like an organ stop?

It still did not entirely ring true but we tried it. We lit fires with every combination of ash box in, ash box out, ash box halfway in; ash box out, brick in. You name it, we watched smoke billow over it.

Perhaps it was the chimney? It had probably been years since it had been cleaned and what better reason for a smoking fire than a dirty chimney?

This sounded like a sensible course of action.

If we could find somewhere to stick a brush.

We searched the roof of the *insert*. For some reason instead of having one large flue, it had six small ones, none of them large enough to take a brush. And there was no access hatch in the chimneybreast or in any of the rooms upstairs. We looked, tracing the path of the chimney to the roof. The only access had to be from the top, via the chimneypot.

Sometimes you can tell when fate has decided that certain tasks are beyond your reach by the number and level of obstacles that are thrown in your path. Some people take heed and give up. Others ignore the omens and press on.

They are called madmen.

And Shelagh was married to one.

"*You're* not going on the roof?"

I didn't like the emphasis on the word 'you're'.

"Why not? We've got the brushes."

"But *you*?"

There it was again. If anything stronger.

But you don't live with someone for twenty years without knowing how to win the occasional argument.

"Do *you* want to go on the roof?" I asked, knowing that Shelagh wouldn't set foot on a ladder unless there were at least six men to hold it steady and an ambulance crew on stand-by.

"No-o."

"Do you want to spend another day trying to find a 'George' who does?"

Checkmate. But was our ladder long enough to reach the roof?

It wasn't. Not by a storey.

We stood in the courtyard and surveyed the roofline. Was there another way? Perhaps via the outbuildings?

I could see what looked like a footstool balanced on the ridge of the outbuilding roof where it met the wall of the house. At that point, it was only about three or four feet to the main roof's gutter. If I placed the ladder up against the gable wall of the far outbuilding, I could walk along the L shaped ridge and use the footstool to climb onto the main roof.

Shelagh looked at the roof and then at me. It was not the prelude to a vote of confidence.

I tried to explain to her that this was the *Sud*, where roofs were dry and low-pitched and covered in householders. I'd read about it, I'd seen the pictures. It was one of the joys of owning an old canal-tiled roof where only gravity held the tiles in place – the need to spend the odd afternoon sitting on the roof, reshuffling tiles and replacing missing or broken ones. It was a way of life. And if an eighty year-old *paysan* could do it – why couldn't I?

I think Shelagh was on the verge of providing me with a detailed list, when I quickly changed the subject back to ladders. And as neither five extra men nor an ambulance were in obvious sight, the subject of my fitness for the task was quickly dropped.

So I propped the ladder up against the gable wall, Shelagh handed me the rods and brush, and up I went. At the top, I paused to test the ridge tiles with a few trial prods. Everything seemed in order. The ridge tiles were stable and I could feel no give as I tentatively edged myself off the ladder and crawled onto the roof.

I moved one limb at a time, straddling the ridge, shifting my weight slowly from hand to knee, sliding the rods and brush ahead of me, feeling out the tiles for any sign of give.

I was not looking to win any prizes for speed or bravery. Even though the roof was dry and low-pitched, it was still a roof and the ground was still the ground.

How things change. When I was young I had no fear of heights. I'd swing from the tops of trees, oblivious to gravity, secure in the knowledge that if I fell, I was quick and agile enough to grab a passing branch.

I sometimes miss that single-perspective certainty of youth. If anyone then had asked the younger me if I realised how dangerous it was, I'd have replied, "of course I do." But the relevance of the question would have eluded me. I wasn't intending to fall so what was the point in asking? All I could envision was success.

But the older me had wisdom. And Wisdom had commissioned Imagination to produce a report on the dangers of walking on roofs. Apparently there were at least fifty ways to break a neck, more if you skimmed through the appendices.

Then I saw the first wasp - something Imagination had neglected to warn me about. It flew into a gap under one of the tiles in front of my left hand. I froze.

Another wasp appeared. And then another. Coming out from the tiles this time as well as going in.

A wasp nest!

Could I pass by quietly without disturbing them?

I edged forward, holding my breath, trying to glide over the tiles without making any noise.

Crunch. A tile shifted under the weight of my left hand and grated against its neighbour.

The next second there were wasps flying around my head and I was up and running. My fear of wasps pushing everything else aside, I made the elbow of the roof in under a second. I could feel the slight give in the ridge tiles, the scraping, crunchy sound they made as their edges rasped against each other. But what did that matter, I was being pursued by wasps!

I didn't stop at the elbow, I leaned into the bend and jumped across the angle, momentum and fear carrying me across the entire thirty yards of roof to the wall of the main house.

Wisdom had left me sometime between the third and fourth wasp. And taken all fifty ways of breaking my neck with it. Leaving me blinkered again, one goal in mind - to escape. I wouldn't have been surprised if I'd snapped a couple of rods together and pole-vaulted onto the main roof. I was in that determined a frame of mind.

"What are you doing!" shouted an incredulous Shelagh.

What was I doing? Hadn't she ever seen a man run across a roof, pursued by a cloud of killer wasp mutant death hornets before?

"Wasps," I said breathlessly as I looked back along the ridge, ducking every time I thought I heard a buzz. I couldn't see any wasps. They must have given up.

Unlike me. I'd reached the footstool. The main roof was only a few feet away...

But would the footstool take my weight? The two steps looked strong enough but the plywood seat had a disconcertingly bowed and rotten appearance.

And the footstool wasn't exactly stable - it wobbled when I gave it a prod. So I slid it back and forth along the ridge until I found

something approaching a stable position. And then looked at it
again. And looked at the ground – some thirty feet below. One
mistake and Shelagh might find herself treated to an impromptu
visual performance of *It's Raining Men.*

But what choice did I have? The killer wasp mutant death hornets
would need at least another ten minutes to quieten down. I had to
press on.

I carefully shifted my weight onto the first step, then even more
carefully onto the seat. Leaning forward I was almost able to stretch
a knee onto the lower tiles of the main roof. I was a few inches
short. Three or four wasps behind me and I might have made it.

I tried several more attempts, hoping that, somehow, either my
legs would grow longer or the roof would drop. Neither happened.

A braver person might have tried a small jump, flexed the knees
and pushed off against the footstool. But that would have meant
placing an extra strain on the plywood, which might have responded
resiliently like a springboard or fallen apart and deposited me on
the patio.

Imagination favoured the patio scenario.

It was then that I noticed the skylight. It was only a few feet away
from my outstretched hand. Someone could catch hold of a section
of pole from there and pull me up. Couldn't they?

They could. A minute later Shelagh's disembodied hand appeared
from the depths of the attic skylight – somewhat reminiscent of the
Lady of the Lake, I thought – and I waved a pole towards it.

Within seconds I was half pulled, half crawling onto the lower
section of the hip roof. Success!

I edged upwards towards the ridge, taking great care to spread
my weight and not crack anything. And scanning the tiles ahead for
any sign of wasps, hornets or nesting giant rocs.

Once on the ridge it was easier, the tiles were larger and
cemented in. And then I was over and off the ridge and heading
down towards the chimney on the far side.

It wasn't too bad. If I didn't look down or scream. And the view
was superb. I could almost enjoy this, I thought, for one wild
moment of abandon.

I wedged my feet against the base of the chimney and started to
assemble the brush. One by one, I attached each section, screwing
the rods together, and pushing the brush down the chimney. This
was going very well.

And I couldn't hear any screams to stop from Shelagh – so either
everything was all right inside the lounge or she'd been buried by a
cave-in.

Suddenly the brush refused to descend any further. I didn't think
I'd reached the fire so perhaps I'd found the obstruction? I started

to work the brush back and forth, pushing, pulling, rotating...

And then...

Oh God! I hadn't, had I?

I withdrew the rods as quick as I could. Pulling the pole up hand over fist until...

I had.

The last section of pole came up by itself. I'd unscrewed the brush. If the flue wasn't blocked before, it certainly was now.

With fate's usual impeccable timing the logs arrived as soon as I'd removed all possibility of using them in the lounge fire. But we did have the kitchen range ... and its fourteen radiators.

Not that we had much confidence in that system, we'd had an old range in England and that had had problems keeping six radiators lukewarm. This one looked of a similar ilk.

But we were nothing if not game. We had logs, we had paper, we had kindling. And soon we had a fire. We had no instructions with the range but there was a lever at the front with a large picture of a chicken on one side and a radiator on the other. Even my non-mechanically minded brain could work that one out so I pushed the lever to the radiator position.

Next we had to set the radiator pumps. There was a cupboard in the adjoining outhouse which gave access to the back of the range. It looked like the London Underground map in there. There were pipes everywhere, connecting, interconnecting, appearing, disappearing.

But at least I could identify two pumps. I switched one on. It whirred. I switched the other one on and pipes started juddering loudly in sympathy. I switched it off. Over the coming days we experimented with every combination of the two pumps at various speed settings until we found one that moved water through the system without an accompanying drum roll on the pipes.

But 3,000 square feet of house with nine-foot high ceilings was not going to be greatly affected by fourteen lukewarm radiators. Even with all the ones upstairs turned off we couldn't raise the temperature significantly in those left.

We tried everything we could to boost the range. We riddled the firebox every few minutes, we had all the air vents set to maximum, we opened the doors of the range, we tried bellows. But still we couldn't raise the temperature of the water in the boiler above 35°C. And by the time the pumps moved the water to the radiators – via what appeared to be close on ten miles of pipes – that temperature dropped to the low twenties.

If we both clustered around the lounge radiator we could keep our hands warm – but little else.

So we gave up on the radiators and moved our lounge into the kitchen. If we couldn't use the range to heat the radiators we could at least use it to heat the kitchen.

Couldn't we?

I turned the range to chicken and we huddled around the oven in the evenings, sat back in our chairs with our feet resting on the hob. It wasn't what you could call hot but it wasn't cold either. With the oven doors open you could almost call it pleasant.

But a kitchen is not a lounge. Even with a settee and a couple of chairs pulled through it wasn't the same. I'd had the lounge cabled for television, I'd set up the speakers for the stereo, all our tapes and records were there.

After a few nights of warmth in the kitchen listening to BBC Radio Four go in and out of phase we moved back to the lounge. We had to get that fire going.

So the next day we bought a flue hatch from a hardware shop in Aurignac and attacked the chimneybreast in our bedroom.

Once started upon a course of action you either give up or see it through to the end. We were not in a giving-up frame of mind. It was us or the fire.

We made a guess as to where we thought the brush might have lodged, drew a square on the wallpaper and then attacked it with an angle-grinder. After all, it would be handy to have access to the flue without having to climb onto the roof.

After an inch of soft plaster we found the brick flue. A few minutes later we were shining a torch into the blackness. Up and down we shone the light, where was the brush?

There!

It was a foot or so below the hatch. I reached in and pulled it out. Success!

It had lodged where the square brick flue of the bedroom met the smaller angled metal flue from the lounge. I couldn't see any other obstruction and both flues looked clean – at least, as clean as any chimney can. Whatever was wrong with the fire, it wasn't the chimney.

Which meant it had to be something else.

Which meant another close look at the fire.

Which meant another five minutes kneeling in front of the *insert* with my head stuck inside the firebox waiting for inspiration to strike.

Could I take it apart? Could I combine the six smaller flues into one larger one? And why was the air being directed up through the ash-layer? For that to work, the ash would have to be less fine.

Like coal.

Was the fire designed to burn coal?

And so began our search for coal. Which, amazingly, does not exist in South-West France.

"Charbon? Pourquoi?" we would be asked by incredulous shop-keepers. Apparently we were living in a log burning region. Wood was cheap and plentiful. Why would anyone want coal?

Further enquiry elicited the response that perhaps someone near Cazeres might stock it. Cazeres being mentioned in the kind of hushed tones that implied it was just the kind of place where anomalous acts such as the burning of coal might still be practised.

A trip to Cazeres was met with further incredulity. *"Charbon? Pourquoi?"*

It was in danger of becoming a catch-phrase.

After turning down charcoal – I think they thought we were planning a barbecue – we returned home, fuelless.

I still do not know what is wrong with our French.

We'd spend hours in preparation. Working out what we were going to say, looking up all the words in the dictionary, cobbling the sentences together. Trying to make sure they elucidated simple responses like *oui* or *non*. And when that was impossible we made a list of all the likely replies and made rough translations.

It was like writing a scene from a play. We had the whole conversation written down and scripted. And then brimming with confidence we'd pick up the phone or march into the office, out would come our first question and everyone would start ad libbing.

Even our simple questions that couldn't possibly merit an answer other than yes or no somehow managed to breach a dam full of unexpected sentences.

It was as though we were standing over them with a gong trying to catch them out – *yes* and *no* suddenly disappeared from their vocabulary. In the end we had to show them the script and point to what they were supposed to say.

"Do you sell coal?"

"Charbon? Pourquoi?"

"No, not '*charbon, pourquoi?*' The only possible answer is yes or no. Look, I've written it down."

"Non."

"Yes I have. It's here."

"Charbon?"

"I know - *Pourquoi?*" And by that time I couldn't think of a good reason for burning coal either.

I think the French are just naturally inquisitive. They want to know the full context of your enquiry before telling you that you can't have it. Then they come up with a long list of what you really need and baffle you even more.

Time to call in the experts.

We'd seen a *cheminée* showroom on the outskirts of St. Gaudens. Perhaps they could help us. Or failing that, know where we could buy coal.

It was a large showroom, abounding with *inserts*, ranges and mock fireplaces of every description. Surely they had to have one like ours?

We checked them all, kneeling down and pushing our heads inside for a good look. What kind of flue did they have, what kind of grate, how did they arrange the ash box.

In hindsight we must have looked pretty strange, knelt down in front of fires and ovens with our heads inside, looking more like opportunist suicides than potential customers.

But we made some interesting discoveries. The first one being that our fire was not normal. All the shop's *inserts* had the flue placed at the highest point of the fire-box. Ours wasn't. Its highest point was at the front by the doors. Which might explain why the smoke was directed forwards and into the room.

And no other design had six small flues or that ridiculously small grate. They used every inch of the fire box – after all they were designed to burn logs, not twigs.

But most important of all we found a catalogue containing all the latest design research on *cheminée* technology. This was exactly what we wanted. It showed us how to install an *insert*. It had diagrams. It had words we could translate. Words unfettered by interlocking 'r's or extraneous questions.

We didn't bother to ask for coal after that. After all, *charbon, pourquoi?*

Back home, I studied the *cheminée* designs in greater detail.

Instead of using up the warm air in the lounge, they suggested taking cold air from outside and ducting that into the fire. Very sensible.

Didn't we have a strange hole in the outside wall behind the fire?

We went outside to check.

We did.

Or, more accurately, we had. We'd noticed it the first day, couldn't work out what it was, couldn't think of a good reason for having it, came up with several good reasons for not having it. And blocked it up.

Could that be why the fire smoked?

More tests. Ash box in, hole unblocked, brick out; ash box out, left leg in...

Thirty minutes later we staggered into the sunlight like a pair of kippers. Clouds of smoke hung eerily inside the lounge, flies coughed on the window-sills.

But we had noticed a difference. With the hole unblocked we could successfully channel cold air from the outside directly into the lounge. The ash box cleverly prevented it from reaching the fire.

The more I looked at the design of the fire the more I came to the conclusion that I was looking at the log-burning equivalent of the toilet at the bottom of the stairs.

This was not a commercially available fire.

This was the product of a creative householder and his tool box.

A creative householder of rare genius. Someone who'd managed to bring all the ingredients of state-of-the-art *cheminée* design and make it his own. He'd taken cold air from the outside, fed it into the lounge, let it circulate for a while then exchanged it for smoke.

The only item he'd missed was the recuperator system to pump the smoke throughout the house.

Perhaps that was next year's project?

The inventor of Meccano[2] has a lot to answer for.

But the evenings were getting warmer. Or was it the fact that we'd discovered the joys of wearing two pairs of trousers? With my track suit bottoms over my jeans and two thick sweaters, it was almost pleasant.

In the latter weeks of March we remembered our ski clothes – even better. We would watch TV in our salopettes. Luckily no one ever rang the doorbell on those nights. I'm not sure what they'd have thought, having the door opened by a couple who looked as if they'd just stepped off a ski-lift.

But we were warm and gradually the nights were becoming warmer too.

And we were not going to spend another winter with that fire. It had to go. Which it did. A few months later with the help of a sledgehammer.

We now have a log-burner and have reintroduced the word warm into our winter vocabulary.

Pipes and *Plombiers*

"Cavagnac? Cavagnac! Le voleur de la Montagne!"

I don't think the plumber liked our house's previous owner.

"*La grande merde! Merde! Merde! Merde! Merde! Merde! MERDE!*"

We waited. I didn't think there were any more *merdes* but there was a lot of muttering and, I suspect, some spitting, along with the mandatory arm waving and even more colourful expletives. From what we could understand our plumber would never have come to our house if he'd known who the previous owner had been.

Eventually we calmed him down long enough to hear about his friend's house and how it had been a Cavagnac, the aforementioned 'Thief of the Mountains' and All-Pyrenean *Grande Merde*, who had caused the damage. Everything had had to be ripped out, and never – *never* – would he have anything to do with that man again.

There was another bout of *merdes* and spitting on the ground. Plus a ritual grinding of the spittle into our tarmac drive with the toe of his boot. This was a pretty impressive demonstration of Gallic dislike and I dreaded what would happen if our previous owner took this moment to return to his old house and pay the new tenants a visit.

Though I suspect it would have been filed away under justifiable homicide – there's bound to be some ancient French *Loi Plombier* that grants all plumbers the right to execute summary justice whenever the wind blows from a particular direction.

It seemed that our vendor's expertise as a designer of fires was only exceeded by his flair for plumbing. After all, plumbing does have far more scope for the creative mind – all those miles of pipes and limitless configurations. It must be something like designing a railway network; I could see the appeal.

But I could see a plumber who didn't.

The problem had started on our first day – as most of our problems had. I think we must have ripped a sizeable hole in the space-time continuum the moment we set foot on French soil. It's the only explanation that makes sense.

Unlike our hot water system.

We had been told that the previous owner had installed a dual system with a summer/winter switch. It sounded clever. The kitchen range heated the water in the winter, storing the water in a tank, and in the summer you switched over to a gas-fired heater.

Very sensible and it may well have worked four years ago when it was last used but it didn't appear to want to work for us. We tried the gas heater first, we connected up our new bottle of Butagaz, turned on the tap and...

Nothing.

Was our system set to summer or winter?

We went in search of the switch.

Unfortunately it wasn't obvious. We were told it lived in the cupboard behind the range but so did about eight others and ten spiders. Eventually, by trial and error, we found something that worked and discovered the gas heater didn't.

So we called in a plumber.

Who arrived in his Citroen 2CV van a few hours later. A slight, smiling sexagenarian wearing bright blue overalls and a beret climbed out. I went to shake his hand and was surprised to be offered an elbow. I'd never shaken an elbow before and wasn't quite sure what to do. Should I grasp it manfully and give it a tug or roll up my sleeves and rub elbows?

I went for the manful tug, always the best option during a First Contact situation. I later learned that elbow shaking was the local custom when your hands were too dirty to inflict on the unwary.

Either that or he was a Mason.

We explained our problem as best we could, resorting to the script on frequent occasions and reinforcing the message with a certain amount of gesticulation. Antlers, however, were wisely kept to a minimum.

It started well. The plumber understood. He'd disconnect the hot water and take the boiler away for tests.

Three hours later he was still trying.

The problem appeared to be that he couldn't shut off the hot water. Every time he thought he'd succeeded, he'd turn on a hot tap and water would appear. It was like magic.

We'd see him in various locations throughout the house, pushing his beret back over his head and scratching his hair, then rushing off into another room and trying a tap or tracing the path of a pipe. I don't think he could believe the number of appliances we had. Just when he thought he'd located every tap in the house, he'd open a door and there were another three.

I think he liked his plumbing simple – exposed pipes which you could trace, useful taps where you could isolate appliances, labels.

Whereas our system had been designed by an artist. An artist with enough copper pipe to match his imagination. We had pipes interconnecting and disappearing into concrete floors and walls, splitting into threes and fours, recombining, disappearing and, for all I knew, breeding in the wall cavities.

Heath Robinson[3] could have taken notes.

But it did have a built-in resilience. You couldn't switch it off. We could probably take a minor nuclear strike on a back bathroom and still have a tap working somewhere in the house.

Our plumber went home, temporarily defeated. But he would be back. Tomorrow.

The next day, our plumber returned, convinced he'd solved the problem. Somehow, the hot and cold water supply had become connected – probably a faulty mixer tap. Did we have any mixer taps?

"Eight or nine," I replied. I'd lost count of the sinks let alone the taps. Several mixer taps later he was still confused. It was then that he found out that Monsieur Cavagnac had been the previous owner.

Several *merdes* later he was still spitting.

We thought he was going to leave us. At one point he walked off into the garden and we thought that was it. He'd abandoned his car and stormed off into the undergrowth never to be seen again!

But then we saw the traditional legs apart stance and realised … He was using our wall. Which just goes to show what he thought of our plumbing.

But you don't have to stay long in France to appreciate that the French have a different attitude to the British when it comes to urinating in public. In Britain, it's an offence. In France, it's a basic human right.

At the top of an alpine chairlift or the edge of a supermarket car park, I've seen it all. In a manner of speaking. Although the top of the Alpine chairlift was by far the greater of the two surprises. The last thing you expect to find at 3,000 metres in the middle of a blizzard is a Frenchman with his legs apart.

Shelagh is certain it's something territorial. An ancient male need to mark out a territory and ward off other males. Though how many males needed warding off at the top of the chairlift I'm not sure. Certainly I didn't feel threatened or imparted with the need to mark an adjacent spot. But then I'm not French. And it was cold.

But I think she may have a point. And it might explain the strange behaviour of our dustmen.

Our property marks the boundary between the communes of Cassagne and Tuco. And every Tuesday morning the dust-cart wends its way up from Cassagne to empty our bins. And every time, the driver gets out, walks up to the tree at the end of our lane and relieves himself. Every Tuesday without fail, bank holidays included. He then climbs back in the truck, turns round, and drives back to Cassagne.

We've never seen the Tuco dustmen, but we have a sneaking suspicion that a similar border ritual is carried out on another day and on another tree.

Having successfully warded off any wandering plumbers from our back garden, our plumber returned. And decided the next step was to dismantle the summer/winter switch. We'd given up on the range by then so it seemed the sensible solution.

Yards of superfluous pipes and taps were removed. It was amazing just to watch. The more I looked at the pipework in our cupboard behind the range, the more I could see a faithful interpretation of the entire London Underground in copper – complete with sidings and points. It was a work of art. But was it plumbing?

Gradually London Underground was dismantled – privatised and stripped down – the hot water tank disconnected and the water drained.

I dreaded the turning on of our kitchen hot tap. But it had to be done. A few swift turns ... and out came the water, as strong as ever.

I thought our plumber was going to cry.

But he didn't, he gave us a resigned smile and proffered an elbow. He'd be back.

Now, I know as much about plumbing as I do about the internal combustion engine but I couldn't see what all the fuss was about. Why didn't he just cut off the water supply to the entire house? Hot, cold or lukewarm, what did it matter? It was the water heater that didn't work, so why not just cut off the water, disconnect it and take it away?

Shelagh told me I was being too simplistic, and proceeded to explain that if there was cold water bleeding into the hot water pipes then we'd never get really hot water. There'd always be an amount of cold being fed into the system.

It sounded plausible – technical explanations always do, for a while – but was the price of really hot water worth a live-in plumber?

The next day dawned with two plumbers on our doorstep. Were they breeding in the wall cavities too?

Luckily not. Our plumber had decided to bring a friend. A local guru, renowned as a man who knew his pipes.

The two of them raced around the house, a blur of bright blue, switching taps on and off, deep in conversation one minute and chuckling the next.

At least someone could see the funny side.

The funniest by far being the cupboard behind the range. The friend couldn't keep away. He kept going back for another look, rummaging through the large pile of discarded copper and giggling.

But eventually they had to admit defeat. This was a pipe too far – even for a guru.

"Chop all the pipes off at ground level and start again," was his advice. Slightly on the drastic side, I thought. We'd only rung up to have a water heater looked at.

But I suppose that's the plumber's-eye view of the world – all pipes should be exposed, easy to maintain and well-labelled. Me, I see nothing wrong in hiding pipes. Or in the occasional scale model of the London Underground. It all adds to life's rich tapestry.

I turned the conversation back to the water heater. Wasn't it about time that someone looked at it?

With the water turned off at the mains, the gas heater was disconnected in five minutes. It then disappeared into the back of the van and with a raised beret, a smile and an elbow the two plumbers disappeared. No doubt with a new story to regale their grandchildren with.

I was left wondering how much it would all cost. Plumbers had a deserved reputation for being expensive and we'd had two and a half days worth. And that was before anyone touched the boiler. God knows what he'd find wrong with that?

Perhaps he'd give us a reduction for entertaining his friends?

It was then that a frightening thought occurred. Our vendor wouldn't have, would he? Surely not? People don't build their own gas-fired water heaters, do they?

I thought of the *insert*. I thought of the London Underground in copper. I thought of bleeding water taps. And worst of all, an exploding plumber visiting his workshop roof considerably quicker than anyone thought possible.

A day later our plumber called. He was alive and had fixed the boiler. A small piece of plastic valve had cracked and broken. He'd replaced it and was ready to put it all back again.

He still wasn't happy about leaving us with a system that bled cold water but was resigned to the fact that life wasn't fair and some things were meant to remain a mystery.

He was a philosophical plumber.

Animals Behaving Typically

"Cat fight!"

"What!" I sprang from my pillow, engaging automatic pilot on the way down, one leg in a pair of jeans, the other still asleep.

What the hell was happening?

"Cat fight!" screamed Shelagh once more from some dark place on the other side of the bed.

An awake eye peered at the clock – 1:35 – the middle of the night. That's why it was so dark.

I staggered across the room in search of slippers ... or the light switch ... or possibly the window. Brain was not quite sure. Legs were even less so. Especially the solitary one, half-buried in a pair of jeans.

I fell down. It seemed a sensible course of action. And it gave Brain an extra few seconds to arrive at an explanation.

Something about a cat fight?

A strange yowling noise burst in through the open window. Oh my God! Now I remembered. The Black Cat! Both our cats had been injured in fights – Guinny had had to have stitches, Gally had limped for a week.

Was the Black Cat back? Was it attacking our cats?

I stopped struggling with the trousers, threw them off and staggered arms out-stretched through the gloom towards the bedroom door. Which immediately flew back and met me halfway, Shelagh having got there first.

Closely followed by Gypsy.

I was somewhere in between. Dazed, confused, half-asleep and under attack from a playful puppy. A predicament lent a considerable piquancy when it's pitch black and your clothes are on the other side of the room.

I grabbed my dressing gown from the back of the bedroom door and stumbled into the hallway, trying to fight off Gypsy, get dressed and find a light switch all at the same time.

And then there was light. At least for a short while – our hall light being on a timer carefully designed to extinguish itself ten seconds before you really needed it to. Like when you're desperately trying to unlock the front door and find your shoes at the same time.

And there's nothing quite so unexpected in a dark hallway as a cold nose slipping under your dressing gown as you bend over in search of shoes.

I screamed.

Gypsy barked.

Strange nocturnal noises wafted in through the cat flap.

Whereupon I was admonished – stop playing with the puppy and go save our cats!

As if I was trying to do anything else.

Gypsy continued to bark and boldly go places where noses hadn't and shouldn't have gone before. I struggled with the door. It opened, I fell out. Gypsy's lead was thrust into my hand, plaintive yowling drifted in from my right ... and then we were off. Man and dog sprinting across the fields towards the sounds of battle. Surely even the Black Cat wouldn't hang around once he caught sight of a giant dog bounding towards him.

"It's coming from over here!" I shouted over my shoulder as we plunged through the stubble of last year's maize crop.

"Is it Gally?" shouted Shelagh.

It was difficult to tell, it was coming from such a long way off. Not so much in the field as over the far hill.

And was it a cat?

I stopped.

And listened.

Wasn't that a cow?

I looked back at Shelagh, standing on the patio bathed in the glow of the outside light. An anxious figure staring fieldwards, flanked by two interested cats.

Two cats?

I looked at Gypsy. She smiled and wagged her tail; this was what life should be like – faithful hound and master stride out into the night to hunt cows by moonlight.

I was not so enthused.

It had started on our second night. I think the local feline population had called an emergency meeting as soon as they sniffed out our arrival – cats having that uncanny ability – and a ginger tom had won the ballot for first shot at the newcomers.

He tried the 'Homeless Cat's Plaintive Serenade Under The Bedroom Window In The Middle Of The Night' ploy – an old favourite and usually a sure-fire winner. Certainly, we'd fallen for it before. But this time we had two cats in residence and felt that our quota had been well and truly filled.

The next night he tried the 'Homeless Cat's Plaintive Serenade From Under The Bed' ploy. A much bolder stratagem and a considerable surprise at two o'clock in the morning. One minute I was asleep, enjoying a cat-free dream, the next I was awoken by a discordant caterwauling emanating from less than one foot below my left ear.

And he was caterwauling in French. I could tell by the accordion accompaniment.

Having a cat flap certainly has its disadvantages. Singing cats unexpectedly gaining access to your bedroom in the middle of the night being one of them. Sharing a bed with a very large puppy has only one advantage. The singing cat didn't stay long enough to appreciate it.

But he did appreciate the cat flap again – at great speed – closely followed by the aforementioned very large puppy.

With the failure of the singing ginger cat, the starving black cat was sent in. Its job was to beg for food. Well, perhaps not so much beg as ask very quietly when no one was around then come back at night and strip the property of everything edible – including Gally's favourite fishy-shaped croquettes.

And the best part of a loaf of bread – the middle part – carefully excavated through its paper wrapper.

Its stomach bulging from the night's endeavours, the black cat then climbed to the top of our fridge freezer and was promptly sick from a great height. Lending a textured wavy stripe to our fridge door.

We could forgive a starving cat the croquettes, perhaps the bread as well. But I think the wavy stripe was going a bit too far.

After that we kept a nightly watch.

And so did our cats.

Especially Gally, who had taken the theft of his croquettes very badly. They were his favourite. And more than that – they were fishy-shaped.

We'd first noticed his penchant for fishy-shaped crunchy bits in Devon. The cat supplement we bought there was composed of variously shaped and flavoured croquettes but we noticed that Gally invariably picked out the fish-flavoured ones. He even developed a rather bizarre ritual of biting their heads off first and spitting them out. Leaving a residue of assorted meat-flavoured stars covered in tiny fish heads.

Guinny's reaction to the invasion of her home was somewhat different. She underwent a transformation … and became … Guinevere, Warrior Kitten.

We first noticed the manifestation of her new identity one night when our evening peace was destroyed by what sounded like a herd of medium-sized elephants rampaging up and down our stairs. Naturally we assumed it was Gypsy and shouted at her to be quiet. A sad black face stared back at us from an armchair on the other side of the room. For the first time in her life the words 'Not Guilty' and

'Gypsy' could be used in the same sentence.

Intrigued, we tracked the noise to its source. And found Guinny – aka Guinevere, Warrior Kitten – and normally such a quiet unassuming cat, performing one of her new training work-outs – charging up and down the stairs, leaping at imaginary foes and raking the wallpaper with her claws.

I think she'd been watching too many Sword and Sorcery films – evil cat burns down young kitten's village, young kitten spends many years learning martial arts, young kitten grows up to avenge attack on village and evil cat gets just desserts.

Unfortunately the Black Cat hadn't seen the film, or if he had he'd slept through the ending. The result being, a fortnight later, a trip to the vet for the Warrior Kitten and a renewed nightly vigilance.

When Gally followed a week later – his back legs having seized up after a particularly nasty bite – our vigilance bordered on obsession.

We slept with the windows open, ears programmed to react to the first yowl of battle.

And anything remotely similar.

Sometimes it was a cow, sometimes a bird, sometimes a bandy-legged cicada with a strange stuttering chirrup. The variety of weird nocturnal noises in the French countryside is truly vast – especially when you're wide awake and really concentrating.

But sometimes it was the real thing. And we'd spend an anxious half an hour accounting for all our cats and often as not trying to talk one of them down from a tree.

Anyone who has ever had to rescue a cat from a tree knows that co-operation from the animal in question is non-existent. And anyone who has ever climbed a tree would also confirm that a dressing gown and slippers are not recommended climbing attire.

And a puppy is no help whatsoever.

I wasn't sure how much more I could take. A decent night's sleep became a distant memory, and the words, 'Cat Fight', a nightly scream. I lost count of the number of times I found myself dragged from sleep and deposited somewhere between the bed and the window, not really knowing why or what I was supposed to be doing other than running somewhere and defending something small and furry.

We tried keeping the cats in at night but that didn't work as no one thought of informing Shelagh's subconscious. She'd wake up screaming 'Cat Fight!' I'd hit the ceiling and various articles of furniture and then we'd have a slow descent into reality.

Made even slower by the all-encompassing darkness and the leg-encompassing jaws of our faithful puppy.

Our one consolation were the words of our vet. It would soon be over, he told us. In the spring, cats fight. It's the season for it.

I hoped someone would tell Shelagh's subconscious.

The cats were not the first of our menagerie to visit the vet. That honour had fallen to Gypsy within the first week. We hadn't been able to have her vaccinated in England due to the export regulations – no vaccinations were allowed in the month prior to embarkation – so she was overdue.

The cats made the most of it, sitting on the patio making little needle signs with their paws as Gypsy passed by, her nose pressed against the inside of the car window. Cats can be cruel. Especially to impressionable puppies.

Once in Aurignac, we dragged Gypsy into the waiting room. I think she could smell the warning signs as soon as we approached the vet's – years of panicked animals having marked the surrounding area. But once inside, Gypsy settled down and apart from the odd verse of nervous singing she was fine.

Unlike Shelagh, who can't be left alone in a vet's waiting room – not when there are leaflets and posters about animal diseases to be worried over. She spent a good five minutes in front of a map of France showing the number of rabies cases by *département*. And mentally crossing off a large chunk of north-eastern France from our list of places to visit. Next came the leaflets – tastefully arranged on a long coffee table in order of skin-crawl, with everything you never wanted to know about fleas, tapeworms, ticks and roundworms.

The tick leaflet was Shelagh's favourite. I'm not sure how many times the picture on the front had been magnified but this tick looked like a minor asteroid with skin problems. And it carried an infection – pyroplasm – which was endemic in France, especially South-West France, and fatal for dogs.

This was something not mentioned in any literature we'd ever read on living in France. And we'd read a considerable amount. By the time it was our turn to see the vet, Shelagh was ready to pack up and return to England.

"Why didn't you tell me about pyroplasm?" she hissed.

"I'd never heard about it!"

"Hmm."

It was a 'hmm' I recognised, a 'hmm' that signified that judgement had been suspended and, unless I wanted to suffer a similar fate, I'd better hope the vet comes up with some conciliatory words. Preferably along the lines of, 'pyroplasm, *pas de problème*.'

I dragged Gypsy along the tiled floor into the surgery – it's a wise vet who keeps his floor well greased – and Shelagh followed behind clutching her tick leaflet.

The vet was a small grey-haired man with a white coat and a

ready smile. And a profound love of animals. We talked for a while about Gypsy's pedigree. At least, we tried. Even though his 'little of English' turned out to be a good deal greater than our *peu de Français*, we couldn't quite explain what a lurcher was. In hindsight, we should have passed her off as a greyhound. We were all happy with greyhound – it's the same word in English and French. But we made the mistake of striving for accuracy and explaining how Gypsy was a deerhound greyhound cross. I toyed with the idea about adding my suspicion that she was also part crocodile but thought better of it – we were having enough trouble trying to find the French for deerhound.

We tried *lévrier de cerf*, a chimera of our own invention; *lévrier* being the name of a Gypsy look-alike we'd seen on a poster on the waiting room wall and *cerf* being French for stag.

The vet stared at us blankly. *Lévrier de cerf*?

We tried a different approach. Lurchers were hunting dogs. *Chien de chasse*? Hunting for the pot? The traditional dog of the Gypsies?

The vet shook his head.

Shelagh was about to give up but I was a person who knew the French for Gypsy – I'd looked it up in case anyone ever asked what Gypsy's name meant. Here was my first opportunity to use it.

Unfortunately *Gitane* is probably more famous as a brand of cigarette than as French for Gypsy. And my attempted explanation that she was *le chien de chasse pour les Gitanes*, probably gave the impression that the English countryside was awash with dogs specially bred to hunt cigarettes.

A little French is a dangerous thing.

The vaccination over, Shelagh turned the conversation quickly towards pyroplasm. Yes, it was a problem, he told us, but there was a vaccination. Unfortunately, Gypsy was too young. We'd have to bring her back in May when she'd be old enough. In the meantime we could spray her, there was a *produit* that you could apply every month that gave some protection.

And we'd have to spray Rhiannon, as horses could catch it as well.

Leaving the surgery, we didn't know what to think. Was pyroplasm such a killer? And yet dogs were so common, most farms seemed to have at least four. Did they spray them regularly? Were they vaccinated? We greatly doubted it. But to read the literature you couldn't imagine a stray dog surviving in the wild for more than a few months.

We decided to investigate further.

Over the next few weeks, we introduced pyroplasm casually into every conversation we could, hoping to hear comforting words like –

it's not a serious problem, you can spray if you like but we never have.

Instead we heard about dead pets and dogs saved from death by last minute ministrations from the vet.

We couldn't find a dog owner who hadn't had first-hand experience.

Shelagh's first, second and third thoughts were to leave for England immediately. She'd had enough. If she'd known that she was endangering her animals by moving to France she'd never have come.

That gradually gave way to a ban on Gypsy's walks into long grass, woods or any other suspected tick haunt. And the pyroplasm leaflet became bedtime reading – ideal material to keep you awake while awaiting an imminent cat fight.

In early April, the worst happened. Presumably, having survived the cat fighting season, we were due for our next test. And what a test it was. Gypsy wouldn't eat her dinner, wasn't interested in biting my leg and decided to spend the day crashed out on her beanbag.

Out came the thermometer. And then in went the thermometer. Even that didn't seem to bring Gypsy out of her lethargy.

Her temperature was over 40°C, way above normal. And her eyes and gums were pale and anaemic – Shelagh knew all the symptoms of pyroplasm off by heart by that time.

She called the vet and made the appointment before thinking the next stage through. How were we going to get to the vet? In early April we were still waiting for the papers to come through for our car, to drive it would be illegal.

But there are laws and there are *laws*. And untaxed driving was not one recognised by the provisional council of the Kennel Club when an animal's life was in danger. And I greatly suspected that murdering one's husband if he objected was viewed as justifiable homicide – if not obligatory.

So, I drove into town, trying to exude a law-abiding aura while deep down feeling like an axe-murderer with a trunk full of severed heads. Every car on the road screamed – unmarked police car – every person – detective on stakeout!

Once in Aurignac, I thought I'd find an unobtrusive parking slot – maybe sandwiched in between two large lorries or buried in someone's back garden beneath a pile of leaves.

But Shelagh would have none of it. We'd park as close to the vet's as we could. Gypsy was too weak to walk far.

The surgery was packed. I began to think that our half past six *rendez-vous* was more of an invitation to a general surgery than an appointment. The waiting room was full of sorry looking dogs.

Including one that looked like a small bear – it was that big and hairy. And so ill. As were they all. I can't remember ever being in a room full of so many quiet dogs. They were sprawled everywhere, panting, lethargic, not caring if the dog on their left was looking at them funny – no singing, no barking, no sniffing.

We waited an hour and a half – watching Gypsy all the time, looking for signs of deterioration, hoping we weren't too late.

And hoping the *gendarmes* weren't on traffic patrol that evening. I could feel our car standing out from all its neighbours, flashing "arrest me!" at every passing motorist. And drawing every eye to the bare patch of windscreen where the tax disc should have been.

At eight o'clock a police siren wailed in the distance and I was up and running. If I got to the car quick, I could move it into a side street.

I ran outside. The siren came closer. I tried a fast nonchalant walk, my hands digging into my pockets, searching for the car keys. Was there time to move the car or should I ignore it and walk past? Deny all knowledge of the car, Shelagh and Gypsy and sprint off home across the fields?

That sounded like a good plan.

Luckily the police car swept past before I made it to the first maize field. They weren't looking for me. I could relax.

Which was when I noticed the abundance of chairs on the pavement. They hadn't been there earlier. But now Aurignac's High Street was alive with people sitting outside their homes, chatting to each other across the street, hailing passers by, pointing out the axe murderer's getaway car with the missing tax disc...

It was an unusual sight and one which I was to become used to over the summer months. I don't know what it says about French television but it does appear to be a rural custom to sit outside your home for a couple of hours in the evening.

I still find it strange. My experience has always been that, given the choice between the front and the back garden, the English invariably choose the privacy of the back garden. And I've never seen people ignore the garden altogether and bring their furniture out onto the pavement. But here they did.

I walked back to the surgery, weaving between the chairs and exuding a law-abiding nonchalance. I'm English, we always run screaming from the vet's on Thursdays – it's a tradition.

Back inside the vet's, we waited, the room gradually emptying as sad bundles of hair were dragged one by one into the surgery. It was gone nine before a very tired vet waved us through for our turn. It didn't look like he'd had a break since lunch.

A diagnosis confirmed a few minutes later when a woman pushed open the surgery door and marched in. It was the vet's wife. In dressing gown and slippers.

You did not need to be fluent in French to understand the gist of her questioning. When are you coming home? Do you know what time it is? Do you realise that dinner has been ready for hours?

He did. And, honour satisfied, she left.

At least we were his last case. He'd had fifteen cases of pyroplasm that day. And expected the same tomorrow. That was on top of his usual workload.

Apparently it was the season for pyroplasm.

And Gypsy had definitely got it. He stepped back from the microscope and invited us to see for ourselves, pointing out the pear shaped blotches invading Gypsy's red blood cells which gave pyroplasm it's name – *pyro* meaning pear.

But we'd caught it in time. Gypsy would survive. Two huge injections later she was being lifted down from the surgery table. But she'd have to come back in three days time, just in case.

Tick checks were intensified after that. We couldn't keep Gypsy out of the long grass entirely but at least we could check her coat when she came back. And our jeans – ticks, apparently, being quite partial to denim.

And we turned more and more towards the roads for our daily dog walks. At least tarmac was safe from ticks.

But not from dogs.

The average French farmhouse, we found, is garrisoned by four dogs. The first of which is typically a terrier – or some other small and fiery breed – whose job it is to race outside at the first hint of an intruder and raise the alarm.

Usually they take one look at Gypsy, gauge her size, and then retreat behind the advancing second wave; who are either border collies or various hunting breeds – spaniels, setters and assorted flop-eared hounds. Their job is to hold the intruder at bay until the arrival of the ultimate deterrent – the *gardien de vache* – who always lumbers in last due to its enormous bulk.

And probably because it takes a while to put all its weight-training equipment away.

The *gardien* is always of indeterminate breed – normally a cross between a small cow and the Hound of the Baskervilles. And its job is to protect the herd – against anything from a pack of wild dogs to a couple of German panzer divisions.

We usually hasten our step at that point and look the other way. Hoping that an English couple and their dog are hardly worth bothering with.

It was coming back from one of these late morning walks one day when Shelagh noticed Rhiannon rolling in her paddock and pawing at the ground. She recognised the symptoms immediately. Colic!

It was Rhiannon's turn to meet the vet.

He arrived within the hour, examined her for a few minutes and pronounced in almost perfect English, "it's zer wind."

"Yes, colic." we agreed.

"*Non*, wind," he insisted.

"Colic?" I repeated, trying a different pronunciation this time, making it rhyme somewhat tunefully with eek.

"*Oui, Colique. Mais* ... zer wind." And he emphasised his point by pursing his lips and blowing.

The wind? We were confused. What had the wind got to do with anything?

But we should have realised. Any country that has a wind that can turn people mad – strange but true: 'the Mistral drove me mad' has been used successfully in a French court to escape imprisonment in a murder trial – can certainly find room for one that gives horses colic.

We listened, amazed. There was a wind, he told us, a very rare wind, that when it blew off the Mediterranean, it left horses writhing in its wake. He'd had several cases already that morning.

Shelagh cast a look in my direction. It was a look of blame. Not only had I been hiding all the articles on pyroplasm but I'd neglected to mention the wind they called Horsekiller.

And, of course, we couldn't have anything as simple as a mere colic-inducing wind sweeping over our fields. We had to have complications. Rhiannon had a strange rash on her shoulder. Was that anything to do with this wind? We'd never noticed a rash associated with colic before.

It's one of the disadvantages of our keyword method of translation that occasionally you hear something only too well – like the phrase 'ten foot long caterpillar' – and whatever words you pad the rest of the sentence with, nothing can produce anything you'd like to hear.

I looked at Shelagh, had I misheard?

I hadn't. I could tell by the mouthed, "ten foot long caterpillar?" that she'd arrived at the same translation.

Then the vet pointed at a fir tree behind us.

"*Là,*" he said.

When someone introduces a ten-foot long caterpillar into the conversation and then points at a tree above your head, you do not take that action lightly. Nor do you stand underneath said tree for long.

We leapt.

I could feel the imminent grip of the ten-foot long killer insect as it reached down from its lair in the trees. But I tried to disguise my panic by mutating the scream in my throat into a strangled cough.

Safely standing behind the vet, we looked back towards the tree.

It must have been an invisible ten-foot long caterpillar.

"Where is it?"

"*Là* ... zer nest."

I could see several balls of white filament dotted amongst the branches. Were they nests? Surely they were too small to accommodate the arboreal cousin of the Loch Ness monster?

"*Processionnaire,*" he continued, struggling in a mixture of French and English. "Many *chenille.*"

The dictionary was quickly consulted. Apparently it was not one ten foot long caterpillar but a ten foot long line of processionary caterpillars joined head to tail, contact with which could cause skin irritations.

And of all the places to roll when struck with colic, Rhiannon had chosen the one piece of ground currently being traversed by a ten-foot long string of orange and black hairy beasties.

Luckily it wasn't serious. Except for the caterpillars – who suffer far more than skin irritation when brought into unexpected contact with half a ton of horse.

Rhiannon was not having much luck on the horse-riding front either. When we first asked about horse-riding in France we were told there was no problem, you could go anywhere. France was a haven for the horse.

I thought it strange that I never actually saw anyone riding a horse in the three weeks I'd spent house hunting but everyone had been so adamant – horse riding? No problem, lots of it.

I began to suspect that perhaps, none of these people actually rode.

The biggest problem where we were was the lack of tracks. Or, more accurately, the lack of usable tracks. There were plenty of *chemins*, they just didn't go very far. Twenty yards in from the road and they fizzled out – usually into thick forest or a fence.

If Rhiannon had been better in traffic this might not have been a problem. But she had an aversion to large lorries, noise, tractors, cyclists, oddly shaped trees, flapping polythene...

She had a very long list.

Shelagh was ready to give up ... until we noticed a stable a few miles away and plucking up courage – and the ubiquitous dictionary – decided to investigate. Maybe someone there would know of a good place to ride.

And so we met Chantal. Very sun-tanned, very blonde and very talkative. Like many of the younger French we met, her English was much better than she let on. And much better than our French.

She'd only just moved to the area herself and was in the process of establishing a livery.

She'd had trouble finding places to ride as well. Although she had found a excellent sandy square in the village to use for exercise. Or so she'd thought. It was just like a purpose-built menage.

That is until she noticed the word *Boulodrome* writ large on a sign by the entrance. She was just thinking 'Thank God, no one saw me' when she became aware of the large number of eyes peering at her from various surrounding windows and gardens.

It's always the same. Do a good deed and the streets are deserted, plough up a *Boulodrome* for half an hour and the entire *boules* committee are having a tea party next door.

She spent the rest of the afternoon with a rake. The French are very particular about their *Boulodrome*s.

But she'd love to have Shelagh ride with her. She'd enjoy the company. Exercising horses was not much fun on your own. Would tomorrow be okay? She had a friend coming down from Toulouse in the afternoon. A young girl, who, though an inexperienced rider, was keen to learn and had a horse at the stables. Why didn't Shelagh join them?

Shelagh could think of two very good reasons – Rhiannon and her long list of things she didn't like to meet while out riding. But it was too good an opportunity to pass up. She'd meet them at two.

It was a long ride to Chantal's. Made even longer by the appearance of seventeen assorted tractors, lorries and flapping fertiliser bags. The latter waving so menacingly from their roadside nests that Rhiannon was forced to tiptoe past on the far side of the road. Nothing could be more frightening than a fertiliser bag where a fertiliser bag shouldn't be.

I've often wondered how Rhiannon would have fared in the Wild West. And where cowboys found horses that could be left loosely tied outside saloons? Every horse I've ever come into contact with would have disappeared before the first foaming pint came sliding down the saloon bar. And as for riding through gunfire – none of our horses would have made it past the first oddly shaped haystack let alone ridden into danger.

But eventually Shelagh and Rhiannon arrived and trotted into Chantal's yard. Whereupon both were immediately besieged by a welcoming pack of assorted dogs.

Rhiannon did not like dogs – they were on page five of her list – especially those that ran between her legs. She liked to maintain a dignified distance between herself and other animals. A personal space that extended to the ground even where she didn't.

A few sly sideways kicks quickly punched the air but the dogs didn't even notice. They were too excited at Shelagh's arrival. They knew a horse in the yard meant a walk was imminent. And a walk meant adventure.

The fact that the ride was to be accompanied by three large excitable dogs was not the only surprise. Veronique, Chantal's young friend, had a gelding.

Rhiannon did not like geldings either. They were on pages one, two, four and six of her list.

And it was more than a dislike, it bordered on the pathological. Put her next to a stallion and she became a paragon of good behaviour – quiet, obedient, calm, a fluttering eyelash or two. But put her next to a gelding and she'd lunge at him with teeth snapping. Or spin round and try to flatten him with her back legs.

Shelagh tried to explain the situation to Chantal as best she could but not surprisingly the intelligence was not immediately believed. That is until Chantal noticed Rhiannon, teeth bared and ears back, pulling strongly in the direction of Veronique's mount.

If ever a horse looked bent upon a course of dire deeds, this was that horse.

After a brief peace conference it was decided that perhaps the best plan was to keep as much distance between the two horses as possible. And not to tell Veronique, who was nervous enough without the added pressure of a psychotic quadruped with a gelding fixation.

So Shelagh was tasked to ride in front, Veronique at the back and Chantal would keep the peace in the middle – and give directions. There was a *forêt domaniale* a mile or two down the road. She hadn't explored it fully yet but from what she'd seen there were some good riding tracks there.

Off they set, down the short drive and onto the road.

And along came Chantal's dogs, tracing energetic circles around the horses and occasionally through their legs.

Naturally, this did not meet with Rhiannon's approval who, in between kicking out at the dogs as they ran between her legs and craning her neck around to keep an eye on the gelding, was becoming somewhat difficult to handle.

Half a mile down the road, the three dogs became four – the fourth recruited from a passing garden.

Persuading cars to slow down for horses on the road had been a recurrent headache for Shelagh all her riding life. But not today. The sight of three horses being circled by a pack of bouncing dogs proved too much for even the most insistent motorist. They stopped. One driver wound his window down. Whether for a chat or to remonstrate about his journey being interrupted was never known.

For as soon as his head moved towards the open window he found a large, hairy dog had got there first, its muddy paws resting on the lip of the glass and tongue slobbering over the driver's face.

But dogs are easily bored and ten minutes later there were none to be seen. They'd disappeared through a gap in a fence and shot off in search of something new – probably a rumour that a giant rabbit had landed in a spaceship two miles away. Dogs are very gullible.

Which left Rhiannon free to concentrate on the gelding, a demonic eye scanning behind at every opportunity.

The road bent and curved its way between thickening woodland, predominantly oak with stands of chestnut and acacia; slender spires of juniper dotted the roadside, the whole knitted together with thorn and briar and huge hanging vines. Dark, abandoned and impenetrable. Except to the deer and wild boar and the occasional hardy *chasseur* and his dog.

It's still strange to see so much wild woodland. Even the National Forests in Britain are largely managed, their paths maintained, the undergrowth cut back, the trees thinned. It's a business. But in rural South-West France so much is just left, an abundance of land and a declining rural population having turned vast tracts of woodland back to nature. With no one to maintain the tracks, the old *chemins* quickly disappeared under advancing woodland. As have the old stone buildings, giving an eerie feel to the place – silent, dark woods, abandoned ruins.

Which turned the conversation, quite naturally, towards eerie topics. Witchcraft for one. According to Chantal it was endemic in the Pyrenees. And worse in the Ariege.

Veronique listened in mounting awe as Chantal detailed the pagan proclivity of the French *départements*. Haute-Pyrenees – witches, Les Landes – witches, Gers – witches. According to Chantal, any *département* with a tree in it was susceptible. It was the curse of the *campagne*.

Chantal had a very vivid imagination.

A grassy track loomed up on the left. A firebreak between the old abandoned woodland and a newer stand of conifers. If anything, the tract of conifers was even more forbidding. A densely planted sea of straight poles gradually merging into a vast blackness twenty or thirty yards in. But the firebreak was inviting, a line of light between two dark places.

The three riders followed the firebreak on its angular path around the plantation and off into a network of smaller rougher tracks. Thick woods stretched deep and dark on all sides and an eerie quiet descended. Gone was the distant hum of tractors and civilisation. And even the sky disappeared under the spreading canopy.

Rhiannon stopped dead, ears pricked and wild-eyed. Her usual reaction when confronted with anything remotely out of the ordinary – like a leaf out of place or a strangely shaped twig.

"What is zer matter?" asked Chantal, moving up alongside.

"She thinks she can see a monster in the bushes," joked Shelagh.

It was only a casual remark. But unfortunately Chantal knew enough English to know what a monster was and enough imagination to give it flesh.

"*Monstre!*" she cried.

"*Qu'est-ce se passe?*" asked a nervous Veronique from further back.

"*Monstre!*" repeated Chantal, now wide-eyed and convinced of an imminent attack from at least one bogeyman.

Veronique did not need telling twice. It may not have been the Ariege but it wasn't the centre of Paris either. There were trees everywhere. How many did a bogeyman need?

She spurred her gelding on, who responded by shooting off in the only direction it knew – straight ahead – nervously pushing itself between Shelagh and Chantal and barging both horses aside.

Which gave Rhiannon the chance she'd been waiting for – a clear expanse of passing gelding flesh. She lunged, teeth bared, missed the gelding, grabbed Veronique and nipped her leg. Veronique screamed and galloped off through the trees convinced that at least half her leg was now residing in the jaws of the aforementioned bogeyman.

Chantal wasn't far behind. She hadn't seen Rhiannon's lunge, she'd been too busy keeping control of her own horse when the gelding burst past. But she'd heard the scream. And that was more than enough.

Needless to say Rhiannon pushed all thoughts of strangely shaped twigs into the rear stable of her mind and set off in hot pursuit of the gelding.

It was a very dense wood.

With very narrow, twisty ill-maintained tracks.

And three desperate horses.

Two terrified riders.

One deeply embarrassed rider.

And four dogs who, drawn by the screams and furious galloping, had decided to forgo the rabbits from Mars and rejoin the party.

Shelagh's screams of "*Pas monstre!*" didn't help, either. Terrified ears quickly discarded the *pas* part and homed in on *monstre*. And if ever there's a greater spur for leaving a dark wood in a hurry than being pursued by repeated screams of "*Monstre! Monstre!*" I have yet to hear it.

There are undoubtedly passages in the French Highway Code covering the etiquette of riders coming out of a forest track onto a main road. Probably something to do with stopping. But when you're an inexperienced rider on a runaway horse and you're being chased by a bogeyman – or bogeymen – and urged on by repeated shouts of *"Monstre! Monstre!"* you do not overdwell on the finer points of road etiquette.

Not that Veronique noticed the arrival of the road. With her eyes tight shut and arms locked in a bear hug around the gelding's neck, she was more concerned with not falling off. And when you've discarded the reins in favour of the limpet style of riding you do not have that many options when it comes to stopping.

Or much idea of where you're going.

Which is why she didn't notice the car.

Now, as in England, motorists in France tend to fall almost equally into three categories. Those who slow down and treat both horse and rider with caution. Those who regard horses as large cyclists (i.e. nuisances who don't pay road tax, have no rights and deserve to be run off the road at the first opportunity). And people who are late, who, if not in actual possession of a note from God suspending all traffic legislation in their vicinity, are confident it's only a matter of time before they do.

As the first sounds of the car horn penetrated Chantal's consciousness, she thought she'd identified a fourth category – the bogeyman. Who, not being a very fast bogeyman, had presumably taken to his bogeymobile in an attempt to catch up with the horses and was now laying in wait where the track met the road.

Of course, she was wrong. It was a fifth kind, the enraged dog-owner, who – convinced his pet had been kidnapped by a gang of mounted animal vivisectionists – had been combing the roads for the last fifteen minutes in an attempt to track them down.

"C'est mon chien!" he cried as, on cue, a hairy mop burst out of the undergrowth pursued by three even hairier ones.

"Give him back!" he continued, or words to that effect. It's very difficult, if not impossible, to accurately interpret an angry Frenchmen in full flow. Individual words cease to have meaning, instead they coalesce into a flow of emotion, waved on by energetic hand signals.

He was not amused.

Neither was Chantal.

When you've just fought for your life to escape the clutches of a bogeyman, the last thing you need is a mouthful of abuse from a motorist. And, being French, she was well equipped to give as good as she got.

Shelagh slipped past the conflagration, out onto the road ... and walked straight into another. Forty yards down the road stood a grazing gelding. It had had more than enough galloping for the day and was now in the process of replenishing its reserves from a roadside bank. A process made all the more difficult by the strange growth on its neck – Veronique – who, arms and legs locked, hung upside down with a tenacity that few limpets could even dream about.

Rhiannon pulled towards her quarry. Shelagh tried to make her stop. Veronique continued to defy gravity.

And in the foreground, Chantal and the motorist continued their wide-ranging debate on dogs, horses, bogeymen and animal experimentation. That is, until the enraged motorist, seeing his beloved pet's face at the passenger window, made the mistake of opening the door for his dog ... and was immediately engulfed by four excited canines.

A run in the woods *and* a ride in a car – could life get any better?

Few things in life are more difficult than persuading three large dogs, all adamant that a car ride had been promised, to vacate the back seat of a car.

Trying to deter a psychotic horse from biting its prey could be a candidate.

As could manoeuvring said prey whilst hanging upside down from its neck with your eyes closed.

It was a difficult day.

Chantal's dispute with the motorist switched tack.

"Give me back my dogs!"

"I don't want your dogs! Get them out my car!"

In the background, two horses danced excited circles as Rhiannon made repeated lunges towards the gelding. Rhiannon pulling for all she was worth to try and get her teeth into the gelding while Shelagh did her best to turn her away and Veronique wished she'd stayed in Toulouse.

The only happy faces beamed from the back seat of the car. What a day it had been! Could they come out again tomorrow?

Three *Fêtes* and a Football Match

Our first experience of a French *fête* came in early June. We'd found the unexpected invitation waiting for us in our post box a week earlier. *Journée Pêche*, it had said.

It took us a while to work out whether this was a peach festival or something to do with fish. Fish was ahead narrowly, as we'd never seen much evidence of peach worship in the village. But we were far from certain – who could tell what old ways dwelt amongst the rural hearths of Gascony?

We read on. It was to be held at Tuco, by the church, a five-minute walk from our house. And the invitation came complete with a menu and a programme of events, starting with early morning fishing – or, possibly, peach picking.

The midday meal seemed remarkable value at only fifty francs. Especially as it included an *apéritif, charcuterie*, salad, paella, *fromage*, dessert, coffee and wine. Plus what looked like a barbecue of whatever the *pêcheurs* caught that morning. Could you catch peaches? And would you want to barbecue them if you did?

Peaches were definitely out. Although the image of wild peach hunters crouching by the roadsides with their long peach spears glistening in the early morning sun lingered for quite a while.

The programme continued into the afternoon with what it called an amicable game of *boules*. The fact that they had to print the word 'amicable' implied to me that perhaps the normal game was far from it. Should we take our coloured plastic set or would that be taken as an insult to the national game?

We were still wondering about the etiquette of using coloured plastic on the hallowed gravel when we noticed the last entry in the day's festivities. *Grillades, Soirée Dansante et Feu de la St-Jean*.

Ah. *Feu de la St-Jean*, didn't that sound suspiciously like the burning of Joan of Arc? And how would the presence of an English couple at the burning of a French saint go down with the locals?

And why were they burning her? Wasn't she on their side? Wasn't that akin to burning effigies of James I on Guy Fawkes night?

Or was this something peculiarly Gascon? I'd noticed the name *Prince Noir* appear frequently in glowing terms in the local tourist guides. The Black Prince built this, the Black Prince killed that. He'd been Duke of Aquitaine and the feudal lord over much of South-West France. And apparently popular with the locals because he knew how to fight and gave a good party.

But was that enough to turn the region against Joan of Arc?

Which is where my history deserted me. Was Aquitaine still in English hands when Joan of Arc was around? Or didn't that matter, was this like the English Wars of the Roses where rivalry became timeless? Certainly, I could imagine a Yorkshire village fete committee looking favourably upon a suggestion that effigies of Lancashire be burnt as part of the coming year's celebrations. But was there the same depth of feeling here?

And if so, would we, as representatives of England, be called upon to cast the first burning faggot?

On the day of the *fête* we strolled down the hill just before noon. The sun was high overhead, the air still and the temperature soaring.

As the church steeple came into sight we wondered what a French village fete would be like. Would there be raffles and stalls? Would we be fined for not bringing our boules?

The first sounds wafted towards us as we neared the church. But from where? We'd expected the meal to be held in the village square. The word 'square' being used here in its loosest term, a more accurate description would be the space between the church and the road. But square or space, the adjective 'empty' was undoubtedly the correct one to apply.

We followed the noise around the church walls and into a place we didn't know existed. A cleared area behind the church which was now full of trestle tables, benches and about two hundred people.

It looked idyllic, an island of bright crushed stone leading down to a meadow and a small meandering river. Over the river, tree-lined hills rose majestically from the valley floor, the hillside flecked with occasional stone buildings, farmsteads and barns, shining off-white in the sun and capped with the uneven reds, pinks and pale yellow of the old clay roof tiles.

And the *fête* had started.

We soon realised our mistake in not arriving earlier. All the shaded seats were taken. Most of the village crowded around a bar area underneath a huge tree, a few sat on shaded benches, no one sat in the full sun.

Which beat down upon the scene with a growing power. Luckily we'd brought our hats, we'd both had enough of sunstroke that year.

The bar was interesting – quite unlike anything I'd seen at an English fete. No beer, no lager, no cider. This was strictly an aperitif bar – plenty of Ricard[4], muscatel and port. But mainly *Ricard*. Which, from what I could see, could either be green, red or cloudy –

none of which appealed. I find something intrinsically off-putting about drinking something bright green. We stuck to the port. Unadventurous but safe.

We were soon found by three English people. There must have been something instantly recognisable about us – the lost look of an English couple abroad. Within minutes we were being introduced to a bewildering number of locals who all seemed to be interrelated. It was quite surprising. Everyone seemed to be someone's cousin or married to someone's cousin or sometimes both. It was like one big extended family celebration.

And very confusing. All the names and faces blurred into one.

By half past twelve a general consensus erupted and, like a flock of birds, the village turned as one and descended upon the benches. We lost our fellow nationals in the rush but found ourselves sat next to a family we later discovered to be our neighbours – they lived about a mile away but farmed the fields adjoining ours. We both had difficulty introducing ourselves. He became the-man-with-the-black-and-white-cows, a fine old Indian name if ever I've heard one, and we became *Les Anglais*.

And the wine flowed.

And a myth burst.

I had heard, probably from the same French lesson that introduced *priorité à droite*, that even the humblest *paysan* was at heart a connoisseur of the grape and would insist upon a fine bottle of wine to accompany dinner.

But I recognised the wine being handed out. Not from its label – detailing its chateau and year – but from the embossed stars on the glass. *Six étoiles*, the brand we bought, six francs a litre and a franc back on the bottle. It was cheaper than water.

And there would be a tidy sum collected on the bottles from what I could see. Litre bottles of red and rosé alternated along the centre of every trestle table – one bottle between two people. And that was just the start, there were plenty of full crates stacked up for later.

It was interesting to note the lack of white wine. In fact I can't recall ever being offered white wine at any *fête* or communal meal since coming to France. It seems that in the *Sud,* if you want something white to drink it has to be *Ricard*.

Or water. Which Shelagh quickly ordered.

I'm a very moderate drinker as a rule, but I do have an occasional weakness when it comes to refusing a drink. I have been known to stop off at the pub for a swift half, and three pints later I'm set in for the night and destined for a curry.

So I was under strict orders: moderation and plenty of water. Which might have worked if it hadn't been for the friendliness of our neighbours. Who kept filling my glass – even when it was three-quarters full. It was like a magic glass, I'd take a sip, struggle over the odd sentence of French and by the time I looked back my glass was full again.

Which made counting glasses extremely difficult.

And laid waste my plan of having two glasses of water for every glass of wine – nobody was interested in keeping my water glass topped up. This was France after all.

With the important business concluded – the distribution of the wine – next came the bread. Armfuls of *flutes* – the larger, fatter version of the baguette – were plucked from sacks stacked in the church porch and handed around. Then platefuls of various cured meats, *jambon*, paté and gherkins.

Then the hats.

Which was quite unexpected, suddenly large sun hats of all description were being passed amongst the tables. I never found out where they all came from. Whether a selection of headgear was kept permanently in the church for just such an occasion or a band of Mexican tourists had just been mugged outside the village.

The sun rose higher and burned the shade into smaller and smaller islands. Even with my hat I could feel the sun ablaze on the back of my neck. I had to keep putting my hand there to cool it down – it was either that or a piece of *jambon*. And I wasn't sure if the *jambon* would cook in its own fat and who wants to become known by his neighbours as the man who cooks bacon on his neck?

I tried moving my neck out of the sun by craning my head or leaning back but Shelagh kept giving me strange looks. Was I developing some strange affectation or about to pass out before the arrival of the second course?

Paella is a strange dish. However much you eat there always seems to be more left on the plate than when you started. All those shells and various pieces of marine detritus that seem to build up out of all proportion to the meat consumed. I've always considered it a dish to inspire new scientific theories on the conservation of matter. Far more potential than apples. Apples fall off trees – so what? Name a tree fruit that doesn't. But Paella? Not only could it feed the five thousand, it could house them afterwards. Pretty little houses made from shell fragments and bits of claw.

I was definitely getting too much sun and wine. Some people know when to stop when the room begins to rotate. Me, I wait until not only can I see housing estates made out of crayfish but I make an offer on the one on the corner.

I wasn't quite there yet. I think its roof needed attention.

It was about this time that I made my big mistake.

As we ran out of things to say about black and white cows and the weather, I started thinking about sport.

Not a good idea.

For many years I'd greeted the arrival of a new soccer season with the thought that perhaps this year I'd give it another go. Take it up seriously again, dig out the boots and get back into training.

And a few weeks later I'd think of a good reason why not to. It was cold or there was something I wanted to watch on TV or I felt a muscle twinge. And after all, there would always be next year.

A promise that gained less credibility as the years progressed.

But wine has the ability to rejuvenate – the mind, if not the body. I wasn't that old. I could still a play a bit, if I put my mind to it.

Strange things began to happen around me. People became excited and fetched other people who became even more excited.

Did I want to play football, they asked? Of course I did, I replied, I love a kick about.

And the wine flowed and the fromage arrived and glazed apple tart and more wine. By the time the *eau de vie* made its rounds I would have agreed to anything. Unfortunately it appeared I already had.

I was sure I had said, "I had professional trials when I was fifteen." However, I began to have a nasty suspicion it had been interpreted as, "I was a professional footballer for fifteen years." A subtle difference.

And as I later found out, I hadn't been invited to a kick about either. There would be no sweaters rolled up for goalposts on the village green. I'd signed up to play for Racing Club, the local team. With my forty-first birthday fast approaching and not having kicked a ball for four years, and then not particularly well, I was about to make my league debut in French soccer.

But with the warm glow of red wine and general bonhomie abounding, what did I care? I loved football and there was plenty of time to get fit for the new season. And there were definite advantages – Racing Club were having a *fête* next week in Cassagne and we were both invited.

My memories of the latter stages of the *fête* start to fade at this point. I remember the coffee coming round and something to do with sugar lumps. Unfortunately Shelagh remembers it all. And frequently fills in the gaps.

I blame it all on the *eau de vie*.

Which is a kind of home-brewed schnapps. And amazingly legal. It's a strange quirk of French law – undoubtedly Napoleonic – that certain French families were given the right to distil liquor. A right handed down through the generations, so that most communities have an *eau de vie* man. Who can generally be recognised by a certain dissolute appearance and a large number of friends.

I am told I had *eau de vie* in my coffee. Followed by *eau de vie* neat. And finally *eau de vie* on sugar lumps – which apparently is the traditional way of taking it. A bit like tequila with salt and lemon, I suppose.

Shelagh tried to stop me but when her own coffee was threatened with topping up she was distracted long enough for the damage to be done. It's amazing how quick people can be with a doctored sugar lump.

We didn't stay for the *boules*. I remember zigzagging up a hill but had to be told about collapsing through the front door.

The next thing I remember was being woken up that evening by a set of blaring car horns. I'd been happily negotiating the purchase of an end terrace crayfish when suddenly the street exploded in a wall of sound. I staggered to our bedroom window half asleep and peered out at two cars and a drive full of people.

Shelagh called up, "it's for you," and promptly disappeared into the lounge with Gypsy. I don't think I had yet been forgiven for the excesses of the afternoon.

But I was sobering up fast. There's nothing like two car loads of strange men appearing unexpectedly at your house to flush the alcohol from your brain.

I opened the door, not sure whether this was the *boules* committee on a dusk raid or a team of Joan of Arc's hit men. I was ready to deny all knowledge of ever owning coloured plastic boules – *Ce n'est pas moi*, I was ready to shout. But I didn't have to. It was the football team. They'd come to fetch me. The bar was open and festivities underway.

I was dragged off.

As I said, I'm not very good at refusing a drink. And even worse in a foreign language.

I thought I heard the words 'Oh God' emanate from the lounge as the car pulled away.

The church square had been transformed since the afternoon. For one thing it was darker. On a more substantive note, the trestle tables had gone, the bar pulled away from the shade of the tree and enlarged considerably. A small stage had appeared with speakers and microphones and someone had lit a bonfire.

Oh my God!

I might have known. I'd seen the film. The newcomer feted, given food and drink and asked to join the football team and then just when he's starting to enjoy himself – it's human sacrifice time. And I had been cast as this year's Joan.

As we approached closer, I could see figures running – or were they dancing – around the bonfire. There was so much noise and so many people in the way it was hard to tell. I was just wondering what the French for coven was when a woman burst into our group and grabbed the face of the man next to me. When she took her hands away his cheeks had turned black.

I was no longer interested in the French for coven.

I was desperately trying to remember the English for that flesh-eating bug that was all the rage a few years back. Didn't that eat people's faces and turn them black?

Or was that a film I'd seen about zombies?

As the woman turned towards me with her hands outstretched, I waited for my life to flash in front of my eyes. But my life had to wait as it was elbowed aside by fleeing alcohol molecules. Two car loads of strange men may sober a person up fast but a head-grabbing woman turning peoples' faces black has the edge every time.

Two hands fastened upon my cheeks. Still no sign of past events or bright white lights. How long did it take to die? How many more alcohol molecules were there?

As the last droplet of intoxication waved goodbye, I plucked up the courage to ask what was happening. I'd been initiated, apparently. As had everyone else around me, it being the local custom to blacken everyone's face with ash from the bonfire. This may have been something symbolic about the ashes of Joan of Arc. Or, possibly, the last vestiges of Al Jolson worship in continental Europe. My French was not good enough to enquire further.

I was given a beer and introduced to Racing Club's captain, possibly to discuss tactics for the coming season, but seeing as neither of us could understand what the other was saying, nothing of great import was decided.

I rued my lack of French. And vowed to do something about it. Perhaps getting involved with the local team would be the catalyst I needed.

And I suppose I should have used the opportunity to clear up any misconceptions. But the alcohol had established another beachhead and I was starting to look forward to playing again – after all it had been a dream for a long time. And I wasn't likely to be given another chance.

And besides, I didn't see myself as forty. Like most people I had an inner clock which ran much slower than chronological time. I had been seventeen for ages, twenty-three for about six years, clung on to twenty-eight during most of my thirties and was now settling down to a young thirty-five. What were a few games of football to a young thirty-five year-old?

And there was bound to be a couple of weeks of training sessions to iron out any problems. If I wasn't good enough, I'd know, and the door to my boot cupboard could be nailed shut forever.

I staggered back up the hill. Not so many zigzags this time. Above me the stars shone bright and the cicadas hummed Al Jolson medleys.

Climb upon my knee – chirrup – sonny boy – chirrup, chirrup.

I turned into the drive of the little crayfish cottage on the corner and disappeared inside.

At Cassagne's Football *Fête*, I was under strict orders – one glass of wine and no Al Jolson songs.

Life can be tough.

But it does have its compensations. As a *joueur,* I wouldn't have to pay a penny; all the food and drink was free.

And there was shade; a grove of huge horse chestnut trees provided a thick green canopy over the picnic area – a much more sensible arrangement.

Otherwise it was very similar to the *fête* at Tuco: masses of food and drink, the whole village decked out in their summer clothes and a grassy riverbank nestling in folds of fields and hills.

It was strange seeing such a diverse assembly of people at a football function. A football meal in England would have been a lad's night out. The more liberal might have invited wives and girlfriends. But here, everyone was invited – the whole village, young and old. And, just as at Tuco, everyone sat down together, everyone enjoying themselves, not caring if they were sitting next to a stranger, a toddler or a grandparent. No sullen groups of teenagers sulked in the corner, wishing they were somewhere else. Everyone mixed in together; all ages, all social backgrounds. If the village had been called Stepford, I'd have panicked.

And, if anything, the food was even better than at the Tuco *Fête*. A huge cauldron of *cassoulet* gently simmered on the edge of the picnic area as the early courses came and went. Wine flowed, *flutes* and dishes were passed around: cured meats of every description, a huge green salad that had just about everything imaginable in it, more wine.

It was a brilliant *fête*.

Although I couldn't help but feel a mite self-conscious as I overheard scraps of conversation about the English professional who'd been signed up for the coming season. Expectations of certain promotion mixed with incredulous stares and the occasional "*C'est Bobby Charlton?*"

And then along came the *cassoulet,* ladled from cauldron to tureen and passed around the tables. And passed around again a few minutes after that. I had a feeling that no one would be allowed to leave until everyone had taken at least three helpings – it was the regional dish, after all.

I was just spooning the last haricot when a brightly-coloured mountain of a man appeared by my left shoulder. After a frenzied bout of hand shaking that somehow managed to involve the occupants of at least four tables – handshaking being contagious in France – we were introduced.

He was Remy, the club's chef.

"The team has a chef?" I asked incredulously. Surely I'd misheard, what kind of team has its own chef?

A French team, of course. And Racing Club had Remy, who cooked the after-match meal.

"After every match?" I was amazed.

"And after training as well."

I was doubly amazed. Most English teams I'd played for disappeared straight down the pub after a game – and six pints and a packet of peanuts later, we all staggered home. But a sit-down meal? And after training as well?

This was definitely the team to play for.

And this was definitely a chef who liked his food. If you can imagine a giant rugby forward fed on lard for a fortnight and then surgically implanted into Bermuda shorts and a T shirt, then you have some idea of the kind of figure that Remy cut that afternoon.

He was enormous. And wore a smile as colourful as his clothes.

"He's Basque," I heard someone say as though that explained everything.

"Ah, Basque," I said. "Euskadi[5]."

It was my one word of Basque – picked up from a documentary – and it produced startling results.

I was grabbed.

A long lost son couldn't have received a warmer bear hug. I wasn't quite sure what Remy said, other than it was very fast, and even more unintelligible than the local patois – the words weren't so much joined together by 'r's as molecularly bonded. But I assumed it went along the lines of – 'Was I Basque too? I thought they said you were English? Aren't you Bobby Charlton?'

As the meal progressed, so did the number of documents I had to sign. There were almost as many forms as there were courses. And this was just the start.

For one, I'd have to have a medical … and insurance … and, being France, an identity card, complete with picture and doctor's signature.

I began to wonder what level of team I'd signed to play for? Had I unwittingly become a professional? Do village teams normally conduct medicals and employ chefs?

And why did Racing Club sound so familiar?

I had vague memories from the early days of European club football. Wasn't there a famous team called Racing Club back in the sixties?

Still, the season was two months away – plenty of time to get fit – and it's not as though they'd throw me into a big match untried.

Or so I thought.

Until someone mentioned the Cassagne *Fête* – three days of celebration and a football match.

Football match?

"*Oui.*"

A friendly. In three weeks time.

I put down my wedge of *Camembert*. I knew just how friendly a 'friendly' could be.

The friendliest of all being a match I'd seen at Culham, just outside Oxford, where I'd taken a short contract many years ago. Culham was home to the Joint European Torus project – a model of European integration, with scientists from all over the community gathered together to accelerate particles to their heart's content.

And then someone came up with the brilliant idea to cement European relations further with a friendly game of football between the scientists and the manual staff.

And to make it fair, the manual staff would field a veteran team – no one under forty.

The big day arrived with blue skies and everyone looking forward to a pleasant lunchtime kickabout. A hundred spectators lined the pitch as the cleanest, most elegant footballer I had ever seen strode out into the middle. His kit looked brand new – ironed and pressed, it shone and dazzled – a perfect replica of the West German national kit. He was the head of the project and, as the match began, it was obvious he'd played before – he was comfortable on the ball, he passed with accuracy and strolled the park like an older, slightly overweight version of Franz Beckenbauer.

That is until he tried a run down the left wing. Never have I seen such a tackle come from such an unexpected source. The right back must have been pushing retirement; he looked frail, spindly and slightly hunched – a bit like Ghandi after a bad bout of glandular fever. The German approached, smooth and silky, the ball twinkling between his feet. And then – wham – no German, no ball, no game.

I have seen hard tackles. I have seen people kicked up in the air. But this was something else. This was football as it used to be played – in the Middle Ages. When heads were used for footballs and fancy-footed foreigners were fair game once they crossed the halfway line.

The game ended immediately. Or, more accurately, as soon as the German came back out of orbit and discovered gravity the hard way. A full five seconds later, he staggered to his feet, grabbed the ball and started shouting and gesticulating. He wasn't playing any more. No one was playing any more. Ever! Sending off wasn't good enough, the match was abandoned.

He stormed back into the building, the ball clenched firmly under his arm.

I never heard what happened to the right back.

But I had a nasty feeling that in three weeks time the whole village would see exactly what happened to unfit forty year-olds who drank too much at village fetes.

I had three weeks to save my reputation – three weeks to get fit.

The next morning, the alarm went off at 6:30. Time to get up. And what had seemed like a good idea the night before, rapidly became less so as the thought of an early morning run penetrated the warm covers of the bed. Perhaps tomorrow. Or in an hour or so.

It was only the greater fear – that of making a complete fool of myself at the village fete – that propelled me downstairs. If I didn't start today it would be worse tomorrow. And if the thought of running in the early morning was bad, it was nothing compared to that of running in the strength-sapping, heat of the day.

A few minutes later I was decked out in shorts and tennis shoes and blinking into the early morning sun. A loosening jog to the top of the hill, I thought.

It started out well. The first forty yards were downhill, I lengthened my stride and the years fell away. Only to snap back with a vengeance as soon as I turned out of our drive and hit the uphill section of road. A few yards later, I heard something thudding in my chest. I think my heart had just woken up and wanted out.

A few yards more and my pace was just on the forward side of reverse, Lungs had joined forces with Heart, and Stomach was wondering what had happened to breakfast. Only Legs were holding out, but a few heavy-legged strides more and even they started passing notes to Head – notes with 'How about stopping now?' and 'We could always try again later' written in large shaky letters.

Which seemed like a good idea. After all, you don't want to over-do things on the first day ... and three weeks can be a longer time than you think ... and wasn't that a muscle twinge I felt just then?

A unanimous Body turned and walked home. I'd barely jogged a hundred yards.

Walking back, I was reminded of a similar experience ten years earlier when I was in training for the works annual Sport's Day. That had seemed like a good idea at the time too – a pleasant day out and the chance to see if I still had the old speed.

But I hadn't run or played any sport for about a year and neither had my colleagues. So, four of us decided to try out a running track we'd noticed on the way to work. Nothing strenuous, we thought, a few laps of the track and a sprint or two – just to settle us in.

We decided to start with a gentle 400 metres. I slotted in at the back, brimming with confidence, knowing I had the speed to kick for home whenever I wanted. I'd run the 100, 200 and 400 metres for my school and, in my head, I was still as fit as I'd been when I was fifteen. After all, people like me didn't need to train – we were naturally fit.

I dropped out on the first bend. By the back straight there were only two left. A minute later bodies were lying at various intervals along the track, chests heaving and lungs complaining. No one had managed to finish.

Now I was ten years older.

As the day of the match neared, I gradually increased my training regime. Very gradually. On the second day, I managed an extra fifty yards before giving up. The third day, another fifty and I jogged back instead of walking.

I started slipping in the occasional sit-up during the day and bought a football and started a few simple routines to drag back my ball skills from distant memory.

By the third week I was managing to walk and run over an undulating seven kilometres of road and track. A very undulating seven kilometres with fast downhill stretches and lung-killing steep climbs that sapped my calves and knotted my long-dormant muscles. But I was getting there.

Practising my ball skills, however, was a problem. There was no flat piece of ground I could use or a decent wall to bounce the ball off. And worse – the heat. Between eight in the morning and nine at night it was like an oven. Walk out the door and the heat hit you, a few minutes exercise and all your energy was drained.

And I had to play football in this heat? A competitive match in mid-afternoon in mid-July? I could barely walk in the heat, let alone run.

I started praying for rain. Perhaps a polar ice cap could melt for the day and set up some vast climatic shift. An Ice Age would be good – just for the day – no need for woolly mammoths.

When the day of the match came I couldn't believe it.

It was cloudy.

And cool.

After three weeks of nothing but cloudless skies and perpetual heat, the sun had taken a day off. Surely there *was* a God.

At three thirty we pulled up outside the Racing Club stadium. It was an impressive sight. There were even turnstiles and the occasional advertising hoarding. And although there was no grandstand there was a sloping grass bank that formed a natural seating area, ten feet high and bordering two sides of the pitch.

And it was already covered in spectators. About three hundred of them.

For me, most impressive of all was the player's tunnel – which looked suspiciously like a drainage culvert. It cut through the grass bank, joining the changing rooms to the pitch. Presumably to cater for those times when the crowd became too thick for the players to push their way through. I think the designers of the ground were possibly a tad on the optimistic side concerning the club's future.

Fifteen minutes later, I was running onto the park in the red and black of Racing Club. With my number seven on the back and a swimming pool manufacturer on the front, I felt very professional.

And very old.

A quick scan of the other players revealed a handful of teenagers, an armful of players in their twenties, one or two in their early thirties ... and me, who, according to which rumour you believed, was either the referee's dad or Bobby Charlton on a goodwill visit.

Unfortunately the truth lay somewhere in between – I looked like Bobby Charlton and played like the referee's dad.

The match began. I had been hoping for one of those slow-paced summer matches, where the players stroll around in the heat, exuding great skill interspersed with occasional bursts of speed. A less accomplished version of the 1970 World Cup finals, perhaps. I was quickly disabused. The game began like an English cup tie – fast and furious with tackles flying in from all angles. It was tiring just watching the ball.

And as for pacing myself, that plan evaporated with the first attack. It was end to end football with no time to settle on the ball. A game I knew very well. Especially the bit about it not being particularly suited to unfit forty-year-olds who hadn't played for four years.

I slotted into position and started playing from memory, running off the ball, creating gaps, tackling back. All the time hoping that I was fitter than I imagined. And that somewhere I had some deep reservoir of untapped stamina – like a spare fuel tank that I could switch over to in time of dire need.

And then it happened. The ball flew towards me. My first touch. Was this the moment I stunned the crowd with unimaginable feats of skill? ... Or the time that stupid Englishman let the ball run through his legs for a throw in?

I think I froze the ball in mid-air with the power of concentration. Certainly there was no way I was letting that ball past me. I brought it down and then set off. Ideally, it should have been one of those mazey dribbles where the ball appears attached by a silken thread to the educated feet of the right winger.

But I hadn't played for such a long time and, besides, the last time I'd dribbled in public had been when I got drunk at the Tuco fete.

Not to mention that a few weeks practising in the back garden dribbling over hummocks and piles of stones is not ideal preparation. A few touches and the ball flew ahead of me. If there'd been a hummock on the pitch it might have been different – but there wasn't. And my back garden hadn't had defenders either – two of whom were now bearing down on me from different directions and both likely to reach the ball before I did.

But football is a game of the unexpected.

The first defender lunged forward and tried to clear the ball but only succeeded in driving the ball against my shins, whereupon it flew towards the second defender, ricocheted off his knees and came back to me. The next thing I knew, I was stepping over bodies, the ball at my feet and the penalty area fast approaching.

If only it had been deliberate.

With my confidence returning, my next move became clear. The hard low cross, whipped into the penalty area with a hint of swerve to curl around the remaining defender and land at the feet of the advancing centre forward. I could see it all.

Unfortunately my right foot couldn't.

I whipped the ball in hard and low, evading the remaining defenders ... and everyone else. It was one of those embarrassing moments when you pray there's someone in midfield backing up the attack.

But there wasn't. Instead, a huge gap had opened up between the penalty area – now swarming with expectant players – and the centre circle. In between – nothing. Except a ball carving a solitary path towards the far touchline.

Which is what you get for trying to be too clever and bending the ball around defenders when the simple cross would have sufficed.

I made a mental note not to try that again.

A few minutes later we forced a corner on the right and I found myself being handed the ball while everyone else shot off into the penalty area.

I would like to say that it was the quality of my cross that created the goal. That I picked out the only unmarked player, placed an unerringly accurate ball into his path and there was nothing else he could do but score.

But you'd need to be my mother to believe that.

In truth, I was concentrating on not leaning back, not hooking the ball, not slicing it and not pushing it too close to the keeper. The fact that I picked out the only unmarked player was entirely fortuitous.

We were one-nil up. Against the run of play and I'd had a hand in it. Three or four beers and a couple of rounds of *Ricard* and I might claim total credit – it hadn't been his shot, he'd merely deflected my corner. A pretty solid deflection from the edge of the penalty area, but a deflection nonetheless.

Alcohol can make great players of us all.

Latoue, our opponents, pulled a goal back, then went ahead and gradually pushed the game further and further into our half of the pitch. A situation not helped by our right back employing a marking system I was unfamiliar with. It wasn't zonal and it wasn't man to man – unless Latoue were playing with cloaked forwards.

Which meant I had to come back and mark the winger and Latoue started pressing harder and I started playing deeper. But I was enjoying it, even tackling back and playing more as a defender – something I used to hate. It was so good to be playing again.

The last time I'd played, I'd felt old and slow, wallowing in the wake of players I could have given a five-yard start to in my prime. But in the red shirt of Racing Club, I felt young again. My stamina may have been suspect, my touch rusty but I'd rediscovered something I'd thought lost forever ... my speed.

All those years I'd played in my thirties thinking that it was age slowing me down when all the time it had been my growing waistline. All those years of living out of suitcases, pub lunches and midnight curries had pushed me to the top of the handicap.

But now, thirty pounds lighter, suddenly I was fast again.

And taking yards out of my marker every time we attacked. All I needed was someone to play the ball through to me.

And eventually someone did.

I did everything right. I took the ball in mid-stride, played it a few yards ahead, let the keeper come out and then slipped it past him. Perfect.

Unfortunately, the keeper did everything right as well. He came out, narrowed the angle, stood up and then threw out a desperate foot at the last minute, deflecting the ball wide with his toe.

I have relived that moment many times since – and score every time. Why didn't I hit it harder? Or higher? Why didn't I take the ball round the keeper? Why didn't I score? I should have, I did everything right!

Which is undoubtedly where I went wrong. Anyone who plays sports knows the devastating power of the unexpected. The miss-kick, the ricochet, the fluke. Like shooting straight at the keeper only for him to open his legs at the last moment and let the ball through; or bounce off his chest, hit you in the face and rebound over his head into the goal.

I have scored them all. Many times.

Which brings me to *The Great Goal*. Something that is still talked about in darkened saloon bars in Bournemouth. Or, at least, it is when I'm there.

I was sixteen at the time and playing for my school on a cold and blustery winter morning. We'd just attacked down the left and their goalkeeper had rushed to the edge of his area to boot the ball clear. Straight to me. I was at the halfway line, a yard or two out from the right touchline, an open goal some forty or fifty yards ahead of me. Could I do it?

Now, I knew what I had to do. If I waited to control the ball or take it closer to the goal, the moment would be gone. The keeper and defenders would be back in position and the danger would be over.

So I hit it, first time, on the half volley as hard as I could. Wham. Old men in the crowd wept. Never had a ball been hit so hard. Or so high. Or so far in the wrong direction.

It ballooned towards the right-hand corner flag, a small speck in the sky fast disappearing into the clouds. Our forwards turned and started their slow walk back to the centre circle. Another attack over, another goal kick to defend.

But I stayed watching. And watching. Was it ever going to come down? And then something strange happened. One of those magic moments when fate decides to take a hand. The speck froze in the sky ... and then began to change direction. Slowly at first, then picking up pace as a strong wind got behind it.

It was moving back towards the goal.

I noticed that the game on the pitch alongside us had come to a halt. One by one players were stopping and looking up, transfixed by the momentous events unfolding above them.

A defender sprinted back towards the goal. It was a race. The ball and him. No one else was close enough to intervene. The ball growing in size as it hurtled earthwards, the defender positioning himself on the goal line, his neck craned skyward.

Surely it couldn't go in? Not from there? The ball was almost directly over the goal, falling from an impossible angle.

Thud. The dull sound of leather on a cranium rapidly losing consciousness. And goal. The ball found the only gap possible to find and still score. The gap between the defenders head and the crossbar. True, he managed to get his head to the ball but that only served to flatten him and catapult the ball into the roof of the net. So creating a win double – goal scored and one of their best players removed from the game all in one stroke.

Which just goes to show the power of the miss-kick. If I'd

connected cleanly the wind would have taken the ball sailing across the pitch and over for a throw-in. But I hadn't. And I'd scored.

Unfortunately, there were no strong winds in Cassagne that afternoon.

But I didn't care, I was revelling in my newfound speed and youth. Flicking balls off the back foot, dribbling past attackers in my own penalty area, being substituted soon after ... it was just like old times.

I'd set myself two goals for the match – one, not to throw up in public, and two, to leave the pitch without the aid of medical intervention. I'd succeeded admirably on both counts.

All I had to do now was survive the after-match meal.

Both teams were invited to drinks and a meal in the old square and, being France, the invitation was extended to all supporters and all villagers as well.

It was a superb location: an ancient church flanked one side, the *Mairie* and Village Hall another, a row of old stone houses formed the third side and a low wall completed the square. And beyond that wall, a grassy bank led down to a tree-lined river.

We arrived just before eight, Shelagh having insisted we go home first – not to change, but to keep me away from the bar. Thirst and restraint never sit well together and she wanted to make sure I was fully hydrated before being allowed anywhere near a bar.

A restraint not shown by any of the other footballers' wives.

As we walked into the square, it soon became obvious that, as the Irish so aptly put it, drink had been taken. A corner of the square was awash with celebrating *joueurs* and assorted hangers on. The *Ricard* was flowing, the conversation bouncing and somewhere hidden behind the pack of bodies was a bar dispensing drinks. What more could a person want?

How about a barbecue?

That was there too, over by the *Mairie,* a selection of steaks and chops laid out on a large grill propped up on stones over an open fire. Remy stood in attendance, a spatula in one hand and a *Ricard* in the other. Resplendent in T-shirt, shorts and apron, he flitted between the barbecue and the kitchen of one of the small medieval stone houses opposite – which I later found out was the team's clubhouse. Was there any end to the advantages of playing for Racing Club?

Before I could find out, I was spotted and a glass was thrust in my hand from one direction as a bottle of *Ricard* appeared from another. I was still trying to find the words for "I'm not sure if I like *Ricard,"* when I discovered I had a glassful.

And so did Shelagh.

In fact, as I scanned the square, the only people who didn't have a glass of *Ricard* in their hands were those who had two. There was *Ricard naturelle*, *Ricard* with green *menthe* and *Ricard* with grenadine – clear, green and red – undoubtedly some country's flag, one of the more aniseed-loving Caribbean nations perhaps.

And it kept coming, from all directions – even Shelagh couldn't block them all and as for me, well, I didn't try. Around us, the conversation rose and fell with the bottles of *Ricard*. Great feats from the match were analysed and exaggerated. It had been a classic game, one of the best, two teams of heroes, everyone agreed.

Above us, the clouds had pushed away and the early stars were twinkling through the fading sunset pinks and blues. The smell of wood smoke and grilled meat filled the square, and laughter echoed from every wall.

When the food was ready, we adjourned to the lines of benches and trestle tables that had been set up next to the church. And on came the floodlights. The whole square illuminated: two huge artificial suns in a deep black sky, and all around us the yellow, stone walls of antiquity – the high-walled knave, the church tower, the gargoyles.

I couldn't think of a better backdrop for a meal.

The *Ricard* was finally put away and out came the wine, litre after litre. The football stories grew in both telling and volume, everyone had a story to tell, an amazing feat of skill to eulogise. A passer-by would have been incredulous to learn the score had only been 3-1. How was that possible with so many shots on goal, so many great players, so many action-packed incidents?

By the time the last steak had disappeared, we were not so much heroes as lions. Two teams of lions pitched in monumental combat, the like of which hadn't been seen since the last time we'd played.

Ah, alcohol, coach to the Gods.

It was about this time that the eldest lion tried to get up from the table and found the exertions of the afternoon had finally caught up with him. His legs had seized. I'd been a little stiff walking from the car to the square but, plied with *Ricard* and given a bench to sit on, I'd forgotten all about it. But now, as I tried to stand up, the pain hit me – from the back of my thighs all the way down to the large number of pain receptors I'd suddenly discovered in my calves.

And my back didn't feel that good either.

Leaning on his lioness, the eldest lion left the table and limped homeward, his mane threadbare but head held high. Above him, moths flitted like dark shadows against the floodlights and cicadas harmonised to a chorus of "Wimaway."

This lion would definitely sleep tonight.

Crime and Poetry

It was supposed to be a routine call to Simon Gardiner, our financial adviser: a few suggestions about possible changes to our unit trusts and a couple of questions about what had happened to the promised quarterly reports. Instead it turned into one of the worst moments of my life.

Our investment bond – the bulk of the proceeds from our house sale, our life savings, the money that was going to fund our new life in France – had just disappeared.

"You cancelled it in April," came the voice down the line.

It was now September. September 22nd. Friday. Three o'clock.

I froze. This was a piece of financial advice I had not been expecting.

"No, I didn't," I replied, hoping that there'd been some kind of mistake.

I could hear a riffling of papers, pages being turned, a note of panic in Simon's voice.

"I ... er ... have the correspondence here. Yes ... April."

I couldn't believe it. This could *not* be happening. Not to me. Things like this happened to other people!

And then I thought about horseboxes and flying roofs, *vignettes* and roadblocks, football and flues ... and realised ... I'm just the kind of person this does happen to.

It was a shock. That sudden shift in my internal picture. I was no longer the person who sat safe and warm watching events unfold upon the television screen. I was the person in front of the camera. The man standing in the doorway as the getaway car mounts the pavement. The man eating his sandwiches in the park when the sniper opens the attic window.

They're all me.

A voice on the line called me back. There was a chance the money hadn't been paid over.

"There was a dispute with the insurer about the valuation of the bond and I think – yes, here it is – it's still outstanding. And we still have the originals of the bond. I don't think it could have been encashed without them."

"But you're not sure?"

"No. It's up to the insurer whether they require the originals or not. It's unusual but..."

He didn't have to continue. Unusual but not unknown. And with my luck...

"And even if the money hasn't been paid out," he continued, "all the investments would have been liquidated."

"In April?" I asked.

"In April," he confirmed.

Just before the stock markets took off. Just before our investment bond began the 17% rise I'd so eagerly tracked for the last six months. It had been our one success story since leaving England. My trump card whenever cars broke down, fires smoked, dogs keeled over and horses succumbed to ten-foot long caterpillars. At least our finances were booming. If we hadn't sold the farm and come to France, we wouldn't have benefited from the surge in the stock markets.

I should have known it was too good to be true. The only other time we'd dabbled in the stock market was a week before the 1987 crash. Would I never learn?

But how could someone get their hands on our money without us knowing about it? Why didn't someone write to us for confirmation? Or give us a call?

There was more shuffling of papers and then the voice came back.

Simon had a photocopy of a cancellation letter we'd supposedly written to Mutual Friendly, the life insurance company that held our money. He read it out.

I listened in growing amazement.

"Thank you for your letter, received here on 7th April. For domestic reasons we will not proceed with this investment at this time and therefore ask for repayment of the monies paid. Please pay this, by transfer and at our expense, to our business account in Spain, this being the wish of us both.

"As our house is in the process of restoration, please address any further correspondence to our hotel, being as above.

"We particularly request that you and your agents respect our privacy in this matter. We do not wish to discuss our change of mind and will contact our agent at a later date to talk over further investment possibilities."

It was very clever. Plausible even. And in three paragraphs it had severed all links between us and our money.

"Where was the hotel?"

"Er, let's see ... Boulogne."

"And the Spanish bank?"

"It doesn't say."

Probably somewhere on the Costas. It had that ring about it. A ferry to Boulogne to set up an address in France, a cheap flight to the Costas to open a bank account.

I still couldn't believe it. Even after everything that had happened to us, this was just beyond belief. I was numbed. Mentally and physically.

Simon said he'd contact Mutual Friendly, inform them and find out the exact status of the bond. He'd ring back as soon as he had any news.

"You're taking this very calmly," he said before ringing off.

"Yes, I am," I said. But I knew someone who wouldn't.

I opened the window and shouted down to the figure bringing in the washing. "You're not going to believe this."

She didn't.

We hung around the phone for the next hour in shock. How and who and why hadn't someone told us? The same questions repeated over and over again.

Then the phone rang. It was Simon. Mutual Friendly had been informed; they were starting an investigation. He'd had their verbal assurance that no money had been paid out but we'd have to write to them for the written confirmation. And we'd also have to make an official request for compensation as the bond had been encashed. All the unit trusts had been liquidated and Mutual Friendly were holding the proceeds.

"How much?"

"They wouldn't say. That's another thing you'll have to ask in your letter."

We were given the name and address of the manager to write to. And could Simon have a copy for his files. And what about the *gendarmes*? Would we be contacting them?

I didn't particularly want to. With our track record of making ourselves understood in French police stations, we'd probably be arrested on the spot as accomplices.

But there was that hotel in Boulogne. They could always check that out.

"Have you got the full address of the hotel in Boulogne?"

"Yes, it's..." He paused for a while, "I'd better spell it." Which he did – the *Hôtel du Midi,* Boulogne sur Save.

Boulogne sur Save? I couldn't believe it. I was there last month playing football!

This was no longer a quick ferry trip from England to set up an address for correspondence – this was someone coming to within fifteen miles of our home.

"Is the letter from the hotel dated?" I asked. If we knew the dates, the *gendarmes* could check the hotel register. Maybe there'd be a forwarding address or a car registration number.

More riffling of paper and then, "I have a copy of a fax here. Let me see ... it's addressed from the hotel on the 29th May and ... sent at 14:37."

But was the fax sent from the hotel? Just because someone writes Boulogne sur Save at the top of a fax, it doesn't mean that's where it came from.

"Was there a fax number for the hotel?"

There was. And that was something else for the *gendarmes* to check.

The rest of the day swept by in a daze. Stunned silences followed by animated discussions of who, what, why and how. Our lives had rarely been touched by crime. We'd had a car stolen and that was it. But now I'd been impersonated. Someone was out there – pretending to be me – staying at hotels, setting up bank accounts, cancelling bonds and doing God knows what else.

The end of Shelagh's tether, never particularly distant since our arrival in France, was now in plain sight. We should never have come to France, it had been a huge mistake, let's put the house on the market and take the next flight home.

Which brought us back to quarantine, horse transport and a picture of hell that we were only too well acquainted with.

Which brought on another cycle of stunned silence and subsequent who, what, why and hows.

The night didn't get any better. I couldn't sleep. I found myself going over and over everything that had happened and all the things that should have happened.

Why had I felt compelled to entrust all our money to the stock market? Why hadn't I left it in the building society or buried it in the back garden?

Or listened to Gally when he'd suggested we invest it all in mouse futures?

The answer was, of course, the dream.

Although some might call it a vision. It was July 1994 and I suddenly awoke one morning with the certain knowledge that the London Stock Market had reached its bottom. From now on, my dream informed me, it could only rise. Whether this came from God or His financial adviser, the dream didn't say. But what I did know was that after years of non-profit dreaming, I was, at last, given something I could use.

Well, that's not exactly true. I'd had a vaguely similar dream when I was seventeen. That time I dreamt that a horse called Hatherop was about to win a race. Which was a pretty strange thing for a seventeen year-old to dream about, as Hatherop was neither a famous horse nor a name that readily tripped off the tongue. I awoke in a sweat and ran to find the morning paper, almost tearing the pages in my anxiety to find the racing pages.

Incredibly Hatherop was running that day and priced at 16-1. That afternoon I stopped off on the way to school and placed everything I had – four shillings – on Hatherop to win.

He didn't.

My faith was destroyed. What was the point of a shoulder tap from the celestial racing correspondent if the information was duff? And I'd lost half my paper round money in the process!

My mood was not helped when Hatherop went on to win his next race – at even longer odds. Shouldn't prophecies be more specific? Have a date stamp or something?

But this Footsie dream was different. I was sure of it.

Shelagh reminded me of the £1,000 we'd invested a week before the 1987 crash. And what about the pound? Three days after we left England on our first house-hunting expedition to France, the pound crashed out of the ERM and nose-dived towards parity with the Franc.

But I couldn't be shaken, after all, I was the person with the vision. So we diverted some of our savings into an index-linked unit trust ... and the stock market began to climb – exactly as my dream said it would.

A month later we bought shares for the first time. I dowsed the Financial Times and decided Southern Electric had a distinct aura surrounding its name. Three months later Southern Electric almost doubles in price and I have the golden touch.

After that, where else could I invest the money from the house sale but the stock market? Which is when I contacted Simon Gardiner at Eastleigh and Howard and asked him for suggestions. He came back with a proposal for a portfolio of unit trusts held in an off-shore investment bond. I'd have the flexibility of selecting the unit trusts whenever I had a suitable dream and the whole would be held under the tax efficient umbrella of an insurance bond issued by Mutual Friendly in Dublin.

That is, until it was even more efficiently cancelled a few weeks later.

I'm not sure which is worse: never having a prophetic dream or having one and then finding your winnings are void – the bookie having legged it before the first bend.

~

There are eight stages to being robbed, I'm told. Denial, shock, guilt and despair are all in there and I was cycling through them all. Was it my fault? Guilt. Why hadn't I rung up in July and asked what had happened to the second quarterly report? Or queried the non-arrival of Simon's promised six-monthly portfolio evaluation? I'd said I was going to. Many times. But the stock markets were doing brilliantly and I didn't want to bother anyone.

Could that be construed as culpability?

Would Mutual Friendly refuse to pay out as I'd been negligent?

Then came anger. Why should the insurer blame me for negligence? It was their fault, wasn't it? There must have been a signature – two signatures – didn't they check them? And weren't they suspicious? Why on earth would anyone take out a bond and then cancel it within a month? Didn't they think it strange? There'd be cancellation fees!

Shit! Cancellation fees. Was that why Mutual Friendly were being cagey about how much money was left?

I ran through to the study and rifled through my desk drawers. How much would they deduct? Ten per cent? Twenty? Insurance companies were renowned for fixing high penalties for early withdrawal.

Papers flew through my hands. Where was that booklet? I was sure it was in this drawer?

I found it, flicked through to the policy details at the back and...

Eight per cent. There was a full encashment penalty of eight per cent for all policies cancelled in the first year. Our life savings, whose value had dropped by seventeen per cent since this morning, had just dropped another eight. God knows what other penalty clauses there'd be. There was nothing else for it – the cats would have to go out to work.

I think that shifted me into despair. We'd been doing so well, I'd watched the stock markets advance, I'd written a program to monitor all our unit trusts.

Which brought me swiftly into denial. It couldn't be happening. It hadn't happened.

I then, somehow, shifted into detection. I'm not sure if it's a recognised stage of being robbed, but I found it. I was going to solve the case, track down the criminals and hand them over to Shelagh, who was mired in the third stage of being robbed – the desire for vengeance and the speedy return of drawing and quartering.

I cranked up my little grey cells. What do I look for first? Motive? That was simple – greed. Our investment bond was a tempting target for any latent thief. But opportunity? Who had known of the bond's existence? A handful of people – Shelagh, myself, staff at Mutual Friendly and Eastleigh and Howard. That was all. It's not the sort of topic that crops up in casual conversation – where did you say your money was invested? And the account number?

It had to be an inside job. I could see it all. Someone at the Dublin office going through the computer files, looking for people like us. People depositing money before moving abroad, people who might not contact anyone for years. People whose only contact with their money was by letter.

It was perfect. The policy details would be on file, the address, copies of signatures. All you'd need do was select a few to make it worth the risk without attracting interest. Open a series of false bank accounts in Spain, change the address for correspondence and cash in the policy. Perfect.

I think sleep finally caught up with me then, my little grey cells whacked from behind by a growing tiredness that lasted until breakfast the next day.

But a great detective cannot be stilled for long. I was sorting through my correspondence files after breakfast, when I came across a letter from Mutual Friendly, dated 9th June. And it was addressed to our real home – not to any hotel in Boulogne sur Save.

I remembered it now. It asked for the return of the originals of the bond as new regulations required all existing bonds to be re-issued. Amended originals would be sent to us in due course. There was a second page for us to sign and send back with the documents.

I stared at the letter. Two months *after* I'd supposedly cancelled the bond, here was a letter from Mutual Friendly talking about sending me a new set of policy details.

If I sent them the originals.

Which we didn't have. Eastleigh and Howard held them. So I'd rung Mutual Friendly and told them. Which meant I'd talked to someone at Mutual Friendly in June about a bond that hadn't existed since April.

And I'd talked to the person who'd signed the letter – Elaine Varley.

Or someone calling herself that.

And I'd referred to the letter. I'm sure I had. And she said something like, "oh yes, Eastleigh and Howard, I know them well. I'll get in touch with them."

Had she got in touch with them?

And if she had, and they'd refused to release the documents, why hadn't she got back in touch with me?

The more I looked at the letter, the less I liked it. I checked it against the other letters I'd received from Mutual Friendly – the logo was different. But did that mean anything? Companies change logos like other people change socks.

I checked the address. They were the same, as was the telephone number. And I remembered talking to Mutual Friendly's switchboard. And asking for Elaine Varley by name. Which meant she had to work there.

Or had an accomplice on the switchboard?

Was I becoming paranoid? The letter might be genuine. I'd worked for large companies – I knew how easy it was for one part of an organisation to work in isolation from others. The change of address and cancellation of the bond might never have reached the section dealing with the implementation of new regulations.

But if the letter was a forgery...

What better way to make us hand over the originals of the bond?

And if I'd had them, I certainly would have returned them. I had no inkling, no reason to doubt the letter.

Would that have been the end of our money? Were we *that* close to losing everything? Only saved by the fact that our financial advisers had kept the original documents?

I struggled manfully with letter composition until midday, most attempts diving straight into the waste bin. I was trying to strike a balance between righteous anger and a cry for help. A kind of 'Give us our money ... please' stretched over two pages.

And I wanted to enclose the letter from Elaine Varley and highlight the implications. I was convinced it was important.

We decided to delay faxing the letter until Monday. If this was an inside job we didn't want our letter sitting on a fax machine all weekend for anyone to see. We knew a shop in St. Gaudens we could use. We'd drive in, fax the letter and then phone Dublin when we got back to ensure it arrived intact and undoctored.

In the meantime, we'd better inform the *gendarmes*.

Which was something I was not looking forward to. I was half expecting to see my face staring out from the wall of wanted posters: driving without a *vignette* and a false 'Get out of Jail free' card – bounty 10,000 francs.

A fear that never materialised.

Largely because we didn't get that far, the police station being closed.

Well, it was lunchtime.

We looked at each other in disbelief. Can police stations close? Does crime stop between twelve and two?

I wouldn't be surprised. Life in the *campagne* does seem to slip into suspended animation between the *déjeuner* hours. I could well imagine families of masked felons laying aside their bags of swag while they dipped into their midday *cassoulet*.

We drove home, refined our script, and returned.

The *gendarmes* didn't want to know.

I could not believe it – perhaps I was stuck in denial – we had a crime to report, a script, an address to check out.

But our French wasn't good enough.

They said they couldn't understand what we were saying. Perhaps our pronunciation was off. Perhaps we were too excited. But we had the words written down! An attempt has been made to defraud us of our money, someone impersonated me, stayed at the *Hôtel du Midi* in Boulogne sur Save. Perhaps they're still there. What was simpler than that?

We'd spent ages on those few sentences, simplifying and honing.

All for nothing apparently.

Could we come back with someone who spoke French?

I felt like a child being asked to fetch a grown-up.

We made one more grab at our prepared script. Perhaps if we just concentrated on the hotel? Forget the fraud bit, we'd leave that to the Irish police.

It didn't work. Isn't there someone in your village you can bring, they asked?

Which is when we thought of Jean-Pierre. He was the only candidate we could think of. Chantal was on holiday, none of the football team spoke English and none of our English friends spoke French any better than we did. There was only Jean-Pierre left.

We'd been introduced to him at the Tuco *Fête*. He was a neighbour of an English couple we'd met, and he spoke English ... after a fashion. He'd learnt it from the BBC during the war when he'd been a radio operator with the resistance.

Would he help us?

He was brilliant. We descended upon him and his wife on a Saturday afternoon, unannounced and babbling. And he took us in, plied us with aperitif and converted our rough script into a bright shining work of art. Apparently our words were too cold – too Anglo-Saxon – French was a language for poets. He'd show us how to write a proper police statement.

For one awful moment I thought he was going to make it rhyme. But he didn't. He just made it flow. Converting our simple facts into a statement *gendarmes* would queue to listen to. For all I know, Gallicizing, 'I was proceeding along the High Street in a north-easterly direction,' into 'the call of the north-east drew my feet through shop-strewn thoroughfares.'

But what did that matter? If it meant the *gendarmes* would take us seriously, he could add music.

An hour later he was still composing. We'd moved through into his office and he was typing our statement into his PC and setting up print formats for his laser printer. The man was a perfectionist.

I was only looking for a French-speaking adult I could point to while shouting at the *gendarmes*, "he speaks French, now go to the hotel!"

But you cannot complain in the face of such dedication.

Unless you're a *gendarme*.

I don't think they were impressed with the sweeping prose. Or the imaginative use of print fonts.

I think they were too busy searching for the bit about my father's birthday.

We stood in the foyer of the *gendarmerie,* watching as first one, then two *gendarmes* picked up the statement, read it, nodded, shook their heads, muttered, and leapt into animated conversation with Jean-Pierre.

Shelagh and I were lost. Words evaporated around us like Scotch mist.

There's something about watching a conversation you can't follow that highlights cultural differences. You have to fall back on non-verbal clues – body language, attitude, volume.

If this had been three English people talking, I'd have classified it as a heated argument. All flashing eyes, raised tones and vigorous hand movements. I'd have given evens for Jean-Pierre spending the night in the cells.

But this was France. Probably no more than a group of poets discussing the perfidy of the criminal classes.

Which was not what we came for.

I tried to steer the conversation back to the hotel. Could someone please check the fax number? Did it belong to the hotel and, if not, who's was it? It might be the perp's personal number.

The station sergeant looked at my piece of paper, thought for a while, and then pronounced that the fax number indeed belonged to the *Hôtel du Midi*.

I was amazed. He couldn't have taken more than five seconds. Did he really have all the local fax numbers filed away in his head? Or just those with criminal associations? Was the *Hôtel du Midi* a hotbed of local crime?

I was so impressed I asked him how he knew it was the hotel's fax number.

"It says so here," he replied and pointed to my piece of paper. *Hôtel du Midi*, fax number 72 34 60 94.

Brilliant. This was a very trusting policeman. I tried to explain to him that this was my note, I'd written it, I'd copied it down over the phone. It wasn't a sworn affidavit from France Telecom!

Wasn't there a police central computer where you could enter a fax number and get the subscriber's name and address?

I was never to find out. The more excited I got, the less sense I made. My brain was stuffed full of all the relevant English words but all their French equivalents had joined Missing Persons. I was close to bursting.

And Jean-Pierre's knowledge of English was not as extensive as we'd first thought.

I think he employed a similar method of translation to mine – though subtly shifted – listening for a word he recognised then filling in the rest from various BBC wartime broadcasts.

I have a feeling he suggested the *gendarmes* visit Boulogne, round up all the Germans and impose a dusk to dawn curfew. I wasn't sure, but at least it would have been something positive.

But police work these days is more concerned with form-filling ... and about the victim's details rather than the unsub's[6] fax number.

Back came the usual questions. Who was I, what was my address, when was my father's birthday? I could have screamed. There was only one address that was important and that was the hotel in Boulogne sur Save!

As I stood, propped up against the station sergeant's desk, reeling off family birthdays, I could see exactly how the private detective was born. I was feeling decidedly Holmesian myself. I knew what needed to be done but I couldn't find anyone prepared to do it. It was frustrating in the extreme.

From what I could understand from Jean-Pierre, the *gendarmes* would visit the hotel – sometime in the week when they had the time – but couldn't do any more as it wasn't a French crime. It was an Irish crime. An inside job at Mutual Friendly in Dublin. And they'd wait for the Irish police to contact them.

We came away from the *gendarmerie* feeling exhausted, all nervous energy drained. There was a hotel less than half an hour away. The road outside the *gendarmerie* led straight to Boulogne sur Save, they wouldn't even have to take a left turn. But no north-westerly call would draw one single step through shop-strewn thoroughfares until the middle of next week.

Aaaarrrgghh!

Pergonini MD

Monday arrived with a flurry of activity. There were people to phone, people to fax, news to disseminate. We grabbed a very quick breakfast and rushed into St Gaudens with our much-honed letter to Mutual Friendly.

And the two suspicious pages from Elaine Varley.

It cost us £20 to fax eight pages. I was astonished and quickly added that to the money we were owed.

Someone would pay.

Back home, we waited ... and waited.

Surely Dublin would have received the fax by now? We'd asked them to ring us as soon as it arrived.

Approaching midday I could wait no longer. I picked up the phone and asked to speak to Trevor Graham, the Administrative Director.

He wasn't available. He was in an important meeting.

About my letter, hopefully.

I left a message and rang off. I'd have to wait until after dinner.

Two seconds after I put the phone down, it rang.

I stared at the receiver. Was this suspicious? I phone Dublin and someone rings me back immediately?

"Hello," I said warily.

"Mr Dolley? My name's Andy Chatfield, I work for Special Services. Trevor Graham asked me to call."

"Special Services?" I know I'd asked for the police to be involved but I didn't think I'd be talking to MI5.

"Yes, Mutual Friendly International Special Services."

MFI Special Services? It didn't have quite the same ring as MI5.

"I've read your letter and I'd like to ask you a few questions, if that's convenient?"

By all means. I was still intrigued as to how he managed to phone so quickly after I'd rung Dublin. Was he there at the time, but wanted to phone back to make sure I was who I said I was?

Or was I becoming paranoid?

"Have you been to the doctor recently?"

This was not a question I'd been expecting.

Was it in code?

Should I fetch Jean-Pierre and ask if he still had his code book? Were there two British airmen hiding in our outhouse?

"Er ... no?" I replied, waiting, breath well and truly baited for the next question.

"Do you know any doctors in Aurignac?"

"No."

"Does your wife know any doctors ... socially perhaps?"

I placed my hand over the receiver and turned to Shelagh who was standing alongside.

"He wants to know if you know any doctors ... socially."

"Who?"

I was beginning to wonder that myself. Why this fascination with doctors? And was he really who he said he was?

"No, she doesn't," I replied, thinking that about wrapped it up on the doctor front.

"Neither of you have any friends who are doctors or know anyone who'd sign MD after their name?"

I could not believe this.

"Why do you ask?"

He didn't want to say. Apparently it was early in the investigation and it was important that answers were uncoloured by context.

But he did provide me with one very important fact. The letter from Elaine Varley was a fake. The letterhead was not genuine and it wasn't Elaine's signature.

I phoned Simon almost straight away. I wanted to verify this Andy Chatfield. And MFI[7] Special Services. Should I expect a phone call from B&Q[8]?

Apparently not. MFI was the parent organisation of various Mutual Friendly companies in the UK and Europe. And there was such a person as Andy Chatfield who did work for Special Services who were indeed carrying out their own internal investigation.

But what on earth caused his obsession with doctors? Was he a hypochondriac? I wanted my context well and truly coloured.

"Ah, I think I might know why he asked that," said Simon.

At last. I couldn't think of one sensible suggestion.

"I've got the letter here. Let me see ... Yes. Your signatures were witnessed by a Dr. Pergonini of Aurignac."

What? This was getting more and more bizarre. First, there was the hotel fifteen miles away at Boulogne sur Save. Now, there's a doctor involved. At Aurignac ... five miles away.

I asked for the name again. I could check the phone directory. It wouldn't be difficult to see if he existed.

Simon read out the full name. It was stamped on the letter. The signature was illegible but the stamp said: *G.PERGONINI M.D Sur Rendez-Vous 31420 AURIGNAC.*

There was no address, 31420 was the post code for Aurignac, so that was no help. And there was no telephone number. Odd for a doctor's stamp.

Even odder were the letters MD – it may stand for doctor of medicine in English but it meant nothing in French. Doctors called themselves *docteur* – that's all.

And *Sur Rendez-Vous* just meant 'by appointment.'

I began to wonder what else this letter said.

Simon read it out. It was a fax to Elaine Varley dated 30th May.

> *Having found my husband's reply to your fax less than complete, here are our witnessed signatures in approval of your payment to my husband's account with Banca Zaragoza. We would prefer payment by bank draft or transfer and are sending the necessary documents to the bank to convert the account to both our names.*
>
> *We have written to our solicitor asking him to forward to you all documentation concerning this investment, and would ask that any correspondence you send us be by normal mail, your last letter having taken a fortnight to reach us.*
>
> *Thank you for your assistance.*

And at the bottom of the letter, underneath our forged signatures was the line - *I confirm the identity, having seen passports, of the two persons who sign this letter. G.PERGONINI M.D.*

So, on the 30th May, someone writes to Elaine Varley saying they've written to their solicitor asking for the bond's documentation to be forwarded, and on the 9th June someone writes to us asking for that same documentation to be sent to Elaine Varley. It fitted.

And would that explain why she wasn't surprised to hear from me? Having already requested the originals in some earlier letter?

And how many earlier letters were there? What did they say? I needed to see them. Could I have copies?

"Have you got a fax?"

I hadn't, which meant a delay of at least four working days for the post to arrive. And I couldn't wait four days – the suspense would kill me.

And then I remembered our estate agent. He had a fax ... and I might have the number.

I ran into the study. My desk was in its usual mess. Twenty seconds later it entered new levels of untidiness as reams of papers were picked up, shuffled and thrown aside. It had to be here! Somewhere! Where was it?

And then I found it, a letter from the estate agent who'd sold us our house. And there was his fax number on the letterhead. He was only a half hour's drive away and I was sure he wouldn't mind. It was a crisis after all.

I ran back to the phone and gave the details to Simon. He'd fax the papers through immediately.

This was getting quite exciting. Even enjoyable. It was like living in your own whodunit. Every day a new letter, a new clue, a new twist. It was better than TV.

I rang David Jarvis, our estate agent. I thought I'd better warn him before his fax filled his entire office with forged correspondence.

But he wasn't there. So I left a message on his answerphone.

And then I went straight for the telephone directory – there's no rest for the amateur detective – what was that doctor's name? Pergonini?

I scanned Aurignac for Pergoninis. Nothing. Not even anything close.

I then checked Cassagne just to see if doctors were ex-directory. Ours wasn't; I could see his entry, with *médecin* after his name. No hint of an MD.

And the name had to be false, didn't it? Otherwise it meant he'd seen our passports – which was impossible, we'd never let them out of our sight.

Had we?

A quick sprint back into the study and a mad search through our box of files. Household Accounts, Insurance, Medical ... Passports! There they were. Both of them, safe and snug. Thank God for that.

Which meant no Pergonini could have seen our passports.

Unless someone used forgeries.

About half past four the phone rang again. It was David, our estate agent. He'd stepped into his office and almost tripped over a box of fax paper that had spewed out from his machine. What had happened? He'd heard my message but was it really true?

I assured him it was and gave him a quick précis of events so far. He was amazed.

And not sure if he'd received the complete fax message. There were pages of my fax interleaved with other faxes all over the place. He'd checked the name on the fax header and rung up Simon to ask for the fax to be re-transmitted. In the meantime, he'd decollate what he could and make sure it went into that evening's post. We should have it tomorrow. And could we keep him informed? He was intrigued to know how it all turned out.

I replaced the receiver and collapsed onto the settee, wound down my internal detective agency and thought about tomorrow. We had the car booked in for a service. I'd have to get the documentation together and prepare a script.

And then I remembered that other garage. The one we'd bought the car from. The one with the dubious 'Get out of Jail free' cards. They'd had Shelagh's passport for a month. February through March.

A garage in Boulogne sur Save.

Fraud and Warp Coils

I wasn't sure if I was sinking into paranoia or just belatedly suspicious. People impersonate us, stay at a hotel in Boulogne sur Save, claim to use passports to verify their identities. All this happening sometime in April and May. And in March, Shelagh's passport spends the month holidaying at a nearby garage.

Coincidence?

I rolled out of bed the next morning, my mind besieged by conspiracies and lurking doppelgangers.

But today was a new day and I threw back the curtains to greet it. The sun was shining, the sky was blue...

And a dustman was relieving himself against our fence post.

It must be Tuesday.

And we had a car to service.

We had considered, very briefly, ringing up the garage to postpone, but we'd had so much trouble arranging it in the first place we didn't dare cancel.

And our car did need servicing – or perhaps, counselling would have been a better word – it didn't like the wet, didn't like the cold and you couldn't do a thing with it in the mornings.

Ten minutes into a journey and it was fine but those first ten minutes – well, it wasn't natural. Whatever combination of choke I tried – in, out or yanked over my shoulder – it was wrong, and the car would stall. Usually as I was trying to pull out into a major road.

Which led us to the conclusion that with winter approaching perhaps it would be a good time to have the car serviced.

Easier said than done.

We'd looked up 'car service' in the dictionary and found the word *révision*. Ok, so far, but as soon as we checked the Yellow Pages and the garage ads in the local paper – nothing. The word *révision* was mysteriously absent. Didn't they do car services in France? Or was it taken for granted and they didn't feel the need to advertise?

We decided to try the local garage. Or what we assumed to be the local garage. It had CITROEN written in large letters above the door but we'd never seen any signs of life within. And the pile of cars outside never seemed to change.

But it was close by and we could walk home if we needed to leave the car there for any length of time.

We had the conversation mapped out as usual. We'd ask, "can you service our car?" and then, according to their *oui* or *non*, we'd either leave or move onto our next question. After all, what else was there you could say about a car service?

Apparently, quite a lot.

We stood in front of the garage, expectantly waiting for the *oui* or *non*, our slip of paper ready to provide the next line of dialogue, and out came several sentences devoid of *ouis, nons* or anything else we recognised. After requests to speak *lentement* and our by now mandatory prefix of *nous sommes Anglais*, we realised he was asking us what needed servicing.

We pointed to the car.

He asked us what part of the car.

"What part of the car?"

"*Oui.*"

I looked at our script. Besides the part where he said '*oui*', I was lost. Were we really being asked to give a list of all the parts we wanted checking?

I tried to get back on script with an attempt to ask for a full service. But this was met with a blank stare.

Out came the dictionary and a frantic search for terms like oil change and brakes and spark plugs and whatever else we could scavenge from memories not attuned to the internal workings of the motor car. Was this some kind of test to see if we merited his attention?

He seemed to like *vidange*, the French for oil change, but nothing else. And he'd do that for two hundred Francs.

We decided to make a tactical withdrawal and regroup back at the house with the dictionary and Yellow Pages. We didn't fancy the idea of having the car serviced one piece at a time – a *vidange* here and a spark plug there.

I scanned the Yellow Pages again. This time looking to see what services they did advertise. Perhaps they didn't use the word *révision* any more? Perhaps they'd anglicised it to *le service* as they'd done with *le parking* and *le shopping*?

I found plenty of garages offering 'service' – but when I checked the dictionary I found this could mean after sales service. But I also noticed the word *entretien* appearing again and again in the ads. I looked that up in our dictionary and found ... car service. I could not believe it! I checked the dictionary again for 'car service' and found *révision* – no mention of *entretien* at all. My faith in our dictionary crashed. What good was it if they didn't cross-reference all the terms? Were we really supposed to check through all the French words just in case there was another word for the one we wanted?

But we did have a new word and with it a new lead.

The next day we decided to take a detour from our normal shopping route and cruise the main road outside St. Gaudens where all the big garages and car dealers were. With any luck we'd find one offering *entretiens* for Citroens.

We soon found one offering *entretiens pour tous marques*. At last! Armed with our revised script, we entered.

"Do you service cars?" seemed on the superfluous side as an opening question at a garage specialising in nothing but the servicing of cars, so we skipped that one and went onto the next.

"How much does it cost to service a Citroen AX?"

"What kind of service?" came the reply, or words to that general effect.

The conversation was wavering but still on script.

"A full service," I countered.

"*Non*." He shook his head.

This was not the right answer. '*Non*' could only be used on questions one, three, eight and nine. I knew – I had the script. And would have pointed out his error if he hadn't then asked me how many kilometres we'd driven.

A glimmer of hope. He may have started ad libbing but he'd asked me a question I knew the answer to – 160,000. And I could see the way back on script. Obviously he wanted to know how many kilometres the car had done to determine the type of service required.

He then asked me how many kilometres were on the clock when we'd bought it? This was not so good. Why would he want to know that?

"155,000?" I answered dubiously, anxiously fingering the script trying to spot the next likely question.

Which was unintelligible. Equally so when he repeated it slowly. I looked at Shelagh and she looked at me. And then both of us looked back at the mechanic.

Who started speaking very quickly and waving his arms. We caught odd phrases, enough to know that something was *très important* and somehow the mileage was the key. It sounded like 'warp coil'.

"Did he just say warp coil?" I asked Shelagh.

"That's what I thought," she answered, relieved, I think, by the fact that she hadn't been the one to raise the question. We might not know much about the internal combustion engine but we knew all about warp coils. But did Citroen really have warp technology?

We turned to face the mechanic with renewed respect.

He was still in the throes of trying to explain what would happen if the warp coil failed while we were driving. But he didn't need to. We'd watched enough *Star Trek* to know that the warp engines would have to be taken off-line and the moment that happened a

Romulan warbird would de-cloak off the starboard bow.

So, we definitely had to have the warp coil looked at. We nodded sagely.

He liked that. Expensive but necessary, he said.

"How expensive?" I asked.

"Perhaps 500 francs." And then he asked us what else needed servicing.

Not again!

"A full service?" I repeated, determined to claw the conversation back on script.

"*Non*, too expensive," he replied.

I couldn't help but wonder what kind of garage we'd walked into. I'd been so used to hearing reports in England about garages over-charging and performing unnecessary work, that I couldn't conceive of one turning down work on the grounds that it would cost too much.

I turned to our back-up list. After our last encounter at a garage, we'd prepared a list of car parts we'd like looking at – just in case.

I opened with *vidange*.

"Oui," he nodded.

Good start. "Brakes," I continued.

"*Non*, too expensive."

What? How could checking the brakes be too expensive! He then went on to explain he'd have to take the wheels off and if the brakes were Ok it would be a waste of time.

"Were there any problems with the brakes?" he continued.

Not really but...

He said he'd give them a road test if we wanted but nothing else unless he found a problem.

We struggled through the rest of our list. Meeting more *nons* and shakes than *ouis* and nods. Perhaps the French only serviced their cars when something fell off.

But we booked our *rendez-vous*. Nine o'clock, Tuesday. Today.

We definitely had to go through with it. Being robbed was one thing but having a dodgy warp coil was something far, far worse.

John, my brother-in-law, came over just before half eight as arranged. I think he wanted to hear the latest instalment of the Crime of the Century. He'd follow us in and then drive us back.

Off we set with the car playing up as usual – I'm sure it knew it was going to the garage. Certainly its behaviour was reminiscent of Gypsy en route to the vet – plenty of complaining and digging in of tyres. About halfway there the engine cut out, just as I was pulling out at a junction. I quickly restarted the car – I was getting pretty quick with all the practice – and was just slipping into gear when.... Crash! There was a thumping noise and the car lurched forward.

The warp coil!

Merde!

I looked at Shelagh and I could tell she was thinking the same thing – of all the times for the warp coil to blow, it had to be on the way to the garage! Why couldn't it wait another ten minutes?

I tentatively tried the engine again – ever the optimist – and was relieved to hear it start. Perhaps it wasn't irretrievable after all? We limped off the junction and found a patch of ground where we could park safely. John pulled in behind us.

I wearily pushed open the door and was in the process of struggling with the bonnet when I heard John apologising.

What?

"Sorry, I thought you'd pulled out. I took my eye off the road for a while and..."

Ran into the back of us.

My first traffic accident. Years of safe driving behind me and then my brother-in-law runs into the back of me while I'm stationary at a road junction.

But at least it wasn't the warp coil.

Which at that moment was a considerable plus.

We surveyed the slightly crumpled back bumper, the smashed tail lights and the boot which no longer fastened. Minor damage. Nothing compared with ringing up a garage and fighting to make yourself understood in halting French – please come and collect the car, the warp engine's blown and there are dilithium crystals all over the roundabout!

So, we resumed our journey. We toyed with idea of adding the damage to the list of things to be looked at by the garage but quickly dismissed the idea. They'd probably say it was too expensive. And John was confident he could knock everything back into shape himself.

We left the car at the garage and arranged to return at four.

Back home, we waited for the *poste*. About ten, the familiar yellow car wound its way towards us and dropped off our mail at our *boite aux lettres* at the end of the drive.

But no thick envelope from David Jarvis.

I was disappointed to say the least. I couldn't wait to read the next instalment. Now I'd have to wait until tomorrow.

Which naturally led to a bout of recriminations. Why had we let him put it in the post? Why didn't we drive to Castlenau last night and pick up the fax immediately? Why? Why? Why?

I think we were lapsing back into guilt.

Luckily the phone rang before we could sink any further. It was Andy Chatfield. Perhaps he'd found another medical query?

But no, this time he wanted to know about a cancellation form. Had we received it?

I didn't know. What would it look like?

An A4 piece of paper with the words CANCELLATION FORM prominently displayed.

Well, I did ask. Not that I could remember ever receiving one.

"When would it have arrived?"

"It was sent on the 22nd of March."

I still couldn't remember. I asked Andy to wait while I went through my files. I'd sorted through all the correspondence from Eastleigh and Howard and Mutual Friendly over the weekend. If I'd received a cancellation form it should be there.

I couldn't see one.

I gathered up the file and took it back to the phone. The earliest letter I had from Mutual Friendly was dated April 3rd.

"That would be the Policy Schedules."

It was. I had copies of the Policy Schedules, an initial valuation of the bond and several pages entitled "Your Right to Change Your Mind."

"Your right to change your mind?"

"Yes."

"That would have accompanied the cancellation form."

I looked again. The pages weren't dated. It was just four pages of information and disclaimers. I remember glancing through it when it arrived. But I couldn't remember if it had come with a cancellation form or by itself or with another letter.

Neither could I remember when it came – I'd binned the envelope – and filed the contents with all the other bond correspondence.

"You don't remember receiving the cancellation form?"

I didn't. But neither could I be certain that I hadn't.

My eyes drifted down the page in front of me. *Your right to change your mind. You have fourteen days from the day you receive this notice in which to change your mind.*

So, someone had exercised that right. And, from what Andy now told me, used the proper cancellation form as well. It wasn't just someone discovering our policy number and forging a letter. It was someone taking possession of a document posted to us.

Or making sure it was never sent in the first place?

Which reinforced my inside job theory. They had the bond details, the cancellation form and fourteen days to set up a false bank account and a new address. Maybe using an accomplice, maybe one person taking a holiday and flitting around Europe. It all fitted.

But not according to Andy. He'd spent the entire weekend in Dublin. Apparently he'd flown over an hour or two after my call on

Friday and spent the weekend reviewing the files. He was confident there had been no breach of security at the Dublin office.

Well, he would say that, wouldn't he? He was internal security, and the further he could push the crime away from Mutual Friendly the better.

I was not convinced. If it wasn't organised from Dublin, how did they know about the existence of the bond, the cancellation form and everything else?

And I was far from convinced about Elaine Varley's part in all this. It was her name on the letter trying to make me hand over the originals. It might not have been her signature but that didn't mean she couldn't have found someone else to sign her name.

I was still thinking unfriendly thoughts about Ms. Varley when the next call came. It was Simon, our financial adviser, had the fax arrived? I explained it had and it hadn't. He said he'd talked with David Jarvis yesterday afternoon and re-transmitted the fax.

And he had some good news. Mutual Friendly had assured him they would make sure we didn't lose out. And although they hadn't committed anything in writing, they seemed to be accepting everything I'd asked for in my letter.

I knew I should have asked for the Porsche!

The conversation swung back to the crime. I think he was becoming as hooked as I was by the excitement of appearing in your own whodunit. We chatted about the case, I told him about the cancellation form and we swapped suspects.

He mentioned how surprised he'd been when he learnt that we'd cancelled the bond but hadn't suspected a thing. He'd only found out about the cancellation in May – Mutual Friendly having respected our apparent wishes not to tell him.

"In fact, Ralph ... you know Ralph Howard, don't you? One of our directors? He wrote to you at the hotel in May to ask what had happened."

And had received a phone call a week later.

From me.

I was astonished. "Didn't he recognise my voice?"

"Oh, the man didn't get through. He just left a message with the switchboard."

"Saying what?"

"Saying that he found Ralph's letter objectionable and that he didn't want to be contacted by phone or letter. He'd be in touch later."

And later that day he was.

By fax.

Apparently, I had been swamped by a personal problem and was too upset to talk about it.

Very plausible again. What better way to break off contact between two Englishmen – personal problems, can't talk about it, enough said.

At half past three, John arrived and it was time to fetch the car. Following an uneventful drive in to St. Gaudens – there being nothing suitable to ram – we pulled up outside the garage expecting to see a red Citroen in the yard with its overhauled warp engines gleaming.

But it wasn't there. It was still inside, lurking at the end of the far bay ... with its bonnet up.

Never a good sign.

Our warp engineer of the previous day came running over the moment he saw us. He had a slightly incredulous look on his face. Also not a good sign. What will it be this time – anti-matter containment field misaligned?

No, instead he asked us about water. Did we know there was no water in the engine?

What?

He flapped his arms a few times and shook his head. For one moment I thought he was going to grab me by the shoulders. But instead he ushered us towards the car, muttering incredulities as he went.

He showed us a gaping split in the water hose and then revved the engine a few times to demonstrate the fountain of water that spurted in time to the engine pump.

"Ah," I said, "perhaps that explains the burning smell last week."

"What burning smell?" asked Shelagh.

"The one last week. I thought the bonnet felt hot."

"You didn't say anything."

"I didn't think it was important." Which was true. I'd smelt a slight burning smell when I'd climbed out of the car but hadn't managed to trace it and it had only been the merest whiff.

And who was I to question the personal hygiene of our car?

As we stood staring at the ruptured hose, we realised just how lucky we'd been. Of all the times for a part to fail, I couldn't think of a better time than a day or so before the car was booked in for a service. What with the news that Mutual Friendly had guaranteed our money, perhaps Fate was, at last, beginning to smile on us.

Even if we did have the boot to fix.

But the car wouldn't be ready tonight. It needed a new part and they didn't have one in stock. Maybe tomorrow, maybe the next day.

Perhaps it wasn't so much a smile that Fate bestowed upon us, as a grin.

Passports and Wandering Irish Con-Men

It was Wednesday, the sun was shining and not a dustman in sight.

I spent most of the early morning with one eye on the window. Where was the post? Had it arrived yet? Had I blinked and missed it.

Just before ten, I caught a glimpse of yellow car and raced to fetch the post. And there it was, nestling in our *boite aux lettres* – one thick white envelope with our estate agent's logo on the front. It had arrived.

There were eight pages inside. David must have decollated them for us as they were now separated and stapled together.

The first page was a print-out of the Spanish bank account details. I quickly scanned for the address ... where was it?

Bossost.

Bossost? That sounded familiar. I couldn't recall why at first and continued scanning down the page. It was in Spanish – naturally – but it wasn't difficult to follow. My name was under *titulares*, my *domicilio* was given as the *Hôtel du Midi* in Boulogne S.S. And the date of *apertura* was given as the 10th of April.

All fairly easy to understand. There were various other numbers printed out. Some I guessed were the Spanish equivalent of bank sorting codes and account numbers. And on the bottom left, almost obscured by the fold in the page caused by the staple, was a handwritten note. An address. *48 San* something ... I couldn't quite make it out. But I could the next part.

35540 LES.

Which is when I remembered why Bossost seemed so familiar. I'd been there. To both places, Les and Bossost. They were barely an hour's drive away, a few miles over the Spanish border. We'd even stopped and walked around the shops. I remembered it clearly. We'd been told about this amazing supermarket at the Tuco *Fête*. Everyone said it stocked the best and cheapest wine for miles. We hadn't been able to find it at first and had combed both Les and Bossost looking for it.

So much for my theory about a cheap flight to the Costas to set up a false bank account. It was all being done by someone staying here. The hotel at Boulogne, the 'doctor' in Aurignac, the bank in Bossost. Everything was within an hour's drive of our home.

We quickly turned to the next page. What else would we find?

It was the cancellation form. Signed on the 10th of April, the same day the bank account was set up.

And the signatures looked very ropey. I turned back to the bank print-out. My signature was on that one as well. Neither looked very good.

Shelagh's wasn't a good match either. If anything both signatures looked as though they'd been written by the same person.

But they weren't entirely random either. I could see that someone must have had sight of our real signatures. It wasn't a good attempt ... but it was a copy nonetheless.

The next page was one Simon had read out to us, the letter dated April 10th that must have accompanied the cancellation form. And my signature had changed again.

It was better.

Another page, another signature. Different again and Shelagh's had become embellished with flamboyant loops.

It was a fax to Elaine Varley, dated the 29th May.

> *Thank you for your fax of 23/5, which we received today.*
>
> *Regarding our repayment, the account is at present in the name of C Dolley only as it is used for business purposes. Ideally, therefore, we would prefer either a transfer or bank draft in one name only, as per our previous instructions. A cheque payment could well take a month or more to clear.*
>
> *However, we do not want to delay things so will try to change the account to both names and will accept payment by cheque if there is no other possibility. The original of this letter follows by post and we have asked our solicitor to post you the Policy Documents which he holds.*
>
> *We look forward to receiving your faxed confirmation that payment has been made in the very near future and thank you for your assistance.*
>
> *For your records I, Shelagh Dolley, am in complete agreement to payment being made to my husband's account.*

This was a very interesting letter. I hadn't registered the fact that the account in Spain was in my name only. Wasn't that a big mistake? Our investment bond was in both our names – wouldn't it have been more sensible to open a joint account?

Unless there was only one person setting up that account.

"Did they get the account changed to a joint one?"

Shelagh's voice came out of nowhere. I was so engrossed, I'd almost forgotten she was there.

"What did you say?"

"Did they get the account changed to a joint one? Like they said there." She pointed at the third paragraph. "If they added my name to the account, how did they do it?"

Which made me think. How did they manage to open a bank account in *my* name? Don't you have to have identification?

Shelagh flipped us onto the next page before I could explore further. It was the telephone message taken from Eastleigh and Howard's switchboard. It was dated May 16th, 10:40am. It mentioned Ralph's 'objectionable' letter. I was becoming quite interested in this 'objectionable' letter – what on earth had it said?

The rest of the message stressed my desire not to be contacted by letter or phone – which must have been a considerable worry to my impersonator. He'd have had no idea how well the people at Eastleigh and Howard knew me.

The next page contained Ralph's long-awaited letter.

Dear Big Nose, it began ... Well, not exactly. In fact it was fairly mild. It noted the fact that they'd only just learnt (May 5th) from Mutual Friendly about the cancellation and was surprised we hadn't had the common courtesy to inform them directly.

What was interesting was the next page. It was a faxed reply to the 'objectionable' letter, dated 16th May. The same day as the irate telephone call. But by the time 'I' sent the fax, I'd apparently cooled down.

It was addressed to Simon.

Thank you for the portfolio update you sent me in early April. You will have learnt that I have since had to cancel the Mutual Friendly European Personal Bond Fund. I do not wish to enter in to any discussion about this, either by telephone or post as I have been completely swamped by a personal problem which was impossible to foresee.

We fully appreciate the work you put in to the package and plan further investments at the end of July 1995. We will be in touch with you then so that neither you nor your firm will lose out as a result of our changed circumstances. Meanwhile, the house being far from finished we are taking a holiday in Spain, as of tomorrow, for four weeks.

Rest assured, we will contact you during July to discuss an investment which I will then be in a position to undertake.

The letter ended with yet another variation on my signature. The best yet.

I re-read the first paragraph. How did 'I' know that Eastleigh and Howard sent me a portfolio update in early April. Had I received one in early April? I rushed into the study to check my files. I couldn't find one.

And why suddenly start calling the Investment Bond the European

Personal Bond Fund? I'd never seen it referred to as that. Had I?

I re-checked my file. I found a couple of European Bonds and one reference to a Pooled Fund Bond. But no Personal Bond Fund.

Was I being pedantic?

I didn't think so. It had to be important to dissect every sentence to try and find out what was known and when, in order to find out 'who'. If I could find something that only one person could possibly know then I had them.

I checked the date of the letter again – the 16th of May – in reply to a letter sent on the 5th of May. Was that significant? If the person was staying at the hotel, they would have received the letter when? About the 10th? Why wait until the 16th before replying? Especially as the phone call didn't sound planned. You don't plan to ring up and have a go at someone in the morning then pen a reasoned letter in the afternoon. No, the phone call smacked of panic, and the letter of damage limitation – did I overdo it on the phone, should I have said something different?

Which probably meant that Ralph's letter was not seen until the 16th. And that 'I' was no longer staying at the hotel.

The letters were being forwarded.

Or collected.

The last page of our bundle was the Pergonini letter.

The doctor's stamp looked completely wrong. Shelagh dug out a letter we had with our doctor's stamp on it. They weren't remotely similar. One was full of information – address, telephone number, diplomas and specialties – and one had 'by appointment.' What was the point in having a stamp like that? It had to be a fake.

And the signature was unintelligible. I knew doctors were supposed to have notoriously bad handwriting but this was an elongated cross followed by a dot. Somehow all nine letters of Pergonini had been compressed into a broad vertical bar which had then been struck through in a final flourish.

Our deliberations were interrupted at that point by the phone.

It was David Jarvis, our estate agent. Had we received the fax yet? I told him we had and that we were just sifting through it.

"I think I may be able to help you," he said.

"Oh? How?"

"I couldn't help but read some of the letters and ... this will have to be strictly confidential but I think I might be able to spread some light on the matter."

This was a surprise. I'd had a week full of surprises and thought myself well beyond the point where there was anything surprising left in the world.

But here was another one.

"Have you ever heard of Peter Kennedy?" he continued.

"No."

"You realise this is in the strictest confidence. I don't want anyone to know I told you."

Fair enough.

He then proceeded to explain that Peter Kennedy was a former associate of his. They'd worked together in Castlenau. He was a family friend of the previous owners of our house and helped with the sale – receiving half the commission in the process. It was also possible – if not likely – that he still had a key.

He was now living in the Gers, David thought. Which is why he felt compelled to ring. He'd heard Peter was under investigation by the *gendarmes* in Gimont. And there was apparently another case in the Tarn involving an English couple where Peter Kennedy's name had cropped up. £60,000 had gone missing there.

And Peter Kennedy was Irish.

This was becoming more convoluted with every twist. I thought I'd had the crime nicely compartmentalised. It was an inside job at Mutual Friendly's Dublin office. A nameless male accomplice hopped on a ferry to France and drove around Boulogne and the Spanish border, setting up bank accounts and false addresses.

But here was someone with a link to our house. Was it really possible that someone at the Dublin office would have a friend who just happened to have a key to our house? Wasn't that taking coincidence too far?

We chatted a while about the faxes and how incredible everything seemed. I told him I couldn't believe that anyone had been taken in by the forged signatures. They changed with every letter.

"Oh, I don't know," he said. "I thought they were rather good."

Perhaps I was overly suspicious, but I couldn't help thinking I detected a defensive note in his voice. As though he'd forged the signatures and didn't like his prowess being questioned.

I was definitely becoming paranoid.

But I fished his envelope out from our bin.

And checked the postmark. Tuesday. Posted at Masseube at 17:15. Very strange for someone who was rushing to meet the last post on Monday.

And Masseube was nowhere near his office in Castlenau. Masseube was in the Gers. Close to Gimont and Boulogne sur Save.

I phoned Andy almost immediately. After all, doesn't 'in strictest confidence' mean 'pass it on as soon as possible?' And besides, this was evidence in a crime. And a lead that could be followed.

Andy said he'd inform the Irish police and they'd check up on

Peter Kennedy. And he had other contacts he could use as well.

Which sounded interesting. Were these underworld informers? Barmen in hotels, who'd only answer questions when presented with a ten dollar bill?

"Have the *gendarmes* visited the hotel yet?" he asked.

Sadly not, I told him. At least as far as I knew. I wasn't sure if they were going to get back to me or Jean-Pierre. I'd check tomorrow if I hadn't heard by then. And pray they'd phoned Jean-Pierre in the meantime – I had zero faith in my ability to make myself understood by the *gendarmes*.

"Did your estate agent say anything about Peter Kennedy being involved in personal finance?"

No, other than fraud. Which I suppose could be loosely termed as very personal finance.

"Do you know any accountants or financial planners locally?" He was off again. Obviously he'd given up on doctors and was now moving through the rest of the professional classes.

"No," I replied, waiting for the follow-up on bankers, solicitors and veterinary practitioners.

I think he must have realised at this point the obtuse nature of his questioning. "You see," he explained, "I'm sure we're dealing with someone who knows the Financial Services Act intimately. This man is not an amateur."

And it wasn't easy to set up bank accounts nowadays, he continued. Most countries had anti money-laundering legislation. Spain was certain to be a signatory to all the international conventions.

Which made me think. How did someone manage to set up a bank account without identification? If governments were so hot against money laundering these days, how did he do it?

"He'd need a passport or a recognised identity card. Some banks insist on a banker's reference as well."

Which is what I'd thought. Credit Agricole had insisted on both our passports.

So how was this account in Spain opened?

I went back and had a look at the bank account fax. Reading and re-reading all the details. Chasing down every word and number.

Which is when I noticed the line of numbers underneath my name on the account. It wasn't a good copy – probably a fax of a photocopy of a photocopy. But I could make out the letters HIF – or was it MIF – followed by ten digits. And it wasn't the account number.

But there was something vaguely familiar about those numbers.

I'd seen them before ... recently.

My passport!

I shot out of the settee and nearly collided with the door in my haste to check. I dug out my passport and threw it open. The last nine digits on the Spanish bank account were my passport number.

I was totally thrown. Up until noticing the passport number, everything could be traced back to Dublin. It was an inside job. They had our bond details, our address, our signatures, the cancellation form. Everything.

But they'd never had my passport number.

Crime suddenly stepped a thousand miles closer. My passport had never left the house – except when I had it in my hand.

Did that mean someone had broken into our house?

Peter Kennedy?

It was a very fraught ten minutes that followed as the two of us brain-stormed the ramifications. We'd have to get the locks changed. Dare we leave the house unattended? How had someone broken in with Gypsy in the house? Had they waited until we'd all gone off in the car? Was the house being watched?

And why had the Spanish bank added a tenth digit to my passport number?

I looked at it again. It had a leading six. Why?

Perhaps it wasn't my passport?

Clearly nine digits out of ten were too much of a coincidence but was there another explanation? One that didn't involve anyone breaking into our house?

More brain-storming.

What happens when someone loses a passport? Could someone claim they were me and that my passport had been lost or stolen? Would the Passport Office believe them – especially if they had a doctor witness their signature on the claim form?

And would the re-issued document have the same number as the original – but with an extra digit, a leading six to show it was a re-issue?

I'd seen enough plausible faxes in the previous hour to know that whoever was impersonating me would be capable of fooling a Passport Office.

So I rang the Passport Office.

~

You would think that someone ringing to report a passport fraud would be accorded a modicum of priority.

I know I did.

But I couldn't get through.

I could not believe it. The Passport Office had automated their switchboard. Some genius had decided to remove all humans from external contact and replace them with a series of messages.

None of which told you what to do if attempting to report a fraud.

I pressed 'one.' I pressed 'two.' I listened. Nothing. No 'other' option, no press this number if you want to speak to a human.

I doubly could not believe it. Who was I supposed to ring? All the telephone numbers suggested on my 'Essential Information for UK Passport Holders' booklet refused to speak to me – they were all hiding behind a line of robots!

Incredulity was too mild a word to describe my feelings as I scanned all thirty-two pages of the Passport Agency booklet. Lots of useful information about safety and customs and two pages of useless telephone numbers!

But there was a section on what to do if you lost your passport abroad.

The British Consulate!

They were supposed to be informed in case of loss.

And they could issue an emergency document to get you home.

And use to open a bank account in Spain?

I was definitely enjoying myself. This was fun. Detection, problem solving, mystery. What more could a boy detective want?

I tracked down the number of the British Consulate in the appendices of my *Living in France* bible, tapped in the numbers and ... found it had changed.

Which is when I remembered that Paris numbers had changed recently to ten digits or was it eleven? I couldn't remember the exact details but what was a missing couple of digits to a great detective? I'd extemporise. Find a few examples of current Paris numbers and make a guess.

I spoke to a fax machine at the British Embassy.

Never an engaging conversation. I probably set off three international incidents and cancelled a couple of licenses to kill.

But I was not beaten. Weren't there consulates in the regions? I'd look them up in the local directory. Amazingly, I found one. The British Consulate, Toulouse.

I got through immediately. Obviously robots hadn't yet reached South-West France.

"I am destroyed," said the female voice on the other end of the line.

Perhaps robots had reached South-West France.

"Er ... hello?" I ventured.

"The silly girl. She destroy me. I find nothing today," she continued, in a distracted and heavily accented English. She sounded Eastern European and what the hell was she talking about?

"Hello? How I help?" she asked.

I explained about a passport being used to set up a false bank account in Spain and asked what happened when the Consulate issued an emergency passport.

She said she didn't know; there was a Passport Section in Paris that dealt with all that, but it would be a waste of time phoning Paris because no one would answer. Switchboard like that, she said. Many lazy girls. She did have a number for someone in the Passport Section but then some silly girl had come in yesterday and destroyed her filing system. She would find nothing today. Perhaps never. She was destroyed, her files were destroyed, all was destroyed.

It's comforting to know that whatever your situation, there is always someone worse off.

Another call came in and she asked me to hold. I could hear much muttering, shuffling of paper and half a conversation in French.

And then 'I have it!' came screaming down the receiver. "Why she put it there?"

I couldn't hazard a guess. Who could tell with silly girls? They come in, destroy you, then disappear.

But I had a name at the Passport Section – Ian Morris – and a number to reach him on.

Mincemeat Men

I think Ian Morris was related to the man in the *Carte Grise* office. I recognised the same fundamentalist view of the world; the passport system was set up to prevent fraudulent claims, therefore they couldn't exist. And passport numbers were never re-used or had sixes added to the front.

I tried to explain to him that we were dealing with someone who could produce Pergoninis to witness all manner of official documents and could he check his records to see if any passport applications had been made in my name in the last year.

He didn't sound very interested. I think he would have preferred a robot switchboard to protect him from the public as well. But I wasn't going to be put off. Could he check the status of my passport with the Passport Agency? Had it been reported missing at any time? Had anyone made any changes to it, tried to add a name, anything?

He said he would but I wasn't going to hold my breath.

So, how had my passport number appeared on a Spanish bank account?

I thought of all the people who had taken photocopies of my passport. The bank, the *notaire*, the mayor, the *Sous-Préfecture*, the *Préfecture*. And the countless staff who, presumably, had access to files at all the above.

And our estate agent, David Jarvis.

He'd taken a photocopy of my passport when I'd made the offer on the house.

And if Peter Kennedy had been an associate and shared the commission on the sale, he'd probably have had access to it as well.

Did someone take my details to a forger and have a false passport made up?

It was somewhat of an anti-climax to be re-united with our car later that day – what with all the excitement over forged passports and wandering Irish con-men. But so what if we were looked upon with incredulity as the English couple who drove without water in their engine? What was that compared with the knowledge that maybe half of France owned a photocopy of my passport – probably hanging on their wall certified as a genuine Pergonini!

Thursday morning arrived with a phone call. It was Jean-Pierre. The *gendarmes* had just phoned. They had a description of our man. Could I come over?

Try to stop me! I was out the door and revving up the warp engines before the receiver settled in its cradle.

This was the breakthrough, I could feel it. I'd almost given up on the *gendarmes*. And on anyone at the *Hôtel du Midi* actually remembering someone from five months ago.

I found Jean-Pierre in his office, which was looking even more crammed than it had before. The man was definitely a hoarder. I thought I was bad but here was a master, sitting in an office that had become a sanctuary for every electrical appliance he'd ever owned. There was hardly space for his desk and two chairs; his shiny new computer system stood out like an island of tidiness amidst mountains of chaos and what looked like old toasters. I moved a pile of manuals from a chair by the door and pulled up alongside him.

He was busy copying out the *gendarmes*' report, translating it into English and adding a pleasing array of print fonts.

I looked over his shoulder. *Rapport de la Gendarmerie*, it began. Yes, a man had been to the hotel during that period (May-June '95). Yes, he received letters there but no faxes. He was of middle height, blond and minced.

Minced? Was that like a gingerbread man only made of meat? I was being impersonated by a mincemeat man?

God knows what the passport picture looked like!

"Is not right – minced?" asked Jean-Pierre, making squashing gestures with his hands.

I dreaded to think and grabbed for the dictionary. *Mince, mince*, where was it? Ah, there, *mince* – thin, slender, slim.

I think I preferred minced – much easier to spot in a line-up.

I read the *Rapport* further. Elegant appearance, well dressed, looked like a commercial traveller. This was a very good description. I was expecting something along the lines of medium build, two legs, hair.

But this was excellent. And there was more. Youngish man, thirty to forty, very good French but slight accent – English. He said he had family in the area.

English!

But would a Frenchman know the difference between an English and an Irish accent?

Jean-Pierre didn't think so. It would be like me trying to distinguish between a Belgian and a Frenchman. Unless one was Hercule Poirot, I wouldn't have an earthly.

I showed Jean-Pierre the bundle of faxes I'd received and asked him about Pergonini. Had he ever heard of a doctor of that name? Did the stamp look as wrong to him as it did to me?

He shook his head. "No, no, no. There is no Pergonini. It is not name."

This was a very positive assertion. I was amazed. How did he know?

"It is not name," he repeated. "Look I show."

He turned to his *Minitel* screen and started typing in Pergonini and Aurignac. The system came back with no matches. I was impressed. This was better than the *gendarmes*. I wondered if it did fax numbers as well?

He extended the search to the *département* and then to all of France. No Pergoninis. Even if our Pergonini was ex-directory, it was hardly likely that every Pergonini in the entire country was as well.

"It is not name," Jean-Pierre reiterated. "Not Italian. Englishman, he may think it Italian but it is not. Pergoni, yes. Pernini, perhaps. Pergonini, no."

I was even more impressed. An impromptu lesson in Italian genealogy as well. I don't think I'd have been as confident about an English surname.

And I was impressed with the *Minitel* system. If it could search for Pergoninis, it could search for Kennedys too.

We tried the Gers first. No Peter Kennedy. Or any other Kennedy. We tried the Haute Garonne, then the Tarn. Still no luck. Did he even exist?

Or was he ex-directory and in hiding?

We called up the *Hôtel du Midi* and checked their telephone number against its supposed fax number. It wasn't a conclusive test by any means – line numbers can be carried from *département* to *département* – but generally the first four digits of a French telephone number form an area code. The Hotel's was 61 85, the fax was 72 34. Not even close. Very unlikely the fax belonged to the hotel.

Which fitted in with what the *gendarmes* had found. Letters had been received at the hotel but no faxes.

I took another look at the *Rapport de la Gendarmerie*. Medium height, blond, slim, well dressed, fluent French with slight English accent.

And thought.

My God!

David Jarvis to a tee!

And what idiot had sent him all those faxes!

I could not believe it. And I was someone who'd spent most of the last seven days not believing anything. But this! Of all the people in the world to choose, I had to have the faxes sent to the man who'd sent them all in the first place!

What must he have thought?

Months of careful planning and suddenly he walks into his office and finds his floor covered in evidence. Perhaps he thought his fax machine had developed a conscience and had entered spontaneous confession mode?

If it *was* him.

What did Peter Kennedy look like? Had I leapt to a conclusion without proof? And was David's hair blond? I'd have described it as more a mousy brown.

I checked the dictionary again. *Blond* could also mean fair. Presumably a light mousy brown could fall into that category. I tried to summon up his face. The description gave the suspect as thirty to forty. I'd have put David Jarvis more in the thirty-five to forty-five bracket but he had the kind of face difficult to attach an age too. It'd always struck me as one belonging to a dissolute public schoolboy. A schoolboy who'd spent the last ten years at an all-night party.

Jean-Pierre printed off a couple of copies of the *Rapport de la Gendarmerie* and I left to tell Shelagh.

And Andy and Simon and everyone else on my list.

I was bursting with news. And bursting to tell people. By the time I pulled up outside our house I was like an incurable gossip after ten years solitary confinement.

But Shelagh met me on the doorstep. The post had arrived. And with it another envelope of faxes from David Jarvis. And a hand-written note, *I'm not sure you got all the pages last time - David.*

I checked the bundle of faxes; the Pergonini letter, the Spanish bank details, Ralph's Dear Big Nose. They were all there. And so was another page. A copy of a fax header, stamped *La Poste*, Castlenau.

Castlenau! The town where David Jarvis had his office.

Headers and Handwriting

That must have been the reason he'd delayed so long in sending the faxes. He'd been sifting through the bundle and suddenly saw the word CASTLENAU flashing neon-lit back at him – probably alternating with the words 'guilty bastard.'

And it must have been one hell of a shock. It was a header page, not part of the actual fax itself, but a page of A4 with all the details concerning the sender, the destination, everything. I doubt he even knew it had been sent as part of the fax.

He'd have taken one look at it, panicked and spent the next day wondering what to do. He'd have to send something as he knew I was waiting. So he removes the incriminating page and posts the rest.

Then another thought hits him. He'd only bought himself a few days. Someone was bound to notice the Castlenau post office stamp eventually. So he invents Peter Kennedy; gives him a job in Castlenau – handy for the post office – and keys to our house. Then he sends the missing page.

It fitted.

Case solved – send for the black cap.

Then I looked closer at the page of fax details.

La Poste at Castlenau was not the only stamp. There was another one for Villeurbanne, wherever that was. Both stamps contained a date and time. Both were dated 16th May. But the Castlenau stamp said 17h. Villeurbanne said 14h15.

The fax originated at Villeurbanne?

I dived for our road Atlas. Villeurbanne, Villeurbanne, I sifted through hundreds of French towns beginning with Ville. Until I found it; Villeurbanne, page 70, *département* 69.

It was a suburb of Lyon.

I checked the telephone code for Lyon – 72 33. Close enough. The fax came from 72 34, Villeurbanne.

Which opened a considerable number of questions. Where did *La Poste* at Castlenau come into this equation? Was someone trying to make it look as though the faxes were local by routing them via Castlenau? To hide the fact that they were coming from Lyon? Or to frame David Jarvis?

And where were the faxes from Mutual Friendly going? Villeurbanne? Was someone going to Lyon to collect their faxes or having them sent on elsewhere?

I rang Andy. I had about five minutes-worth of solid facts to impart. He said he'd add David Jarvis to his list of names to check out. But he had some bad news from the Irish Police. They'd asked the Spanish police to investigate the bank account in Bossost and had been told it would be at least four weeks before they could even think about it. They were far too busy.

So much for international co-operation.

In all the excitement I forgot to ask what fax number they'd used to contact my impersonator.

I'd have to save that for next time. Meanwhile, I'd gather everything together and try to construct a time-line of events. There were too many stray faxes and telephone messages running around in my head. I needed to put everything down on paper and impose some sort of structure.

The first question was when did it all begin?

Looking through our bundle of faxes, it looked like the 10th of April. That was the day the bank account was opened and the cancellation letter signed. But the letter accompanying the cancellation date talked of the 7th of April – *Thank you for your letter, received here on 7th April.*

A letter supposedly posted sixteen days earlier.

Was there any significance to the 7th of April? Was that the day it all began, our house broken into? Or was the date irrelevant? The cancellation letter never sent but intercepted before it left Mutual Friendly on March 22nd?

I still couldn't see how anyone other than an employee of Mutual Friendly could know about our bond. Even if David Jarvis or Peter Kennedy had duplicate keys to our house – why target us? We don't look well off. I can't stand in a shop doorway for more than five minutes without people giving me money.

And when could they have broken in?

We were under virtual house arrest during March and April. Our car was off the road, we had a dog who barked if a butterfly landed in a field three miles away. And we never discussed our finances with anyone.

Not obvious prey for passing felons.

Unless...

Our post box was at the bottom of the drive, fifty yards from the house and out of sight.

And unlocked.

We hadn't given it a second thought. It was unlocked when we moved in, we assumed it was the local practice. And handy for sending letters – we'd leave them in the box and the postman would collect them.

And there had been a succession of strange cars parked nearby throughout the early spring.

I remembered commenting on it at the time. We'd see people park, climb out and then wander into the field opposite, looking at the grass. We thought they were mushrooming.

Were we wrong? Were they waiting for the postman?

It was all too possible. They could wait until he drove off, walk up to the box, take the letters out, check through them...

But that still implied a knowledge that there was something worthwhile to look for.

And a considerable risk. If they were coming every day they'd risk being noticed. And if it was someone we knew they'd risk being recognised.

I remembered seeing David drive by during March. I was in the far field and saw his car. It was easily recognisable as you rarely see large white BMWs. Most of our neighbours had battered 2CVs or drove tractors.

I remembered walking back to the house expecting to see him parked outside. But he wasn't. Instead he'd dropped a letter off at our post box.

Which meant he knew it was unlocked. But it also showed how easily he and his car stood out. And I'm sure I'd never seen him parked close by.

Another lock was added to the list of security items to buy at the hardware shop. And wouldn't it be a good idea to find out if any other post went missing during that period? Get a list from Simon and Andy of everything I should have received and check it against my files.

My list of actions grew as the day progressed. I'd also need a complete list of all faxes – where they came from and where they were sent. Were there other fax headers like the one from Villeurbanne?

And was that fax really sent from Villeurbanne? The more I looked at the header the less I was convinced. The top portion looked like an application form. It had a handwritten section with my name and the hotel for the sender's name and address, followed by Eastleigh and Howard and their fax number as the destination. And this top portion contained the Castlenau *Poste* stamp.

The bottom section had the Villeurbanne stamp. If it hadn't been for the fact that the times were the wrong way round I would have been certain it originated from Castlenau.

Which could be checked. I could even do it myself. Take the header to the Castlenau *Poste* and ask them.

Maybe even ask them if they remembered it being sent?

And for a description of the man.

I could feel a Holmesian surge pulsing through my body. I wanted to do it. This was my destiny.

But it was also a long way. And I'd have to have a script. And what were the chances of making myself understood?

But there was something I could do. The fax header contained handwriting. I had some handwritten notes from David Jarvis. And I could check the typed letters as well – look for unusual phrases or spelling mistakes, something that could identify the author.

Thirty minutes later it was not looking good for David Jarvis. He used a closed four. So did the unsub. There were also similarities with the way he wrote 'u' and 'g'. But was that conclusive? I didn't think so.

I'd also noticed that all the forged letters ended, 'Yours Sincerely', with a capital 'S' for sincerely. Was that common? I didn't think so. I emptied my correspondence files and checked. David Jarvis used a capital S, I couldn't find anyone else who did.

Unfortunately it was a very small sample. Was one out of four admissible in a court of law?

I was in the process of designing further tests – wasn't there one you used on Shakespeares? Some program that counted the words in a body of text and checked the size of vocabulary and length of sentences?

But I was interrupted. Shelagh wanted to know what would happen if someone ran up debts against this false bank account in Spain? Would we be liable?

I hadn't thought of that.

It was illegal in France to write a bad cheque. Do it twice and you were banned from holding a bank account. What the hell would they do in Spain? Throw you to the bulls at Pamplona?

This added an entirely new dimension to our plight. Anything could be happening with that bank account. It might have loans drawn against it, money laundered through it. Anything.

Hadn't I seen something on TV about people having their lives ruined in similar circumstances? People suddenly finding themselves unable to obtain credit, having their house repossessed, finding their names erroneously placed on credit blacklists. All because someone had fraudulently used their name and details, run up debts and then disappeared.

Was that going to happen to us?

I rang Andy. He sympathised. It was so frustrating. The English police didn't want to know even though false British passports were probably involved. The French considered it an Irish crime. The Irish maintained that that hadn't been proved and it looked distinctly French to them or failing that Spanish. And the Spanish were on holiday for four weeks!

The bank was only an hour's drive away, we could go there ourselves.

It was tempting.

Very tempting.

"It wouldn't cause you any problems, would it?" I asked. I'd seen so many American police shows where cases were thrown out because of procedural mistakes. I didn't want to risk anything similar.

"No, not at all." He seemed pleased. "If you're sure you want to do it?"

I was sure. We had to know what was happening. If nothing else we could freeze the account. And we might be able to find out how it was created. What identification was used? Was it really my passport? Could anyone identify the man who opened it?

I put the phone down. I'd been deputised.

Sherlock Holmes and the Case of the Missing Toilet

Shelagh's eighty-year-old mother, Nan, was arriving on Friday, so we had to put off our excursion into Spain until Monday. But a Great Detective never sleeps. And he never waits until Monday.

We'd stop off at Castlenau *Poste* on the way back from Tarbes airport.

Shelagh disagreed. This was not a good plan. It was going to be tense enough without openly looking for trouble. I could tell she was not looking forward to her mother's arrival.

Like many daughters she had a tense relationship with her mother. A tenseness that, like gravity, increased according to the inverse square of the distance between them. On the phone they were fine, in the same room ... the air crackled with potential. Shelagh was the agent for Order – she had routines, she wrote lists, she planned, she liked to be in control. Whereas Nan was the agent for Chaos – someone who despised lists, never planned and had an uncanny ability to wreak havoc with the slightest of touches. It was never intentional. It just happened. She was a catalyst. And Shelagh couldn't shake the idea that within five minutes of her mother's arrival, Tarbes airport would be put on emergency alert and five cars would disappear in controlled explosions.

It wouldn't happen, of course. But Shelagh was convinced it was only a matter of time. More likely it would be Nan losing one of her bags. Shelagh would be despatched to find it for her. We'd have half the airport turned upside down and then Nan would remember she'd decided not to bring it with her. She'd have a good giggle and walk off in search of the car and Shelagh would quietly tear her hair out by the lost luggage counter.

It was always like that. Sometimes it was a bag, sometimes an ear-ring. But there was always something. And in less than two hours her plane would be landing.

We decided not to take Gypsy with us to the airport. There wasn't really room in the back and dogs, mothers and long car journeys don't mix too well. Still, if we wanted to return to a house free of any unexpected little additions to the upstairs carpets, we'd have to let her out into the garden before we set off.

Gypsy is not stupid. She can recognise an imminent car journey when she smells one, and was not going to be left behind. She ran straight for the car door and stayed there, leaving her post only when chased around the car. And then only to take up a new position at the door on the other side.

"We'll have to take her," I conceded.

"No," insisted Shelagh. And ran three more laps of the car and executed two wild lunges. All to no avail. Gypsy would be coming with us.

And it was all my fault.

I'm never quite sure about the intricacies of attaching blame in family disputes – it's something that apparently only wives are privy to. I think it's similar to the ownership of pets. If a pet is well-behaved she's mine, if she's bad she's yours.

I think I'd just been given custody of Gypsy.

Forty-five minutes later, the beast in the back seat started to cry. She's bored. When are we going to stop? And I need to go to the toilet.

I think dogs and children occupy the same rung on the evolutionary ladder when it comes to long car journeys.

"You had your chance before we set off," admonished Shelagh. "But, oh no, you wouldn't use it, would you?"

I didn't think Gypsy understood English that well. But neither did I think it opportune to intervene. Shelagh was tense enough. I think she could sense that somewhere overhead her mother had just forced her way into the cockpit of the nine o'clock from Manchester and was passing around snaps of her neighbour's cousin's friend's brand new baby granddaughter.

Ten minutes of incessant crying, whimpering and unexpected cold wet noses in the back of the neck later, we gave in. We'd stop at the next lay-by.

Whereupon Gypsy forgot all about her bladder and decided that pulling paper bags and food wrappers out of rubbish bins was just the sort of thing to take the boredom out of a long car journey.

All doubts concerning the ownership of Gypsy were promptly removed. She was mine. Always had been. Always would be.

The last forty minutes of the journey proceeded peacefully. The black dog from hell sat quietly in the back and Shelagh simmered quietly in the front.

We pulled up outside Tarbes-Lourdes airport with twenty minutes to spare. Plenty of time.

And soon even more time. The nine o'clock from Manchester had been a figment of our imagination. Most people called it the ten o'clock.

We had an extra hour at the airport.

"I asked her to check the times!" cried Shelagh.

And we'd reminded her that France was an hour ahead. Was she sure that the time she'd given us was the correct local time?

"Of course," had come back the reply.

I calmed Shelagh down and suggested there was nothing we could do but wait so why not make the best of it. It's easy to be calm and reasonable when it's someone else's mother.

We settled down in the terminal building and waited.

And watched.

There were nuns everywhere.

Strange, since coming to France we'd often commented on the total lack of visible clergy. Every road junction had its religious statue, every hamlet its church ... but we'd never seen a single priest.

Now we knew why. They were all here en route for Lourdes. The terminal teemed with monks, nuns and all manner of priests.

If only I'd brought my I-Spy[9] *Book of Catholicism* with me. There were 500 points in the foyer alone.

Put a family in a car for more than an hour and conversation inevitably turns towards toilets. Who's been, who hasn't, who should have, and when.

Ours was no exception.

Except for the subtle difference that Shelagh's mother only conversed about such matters via an interpreter – preferably a telepathic one.

So when she asked "Are we there yet?" what she really meant was "I am in need of a toilet."

Unfortunately the only telepath in the car was big, black and hairy and still sulking after the incident with the waste bin.

Five minutes later came the next coded query. "Is it much further?"

Following that came a "How much longer?" and a despondent "Oh."

Eventually Shelagh cottoned on to the fact that something was amiss. "What's the matter?" she asked.

But that was far too direct a question to extract anything other than a "Nothing ... really."

I believe teeth are extracted more readily.

A quick bout of twenty questions ensued. What is it? Are you feeling sick, do you want us to stop?

And finally. Do you need a toilet?

Of course it didn't end there. If a hitchhiker had asked us to stop at the next toilet, nothing more would have been said. But we were family and families needed to know. Why didn't you go on the plane? I couldn't. Why not? You know. No, I don't.

But at least we were approaching Castlenau, Shelagh could find a toilet while I went to the *Poste*.

I entered the outskirts of Castlenau with the words – Why didn't you go at the airport then? There wasn't one at the airport! Yes, there was! No, there wasn't! – ringing in my ears.

It is one thing being a Great Detective in the safety of your armchair but an entirely different matter driving into Moriarty's back yard.

I entered the car park at Castlenau in two minds. Do I park out of sight? Round the back, away from the other cars? Or do I park in the front? Where everyone else was.

Which drew the least attention? To be one of the crowd or on your own? In view or in the shadows?

I snaked and swerved across the car park as each gambit pushed itself to the fore.

"What are you doing?" shrieked my front seat passenger. "Watch out for that woman!"

What woman? Eek!

I swerved ... and missed her ... just. I could have been playing football – tricky winger sends startled shopper the wrong way then swerves past her at the last second.

Shelagh was beyond words at that point. Her mouth was open but nothing was coming out.

Which, on the whole, I regarded as probably for the best.

It's not as though the pedestrian had been in any danger. I was only crawling along. But I suppose things always look more frightening from the front passenger's seat. And visions of shoppers somersaulting over the car bonnet easier to envisage.

I decided it was probably safer for everyone concerned if I parked around the back.

However, it was a very bright day and I was momentarily blinded as I left the dazzling sunlight for the deep shadow. My eyes couldn't adjust in time, I thought I saw something, braked, swerved and finally came to a halt amidst a minor sea of broken glass.

Oh my God!

Naturally, I did what any other driver would do when confronted with such a situation.

I blamed the passenger.

"Why didn't you warn me about the glass?"

"What glass?"

"That glass."

I opened the door and looked out. Masses of it. Little fragments of green. Smashed beer bottles. Heineken, 25cl.

Even in moments of stress, a Great Detective is still a Great

Detective.

Luckily, nothing was punctured. And a hands and knees search under the car cleared all remaining sizeable shards away from the tyres.

But the car did look more abandoned than parked. Slued, as it was, across several car parking spaces and at a jaunty angle to the wall.

And slued it would have to stay. I'd had enough car parking for one day and I had a Post Office to find.

I'd never felt so self-conscious before. Castlenau wasn't a large place. It was a small town. A high street, a couple of squares, a network of side streets. And around any corner, at any moment, could come David Jarvis.

I wasn't sure how I'd react. Would I confront him ... or run? He could be innocent, he could be dangerous.

All things considered, I thought it preferable we didn't meet.

It took a while to track down the *Poste*. I thought I'd been very clever. I'd noticed a hotel called the *Hôtel de la Poste* and deduced the post office couldn't be far away. Elementary, I thought to myself, and I would have been right too – if I'd arrived in 1972. Unfortunately the *Poste* had since moved to a new building.

I placed detection on hold and asked directions.

It was a small post office: two counters and enough room for a small conga line. And on the wall a poster advertising something called *Posteclair* – a fax service.

This was encouraging. I placed the copy of the fax header on the counter and asked, "can you tell me if this fax originated from here or Villeurbanne?"

The woman studied the page for a short while before pronouncing, "*ici.*"

"You're sure?"

"*Oui.*"

This was much better than I'd expected.

"But the stamp here says 17h. Villeurbanne says 14h15?"

A shrug. Followed by something I couldn't quite catch.

I asked if she could say it again more slowly.

"The stamp always says that," she exclaimed and showed me the stamp – Castlenau, 17h. They never changed it. It's always five o'clock in Castlenau.

Which I thought sounded pretty nifty as a song title.

"Do you know who sent this fax?"

I knew this was pushing my script to the limit but I was on a roll. And amazed I'd reached so far without meeting a blank stare or a *non*.

"*Oui.*" she replied.

I hardly dared ask the next question.

"Who?"

"This man," she said pointing at my name on the fax header.

The French are definitely a very trusting people.

I tried to explain to her that that was me but I think I just made things worse. If it was me, why was I asking who sent the fax? Was I stupid or just forgetful?

"I'm English," I explained.

"Ah." she smiled, "*Anglais.*"

No need to say any more.

But I had solved the riddle of the wandering fax. All international faxes from the Castlenau *Poste* were routed through an agency in Villeurbanne. So there had been no attempt to disguise the fax's source or lay down an elaborate plan to frame anyone.

Outside the Post Office, I was just digesting this new piece of information when I saw two familiar figures walking along the pavement towards me: Shelagh and her mother.

"I thought we were going to meet back at the car?" I said as we moved into hailing range.

"We haven't found a toilet yet," came back the terse reply. I could tell by Shelagh's tone that the search was not progressing well.

"We'll have to try a cafe," I suggested.

Nan's eyes lit up. The thought of having a coffee, perhaps staying for a meal, was a pleasant one to contemplate.

But not for Shelagh. She had a meal waiting at home. And she'd been to restaurants with her mother before. The words – I can't eat that, I don't like them and I'm not touching those – still chimed through her memory.

Anything with red meat or remotely concerned with internal organs was out. Pasta was inedible and vegetarian dishes were a cheat. And no sauces.

Which just about closed the book on French cuisine. It was difficult enough struggling with a menu written in French without having a fatwa against anything tasty.

We found the nearest cafe and ordered three coffees.

And waited for Nan to come back from the toilet.

Which she did unexpectedly quickly.

And with the words, "I can't stay here," pushed passed us and headed for the exit.

Something had happened.

Shelagh managed to head her off at the door and tried to find out what was the matter.

"You know."

"No, I don't."

Silence.

"Was there someone in there?"

An inkling of possibility. Was it one of those mixed toilets? Had Nan walked in and found a man in the Ladies?

She wasn't saying.

We had another bout of *What happened? You know! No, I don't. Yes, you do* – which I stayed out of and quietly sipped my coffee.

Eventually a quiet voice whispered the terrible truth. "Somebody stole the toilet."

Even a Great Detective's mind can boggle. And mine was no exception.

Why would anyone want to steal a toilet? And how? It's not the sort of thing anyone could sneak away from under your nose. Well, perhaps not your nose but under your...

I was told to shut up, I was making things worse.

Shelagh went in search of the missing toilet and I was told to stay with Nan.

And then came the answer.

The cafe had one of those hole-in-the-ground affairs. Which, now I came to think about it, did look suspiciously like the aftermath of a daring sanitary appliance raid.

We tried to explain the idiosyncrasies of French plumbing to Nan but there were certain standards that could never be compromised. A hole in the ground would always be a hole in the ground. Never a toilet.

We downed three very quick coffees and left.

But we had to find a toilet.

Which meant another cafe.

And another three coffees.

I suppose we could have marched in, used the facilities and left but it didn't feel right. So I hovered by the bar, checking the menu while Shelagh went to inspect the sanitary ware.

Which apparently passed the test. Shelagh appeared with a relieved smile and waved Nan over. And I ordered the coffees.

"*Anglais?*" the barman asked as I passed him our order.

"*Oui,*" I replied, wondering if it was my accent or our pre-occupation with sanitary ware that gave us away. Most customers chose a restaurant by their menu. Only the English check the toilets.

And soon I was doing likewise. Two cups of coffee in quick succession had taken their toll.

Safely ensconced back at home, I reflected upon the events of the day. It hadn't been an overwhelming success. The Great

Detective had intended to enter Castlenau like a shadow in the night – arrive, detect and quickly depart – leaving no trace of his ever having been there.

Instead, he'd terrorised half a car park and placed every restaurant on red alert – watch out, health inspectors!

But that was in the past, Shelagh had let slip that we knew other English couples in the area and Nan wanted to meet them. Immediately, if not sooner.

I could feel another attempt to convert us to coffee mornings and house parties coming on.

Mothers never give up.

I was just in the process of ringing round with the first batch of invitations when I remembered that Lynne probably knew David Jarvis better than most people. I remembered her saying once that she'd been one of his first customers. He'd only been in business a few months and they'd kept in touch ever since.

Had she ever heard of Peter Kennedy?

I asked, nonchalantly slipping the name Peter Kennedy into the conversation.

"Oh, Peter. I haven't seen him for a while."

"What? You know him?" I tried not to sound surprised but I was too shocked to carry it off. I'd been so sure he didn't exist.

And I had to ask. "What's he look like?"

"Peter?"

"Yes."

"Oh, very much like David, really."

Small, well dressed, minced?

"Yes."

Fair haired, fluent French?

"Yes. Do you know him?"

No, but I had a nasty feeling he knew me.

Sherlock Holmes' Darker Brother-In-Law

Even Great Detectives are allowed a break on their birthdays. I was allowed cake as well.

Two of them.

I could tell by the disgruntled, "oh," that met the mention of Shelagh's imminent chocolate cake that something was amiss. And when Nan answered, "nothing," to the question, "what's the matter?" my suspicions were confirmed.

"Where is it?" I asked her.

"What?"

"The cake."

Silence.

But I knew. Nan being the only person who regularly, and secretly, carries six pounds of fruitcake and a slab of icing in her hand luggage.

I used to think it was because she'd seen one of those disaster films where the plane crashes and the survivors have to draw lots on who's to be eaten first – six pounds of fruit cake being worth at least a couple of legs on the open body parts market.

"You haven't brought a cake with you again, have you?" cried Shelagh.

This is the joy of families – everything you do is remembered, catalogued and used in evidence against you later.

Shelagh reminded Nan of the incident of the suitcase that wouldn't close on her trip to Majorca. Of how she found not one but two slabs of fruit cake buried amongst her clothes. And how they agreed she'd never do it again.

"*You* agreed!"

"*We* agreed!"

From there the conversation dwelt on the wisdom of eighty year-olds travelling light and an Englishwoman's inalienable right to bake.

"But I wanted to make a birthday cake!"

"You could have made it here! If you'd said, I'd have got the ingredients ready for you."

"I wanted it to be a surprise."

"It still could have."

"No, it couldn't."

"Yes, it could."

And so on. From that point the conversation became interesting only to the participants as previous grievances – and there were nearly forty years of them – were aired in quick succession.

I'd heard them all before so I slipped quietly out. I knew if I stayed there was the distinct possibility I might be asked to arbitrate and I knew that families and arbitration did not mix.

I still remember the incident of my mother and the two sweaters. I thought I'd been clever – wearing one of her two presents to pick her up at the station. Instead I walked straight into: "What's wrong with the other one? Don't you like it? I can change it if you want."

I was not going to be asked to choose between two cakes.

I left to the strains of, "you used to be such a nice little girl," followed by the plaintive wail, "you never let me have a puppy!"

Shelagh spent the rest of the weekend doing a passable impersonation of a Chernobyl reactor minus its concrete cover, while Nan occupied her time making the kind of helpful suggestions that only a mother can.

I kept a low profile.

And thought about Monday.

I decided we'd need more than a script for our rendezvous with the bank. We'd need a letter. Something we could hand over and set the scene before we launched into a series of questions about how the account was set up, did he remember the man, were we in debt?

For one thing, I was worried about who the bank would recognise as the true owner of the account; the person who opened it or the person whose name he used? Would we drive all that way only to be denied access to the account details?

I thought the best idea was to present all the facts, produce every scrap of identification we possessed and mention the *gendarmes* as often as possible.

And hope the manager spoke French.

Of course there was the remote possibility that he spoke English. But it's hard to be that optimistic when you've been impersonated, robbed, abandoned, and shunted by your brother-in-law.

Monday came and we were ready to leave early. We had thought we were going to travel alone. But had reckoned without Nan. Gypsy wasn't the only one who ran to the car door whenever a journey was in the offing.

If there was a trip to Spain, she wasn't going to miss out. I tried to explain that this was not a sightseeing visit. We had to track down a bank and talk to a bank manager. That was it. No shopping, no restaurants – with or without toilets.

It didn't work.

Neither did our suggestion that she take advantage of the gorgeous weather and a well-stocked fridge meet with any favour. Apparently sitting in the sun all day was classified as a 'dead day.'

I had forgotten about 'dead days.'

It was Nan's classification of life. She believed that at eighty you should live each day as if it were your last. And days that did not come up to the mark were 'dead days.'

Sitting in the sun doing nothing was a 'dead day.' As, apparently, was watching television or reading a book.

Sitting in a car outside a bank, however, was, surprisingly, not a 'dead day'.

Gypsy wasn't so lucky. No amount of crying or circumnavigation of cars would buy her place in the back seat. She'd need a rabies vaccination to be allowed into Spain. I mused momentarily whether there was a similar regulation for mothers-in-law. But, wisely, kept the speculation to myself.

Guinny was never so reticent. She caught Gypsy's eye and expertly demonstrated the length of the rabies needle and suggested she book an early visit to the vet.

We drove away to the accompaniment of a howled lament.

And a dog's head protruding from the cat flap.

It's an easy journey into Spain, fast dual carriageways to begin with followed by a gentle climb up a mountain pass. It would take barely an hour.

But an hour was apparently too long for some people. Or, more accurately, some people's bladders.

"Can you stop at the next wooded bit?" enquired my front seat passenger, aka Shelagh.

Which, of course, made the landscape immediately change. All 'next wooded bits' promptly disappeared and wide open rocky bits pushed themselves to the fore.

I slowed to a crawl. My eyes darting from side to side, checking out anything that looked like a track or a side road or something that might lead towards a bush.

"Are we there?" piped Nan from the back seat.

Was this another coded query? Had another bladder tightened?

Apparently not. The car's slowing had aroused thoughts about shopping. What were the shops like at Bossost? Was it a big place? Was that where the big supermarket was?

I again produced the party line that this was not a shopping trip, it was a quick visit to a bank and an even quicker trip home.

The party line did not play well to the back seat electorate and it was with immense relief that I espied a small copse up ahead and pulled over.

Sherlock Holmes never had this trouble. Mrs. Hudson never waylaid him on his doorstep and insisted he take her shopping. Or drop her off at Honiton for a cream tea on his way to Baskerville Hall. And he never had to stop for Watson to relieve himself behind a bush. Come to think of it he never had Mycroft run into the back of his Hansom Cab either.

Which is the difference between fact and fiction; fictional detectives can ditch their families before the turning of the first page. Real detectives have to live with them, find them wooded bits on demand and promise a long stopover at the supermarket on the way back.

We snaked higher into the Pyrenees; passing tiny villages, the house roofs steepening as we went, grey slate replacing the warm pink terracotta tiles of the valley floor, grassy meadows clinging to steep valley sides, the vast flat fields of grain and sunflowers a distant memory in the rear-view mirror.

The road turned and climbed, following the Garonne, sometimes on its left bank, sometimes on its right. The river flowing fast, flecked white over a bed of boulders and giant stones. Everything closing in upon itself; the sky, the fields, the houses. The valley sides steepening into huge rock faces and sheer cliffs. Untouched natural beauty interspersed with quarries and clouds of rock dust. One village we passed through was caked white. The road surface, the house fronts, the roofs – all covered in a permanent wash of white from the neighbouring factory and the procession of heavy lorries.

The pass continued dotted with bends and houses. Some tucked so snugly into the folds of the valley that they could never see the sun. I wondered why anyone would build there. Who would want to live in a house never touched by the sun? Even on a sunny day the house looked cold and damp – the stone walls and slate roof glistening dark, grey and moist.

We passed the little customs post near the border – empty as usual. I think they only manned it during lorry strikes. Which seemed bizarre to me – to wait until the frontier's blocked before manning the customs post.

Two miles later we crossed into Spain. The road signs changed and the Garonne became *La Garona*.

We decided to visit Les first. It was on the way to Bossost and I wanted to check out the handwritten address on the bank statement.

Maybe the bank was in Les – a sub-branch of a larger branch in

Bossost? Or the address might belong to a hotel – a temporary address given by my impersonator to the bank staff. Either way it had to be checked out.

The road widened and flattened as we entered Les. We'd reached the top of the pass. Hotels, restaurants and large white houses shone in the sun, their gardens alive with late summer greenery set against the hazy browns of the surrounding peaks that stretched around us for miles.

It was a lovely spot, high up in the mountains and bathed in sun, the peaks set back and forming a natural bowl.

I slowed the car as we peered at the numbers on the houses and strained to catch a road name.

And then there it was. The address we'd been looking for – 48, San Agueda.

It was a bank.

The bank.

The Banca Zaragoza.

We found a space a few houses down and parked, gathered up our letters, dictionary and faxes, told Nan we wouldn't be long and hurried inside.

As we approached I ran through several scenarios – what would happen if he didn't understand French? Should we race to the nearest town and buy an English-Spanish dictionary? What if they didn't have one? Buy a French-Spanish one and hook it up in tandem with our English-French?

I pushed the swing door open and walked inside. It was a small bank, no grills or bulletproof glass – just a counter and a waiting area. And only one man on duty – a short, dark-haired man in a white shirt.

We approached the counter with mounting trepidation. Would he understand one word we said?

I handed over the photocopy of the bank account details and asked in French if the account was here.

"*Oui,*" he said excitedly.

I handed him our passports and our very detailed letter of explanation which he read with a growing number of nods and exclamations. He knew it, he told us. Head Office, huh! They told him it was okay, but he knew.

"All the time, I knew it!" he repeated.

This was looking very hopeful. Something must have happened to make him remember the account so vividly.

He produced a folder, placed it on the counter and started flipping through the pages, muttering to himself.

And then he smiled. He'd found what he was looking for. He unclipped two pages from his folder and placed them on the counter in front of us. They were photocopies of passports. One was mine, one was Shelagh's.

But with different faces.

Neither were easy to recognise – the photocopies were poor, they were more silhouettes than pictures – but there was something familiar about them. Especially Shelagh's. I couldn't quite fathom it ... then...

There are few things that test the bonds of family greater than seeing your sister's picture on your wife's passport.

One is finding your brother-in-law's on your own.

The Day of the Gendarmes

There are no words to adequately describe the shock of seeing those two passport photocopies. My threshold of disbelief had been battered and stretched considerably over the previous ten days, but this was something else.

I don't know what I'd expected to find. I suppose I'd expected to find a passport and it would have had a picture on it. Logically the picture of the small, slight, fluent French speaker who I'd assumed had set up the account.

But my brother-in-law? Who was neither small, slight, fair nor fluent in French.

And had a beard.

I pointed to the police description of the man at the hotel and asked if this was similar to the man who had opened the account.

"The same." he agreed.

I looked again at John's picture. I suppose it was more of a black blob than a picture but then this was a photocopy. Surely, having seen the original, no one could mistake him for the small, slight, fair-haired man who'd opened the account?

Except no one *had* seen the original. The account had been opened with the photocopy!

I was beyond amazement. Someone had opened an account in my name with a photocopy of a passport? Someone had just crossed the border from France into Spain but instead of producing their passport took out a photocopy they'd prepared earlier? Sorry, I've left the passport in the car, here's a bad photocopy I carry around just in case?

And what a bad photocopy it was. Probably a photocopy of a long line of photocopies. It looked like he'd pasted my brother-in-law's picture over mine and copied it until the picture was un-recognisable.

Except to a close relative.

In my head, I could hear all the experts back in London talking smugly about the anti money-laundering conventions and how impossible it was nowadays to open a bank account without proper identification.

Obviously not if you have access to a photocopier!

The bank manager must have noticed our shock and ushered us into his office at the back, sitting us down and asking if we wanted him to call the police.

Definitely.

I looked again at the passports while he phoned. Why would anyone use Jan and John's pictures on our passports? I trusted them implicitly. There was no way they would be involved.

So how had their pictures come to be on our passports?

They had bought their house through David Jarvis. Which meant both he and Peter Kennedy would have a copy of their passports as well as ours. But so would our bank – we both banked at the same branch. And applied through the same *Sous-Préfecture* and *Préfecture* for our *cartes de séjour*.

Only the Mayor of Cassagne could be eliminated. He was the only one who hadn't copied both sets of passports.

I heard the manager say, "oh," rather loudly and replace the receiver.

"*Une problème,*" he started, apologetically. I yearned for the days when all we ever heard was *pas de problème*.

"*C'est la Fête des Gendarmes,*" he continued.

He didn't need to say any more. I'd lost the capacity to be surprised. It was *Gendarmes* Day. Of course! The police were on holiday. Silly us, why hadn't we realised?

And the *gendarmes*?

On their way to the restaurant.

Where else.

Did I need further proof? It wasn't Moriarty I was up against, it was Brian Rix. Who else could it be? This whole affair had Whitehall Farce stamped right through it – it was a miracle everyone still had their trousers on!

Of all the days to visit Les, I had to choose the one day – October 2nd – when the entire police force bunk off to the restaurant!

And what the hell was a *Gendarmes* Day?

Was there a *Fête des Voleurs*? Did all the thieves congregate at a restaurant for a day of celebration and spontaneous pick-pocketing?

The manager volunteered to take the matter up with police the next day. I suggested he didn't phone too early.

I was still wrapped in disbelief when Shelagh pointed out the difference in the two passports. Hers was a Visitor's passport.

And she'd grown two inches.

I checked my passport again. Only the picture was different. All the details – name, date of birth, place of birth – were correct.

But not Shelagh's.

It was a composite of three passports.

Shelagh's name, Jan's picture and someone else's address, height and year of birth.

Was this a breakthrough?

The address was given as 44B East Street, Bexley, London SW4 6ET. Nowhere we'd ever lived. Or ever been near.

And someone had taken three years off Shelagh's age and added two inches to her height. Was this an attempt to manufacture a new identity?

The more I looked at the passport, the more false it appeared. Unlike the modern full passport the Visitor's passport was handwritten – but this was written in two hands. In fact, looking closely you could make out sections where the old words had been snowpaked[10] out and the new words didn't quite fill the space. The address had been changed. As had the day and month of birth.

Which meant the year was correct. And the height.

But why use this Visitor's passport when everyone who had a copy of my passport also had a copy of Shelagh's?

I'd have to get in touch with Ian Morris at the Embassy again. Which, I could imagine, would just about make his day.

But the passports were not alone in the bank's files. Just when we were recovering from one shock, the manager handed us another.

A Bankers' Power of Attorney from me to Shelagh; three pages of French and Spanish transferring the account into Shelagh's hands. It was dated 30th May and witnessed by a *notaire,* one Christian Arnaud of Boulogne sur Save.

And it was stamped. An official notarial stamp. Not G. Pergonini MD, but the real McCoy.

It took a while to read and digest. Was this an attempt to switch the account, not so much into a joint account, as Mutual Friendly had been told, but into an account for a woman to use? And was that the reason for Shelagh's composite passport? To change Shelagh's age and height, to pave the way for the arrival of a woman?

In which case, why not use her picture as well?

Or would that have been too risky?

The crime was certain to be discovered eventually, they couldn't afford to use their own pictures ... so they use someone else's. Someone with links to the victim, someone with opportunity.

Jan and John.

They'd set them up to take the blame!

The manager joined in the speculation. I think we'd brightened his day. His name was Miguel and from what we could understand he'd been suspicious from the start. He'd allowed the account to be opened and a small sum deposited – about £50 – but insisted the full passport would be needed to withdraw any money.

He'd passed on his concerns to head office but when they received the power of attorney with the notarial stamp and an attestation by a French notaire that passports had been seen and signatures witnessed – they told him he was being overly suspicious. As long as a valid British passport was eventually produced, the account was to be processed as any other.

But no one had ever returned.

This was a great weight off our minds. So we were not in debt?

"*Non.*"

And we had £50. And I had a valid British passport. Could we?

"*Non.*"

The account had just been frozen.

I still wonder what happened to that money. We certainly never saw any of it. Whose was it? The bank's or the person who illegally deposited it?

But there were more important matters to discuss. Would he be able to recognise the man if he saw him again?

He would.

And if we brought him a photograph?

He'd be able to identify the man.

This was brilliant. Who needed the *gendarmes*? We were doing fine without them.

We chatted some more; I wanted to know if my impersonator had left any other forwarding addresses or fax numbers – something we could use to track him down.

He didn't think so. There was an envelope, but he didn't think it had a sender's address on it. He fished it out of his file. The power of attorney had been inside in it. He handed it over.

It had a printed logo: C & S DOLLEY, Horses of Quality, Seville – Toulouse.

What!

Miguel explained that that was what the man said he did – bought and sold horses. He was opening the account because he was on his way to buy some Andalucian horses. He'd be transferring a large amount into the account to finance the deal.

I was amazed. We had our own personalised envelopes. We bought and sold horses. Was there no end to what we did?

And was the horse motif relevant? Did that imply that someone knew us well enough to know we had a horse? Certainly David Jarvis did. I told him. He knew we were looking for a property with enough land for a horse.

Which presumably meant that Peter Kennedy would know as well?

We asked if Miguel could let us have photocopies of the passports and the power of attorney – which he agreed – and could he write his name, address and telephone number on our pad in case the gendarmes wanted to interview him.

It was with a real sense of achievement that we left the Banca Zaragoza. We'd frozen the account and we had several new leads; a notaire who may or may not exist, an address in London, a British Visitors Passport number and, most important of all – a witness.

All we had to do now was obtain pictures of David Jarvis and Peter Kennedy...

And find Nan.

Who'd disappeared.

Supermarkets, Faxes and the Irish Connection

As usual I could not believe it. I don't know why. Looking back, I should have expected something similar. The car, either devoid of elderly relatives or towed away by a gang of marauding Visigoths. After all, it was *Gendarmes* Day.

We looked at each other. And then back at the empty car. We'd asked her to stay put. We'd told her we wouldn't be long. If she was so determined to look around Les why hadn't she said something?

We looked up and down the street, scanning doorways into the distance. Perhaps she'd just nipped out to stretch her legs?

Nothing.

Perhaps she'd left a note?

She hadn't.

We knew she couldn't have been kidnapped – we weren't that lucky.

Our deliberations were interrupted by a commotion from a building a few doors away.

It was the *Gendarmerie*.

For one awful moment I thought we'd found Nan. I could envisage several burly Spanish policemen dragging Nan out of the station en route for the border and a forced deportation.

Luckily, I was wrong. There were no cries of 'Hands off Gibraltar!' or 'It's the border for you, chummy!'

Instead, we'd stumbled upon the beginning of a procession.

We watched as fifty – or was it nearer eighty? – immaculately dressed *gendarmes* – some in green, some in black, all of them armed – marched out of the station and into the centre of the road.

It looked as though every *gendarme* who had ever visited Les, had a friend called Les, or knew someone who'd once driven down its High Street, was out there marching.

And heading for the nearest restaurant.

We wondered what was happening at the other end of town. Was there a gang of masked felons waiting outside for the signal to come marching in and sack the place? Was Les about to disappear under a wave of blue and white hooped jumpers?

And where, amidst all this chaos, was Nan?

"She's done it again, hasn't she?" said Shelagh.

"What?"

"This! She's only been here five minutes and she's emptied the police station!"

I think Shelagh was going a tad over-the-top concerning her mother's impact upon world events. There was only one person residing at the hub of world misfortune and Shelagh was talking to him. Who else would choose *Gendarmes* Day to visit Spain? If anyone topped Fate's hit list, it was I.

We followed the marching feet of law and order towards the centre of town. After all, where else would Nan be? Tourist shops held the same attraction for Nan that magnets reserved for the more impressionable iron filings.

And Les was a tourist resort.

A typical small Pyrenean resort – plenty of restaurants, hotels and gift shops. And wine. Loads of it. Like many of the resorts near the French border it took advantage of the price differential between French and Spanish wine. Huge wooden vats filled every food shop. A few shelves of provisions and then barrel after barrel of *Tinto* 10%, *Tinto* 12%, *Tinto* 14%, *Moscatel, Porto* and *Misa*. This was take-away country – bring your own container and choose your barrel – with the price dependent on alcoholic strength rather than name or vintage. And it was all incredibly cheap.

I find it a comforting thought that as thousands of Brits queue for their cheap booze at supermarkets near Calais, the French are doing likewise at the Spanish border.

I wondered where the Spanish went? Andorra?

Which begged the question – where did the Andorrans go?

Or were they too drunk to care?

We scanned the cheap wine shops, walked amongst the bric-a-brac displays, the gift shops, the cafe tables. We peered down the narrow alleys between supermarket shelves.

Until we found her. Staring at a label on a bottle of sherry, trying to work out how many pesetas there were in a litre.

"What does this say?" she said as soon as she noticed our arrival, "I can't quite make it out."

I spent the next ten minutes working through the shelves, converting pesetas to pounds, litres to pints, pounds to francs and then back again. And tapping my foot. I wanted to get back home as soon as possible. I had people to phone, information to impart, addresses to check out.

But Nan had a more pressing problem. Should she buy the litre of the cheap medium Sherry or go with the more expensive brand she recognised?

"What do you think, Shelagh?" she asked.

I could tell exactly what Shelagh thought and it had nothing to do with the comparative merits of fortified wine. Both bottles were quickly grabbed and with the words, "consider it a present," marched to the check out.

From there we almost made it to the French border.

Almost ... but not quite.

Nan had the scent.

"Ooh, look at that! Is that the cheap supermarket you told me about?"

Unfortunately, it was. We spent another forty minutes pushing trolleys and calculating prices. I didn't think one small person could buy so much sherry. And after the sherry came the brandy and aren't those liqueur bottles nice and ooh, what's that over there?

I didn't think I'd ever see France again.

With Mrs Hudson safely ensconced counting sherry bottles in her room, 221b Baker Street could return to normal. I had an address to check.

And an old London A-Z.

There was no East Street in Bexley. At least not in 1980. I suppose there was always the chance that there was now – but hardly likely. Local councils didn't go in for East Streets these days; new roads were more likely to be Mandela Avenue or McCartney Plaza.

And the postcode didn't match the address – Bexley was nowhere near SW4. I wondered if it was worth trying to locate the address that did match the postcode but thought, on balance, it probably wasn't. Looking closely, the postcode looked like it had been altered as well – though 'London' and 'SW' looked unchanged. Which would tie up with the issuing post office being Putney, London SW15. Certainly the stamp looked unaltered.

I felt that I'd progressed the address as far as I could. It was time to ring Andy.

I think he was impressed. I'd given him something concrete to check out – an address and a passport number. And the use of the *notaire* might give us another lead. And what about the Bankers' Power of Attorney? Didn't that imply a female accomplice – the account being changed so that she could withdraw the money?

We pushed theories back and forth. Nothing ever seemed straightforward in this case. Why not simply add Shelagh's name to the account? Why complicate matters by drawing up a three-page power of attorney? It seemed so unnecessarily over the top. And it drew in another person – a notaire – someone else who, if they existed, would be a witness.

Andy had some news as well. He'd heard from the Irish police. Neither David Jarvis nor Peter Kennedy were known to them – no criminal records or nefarious associations – and the same went for the UK police.

I decided it was time to move down my checklist. What about

those fax numbers? And more especially, what number did Mutual Friendly use to contact my alter ego?

The number began, 62 04. Which meant it wasn't Villeurbanne. Or the Castlenau Poste. I jotted it down to check out later.

And the other fax numbers? The ones my impersonator used to send the faxes?

Andy reeled off a list. The same four numbers repeating themselves - area codes 42 33, 72 34, 78 35 and 62 04. Quite a collection. What did they all say? How many different ways were there to say – I cancel my bond, give me the money?

Apparently a lot. Andy read out one dated June 9th – the same day I received the request for the bond originals. It was from Shelagh, apologising for the delay in sending the originals but the solicitor had sent them to the old address by mistake. I was driving from Seville to collect them.

I wondered what I'd done with the horse. And also wondered how my impersonator kept track of all these comings and goings. Did he have a storyboard? Chris is in Seville, buying horses. Shelagh is in Spain on holiday. The solicitor has the originals. The house is being renovated.

I was almost impressed.

I said goodbye to Andy and immediately dialled Simon. I might as well get his list of fax numbers while I remembered.

He had a similar list. The same four numbers cropping up again and again: Villeurbanne and three others.

Which is when I thought to ask if these other numbers came with header pages – like the Castlenau *Poste* fax.

They did.

Some of them.

Gradually we constructed the list. 42 33 was the Paris Louvre CTT – a bureau like Villeurbanne used by the Mauvezan *Poste* for routing its international faxes.

And the Mauvezan *Poste?*

That was the owner of the fax number beginning 62 04, the fax number Mutual Friendly was told to reply to.

Mauvezan. A town fifteen minutes from Castlenau. A town which just happened to be where David Jarvis banked.

I remembered him telling me on the first day we met. We were talking about climate and altitude and I remember him saying how he could notice the difference some days when he drove to his bank, Mauvezan being a couple of hundred metres higher than Castlenau.

I wondered where Peter Kennedy banked?

Next, I asked Simon for a list of all the letters he'd sent me. I pulled out my own file and we went through them starting in

February. There was one missing. Sent on the 29th March. It was a single page headed Mutual Friendly European Personal Bond Fund.

Why did that name sound familiar?

I rummaged through my growing list of notes. I'd covered pages of notebooks with numbered items of importance – things to find out, dates and times, fax numbers...

And names ... there it was – Mutual Friendly European Personal Bond Fund. And underneath I'd written – *where did he get this name from, it doesn't appear anywhere else?*

He'd got the name from Simon's letter of the 29th. A letter I'd never received.

And a letter that had never been within a hundred miles of Mutual Friendly and their Dublin office.

Did that rule out the need for an accomplice inside the insurers?

Simon wasn't convinced. It was too much of a coincidence, wasn't it? If no one knew about the bond, why would anyone target our mail?

And why hadn't Elaine Varley questioned me when I rang her about a letter she'd never written? I'm sure I even quoted the date it had been sent.

"And why did she keep asking for us to release the originals when she knew the case was going to arbitration?"

"What?" I didn't know that.

"Yes, let me see ... there were faxes on the 24th of July, the 26th, the 8th of August ... a phone call on the 24th. And she didn't ask for the documents to be sent by courier. Which is very strange."

Was it? I had no idea how these things were done.

"It's the usual procedure. And I know she went on holiday to Spain."

Spain? I wondered when? Was it possible she was the woman who was going to withdraw the money from the account? But couldn't, as Eastleigh and Howard never released the originals?

I decided to ring Andy again. Had he investigated Elaine Varley as thoroughly as he would have if she hadn't been an employee?

I told him about the phone call and the faxes to Eastleigh and Howard.

He was surprised. He had nothing on file. According to his papers, Elaine Varley had not been in contact with Eastleigh and Howard during July or August.

Women and Passports

This was getting even more exciting – every phone call a new revelation, every day a new prime suspect. I wasn't sure which lead to follow next.

As I was by the phone I thought I might as well check out this Boulogne *notaire,* Christian Arnaud. I leafed through the directory, trying to remember if Boulogne sur Save was in the Gers or the Haute Garonne.

It was in the Haute Garonne.

And so was Christian Arnaud.

Arnaud, Christian, *notaire* – the entry proclaimed.

Should we go and see him?

Shelagh didn't think so. Not yet. First, we needed photographs of David Jarvis and Peter Kennedy. Then we'd have something to show him.

But how could we obtain a photograph?

It wasn't going to be easy. You can't ring round mutual acquaintances saying, "hello, I'm collecting pictures of David and Peter. Have you got any?" without exciting peoples' interest. And the possibility of the information getting back to them.

No, we had to obtain the pictures ourselves. We knew where David Jarvis worked. We knew what time he arrived at his office. We had a camera.

We even had a telephoto lens.

What were we waiting for? And if the bank manager identified David Jarvis the case was solved. We wouldn't need to find anyone else.

Conversely, if he didn't identify David Jarvis, wouldn't that be as good as pointing the finger at Peter Kennedy?

It was decided. It was too late to do anything today but tomorrow we'd go to Castlenau. He'd told us he always opened his office at ten, we'd be waiting.

In the meantime, there were other leads to follow. The composite passport and the power of attorney – why go to all that trouble?

We pushed ideas around our heads. Why change the account to allow withdrawal by a woman? Was it something to do with having to produce a valid passport? Was there something a woman could do that a man couldn't? Something to do with passports?

Marriage!

A woman could change her name.

"But not her first name," Shelagh quickly pointed out. And what were the chances of having an accomplice called Shelagh?

Unless there were Australians involved.

I was told to shut up at that point. This was a serious matter and even if you had an accomplice called Shelagh, you'd still have to produce proof of marriage.

"Like a marriage license?" I countered. Like the marriage license we'd given David Jarvis to copy? He'd needed it for the house purchase. And he'd taken copies of our birth certificates as well.

And what would you need to change your name on a passport – a photocopy of a marriage license and a doctor's signature? David Jarvis could produce both. All he'd have to do was change a few dates and the maiden name, photocopy the result and slap on a Pergonini signature.

What other checks would the Passport Office make?

As many as Banca Zaragoza's head office?

The more I thought about it, the more ways I could see of validly obtaining a passport under a different name.

Changing your name by deed poll[11]. How would the Passport Agency handle that?

Or getting hold of a certified copy of Shelagh's birth certificate – we'd done it ourselves before coming to France; we'd been told it was necessary as the French insisted on all official documents being less than three months old.

All we had to do was write to the registrar who issued the original certificate and enclose a cheque for £5.50. No one asked for identification. We could have been anyone.

And if someone had a photocopy of our birth certificates they'd know the issuing registration districts. All they'd need was £11.00 and they'd have valid birth certificates in both our names.

And how difficult would it be to alter a date of birth to throw off any Passport Agency duplication checks?

When you've seen a bank account opened with a bad photocopy of your brother-in-law, you begin to take a less than rose-tinted view of the capabilities of eagle-eyed officialdom.

Nothing would surprise me any more.

So, I phoned Ian Morris at the Embassy. I could tell he was pleased to hear from me by the sudden intake of breath as I mentioned my name.

"I have some more questions about passports," I began and told him what we'd found in Spain and roughed out our latest and most plausible theory about how someone called Shelagh – or someone who had changed her name by deed-poll to Shelagh – could obtain my birth certificate for £5.50 and marry someone pretending to be me and then have all the documentation required to obtain a valid passport in my wife's name.

Silence.

"Are you still there?"

He was – just – but he had the air of a person who would not look unfavourably upon a fire drill within the next three minutes. If not a minor bomb alert. Preferably in the switchboard.

In the meantime, he reiterated the party line, the passport system was foolproof – even against Pergoninis. I countered with "What about Spain then?" and he informed me that the Passport Office was not Spain.

So, I switched tack onto the British Visitor's Passport – could he trace the number for us.

"It won't be easy," he said and went on to explain how the Visitor's Passports were issued by individual post offices, how there was no central registry and how it would mean writing to Putney and asking them to look through their records.

I agreed with him that that sounded very onerous indeed – especially the bit about having to write a letter – couldn't he get someone to help him with the spelling?

The phone call ended soon after that – I think robots seized control of the switchboard. But it didn't make much difference; by then I'd realised that any progress we were going to make was not going to come via third parties.

"A cup of tea would be nice."

"Pardon." I hadn't noticed Nan coming into the room. I'd been too immersed in detection. Was the missing letter from Eastleigh and Howard significant?

"A cup of tea," she repeated.

"We haven't got any tea, mum," answered Shelagh from the other settee. I looked up. I hadn't noticed her arrival either. I thought I'd been alone. I scanned the lounge for further life forms. A dog and two cats stared back. Where had they all come from? And was this a good sign – the Great Detective being caught unawares by a mass invasion of his consulting rooms?

"Would you like a coffee?" Shelagh asked her mother.

"I'd prefer tea."

"But we don't have any."

"Ooh, Shelagh, I saw it there the other day!"

"Where?"

"In the cupboard."

"You can't have. We haven't got any."

I could tell Nan didn't believe one word of Shelagh's denial. And knew from experience exactly what would happen next – all the kitchen cupboards would have to be emptied, their contents checked, suspicious tins opened and traces sent away to Tetley's for analysis.

Shelagh would get annoyed, Nan defensive, coffee would be refused and someone would have to climb into the car and drive to the supermarket.

That someone being me.

By my reckoning I had about five minutes to solve the riddle of the missing letter before the car keys were thrown in my direction.

I moved quickly into the study.

Was the missing letter significant?

I'd have to wait four or five days to read the contents but was its date important? If the letter was sent on the 29th March it would have arrived about the 5th.

I checked through our diaries, calendars and note-pads by the phone – what were we doing the week of the 5th? Were we out, did anything strange happen? I checked our bank statements to see if we had made any cashpoint withdrawals and if so from where?

Then I remembered.

The Bank Statement!

The one that went missing!

Wasn't that sometime in April?

I shouted to Shelagh, "you remember that bank statement that went missing?"

Shelagh couldn't remember. Or was too immersed in kitchen cabinets to reply.

"You know! The one that came out of sequence. I was about to write to the bank when it arrived."

It had been a month late. Exactly a month late. I remembered now. It had to have been April because I'd been waiting for the statement to check some large withdrawals we'd made in March – I wasn't sure if I'd written them down correctly.

I pulled out the statement. It was dated April 5th and it should have arrived a few days later. But it had arrived in May. I hadn't thought that much about it, I'd assumed the bank had mis-filed it and suddenly noticed it when the next statement was due.

But if it hadn't been mislaid?

Two letters due around the 6th; one never arrives, one turns up a month late.

Could the Cancellation Form have been a third letter?

It was pushing the time frame. The Cancellation Form was supposed to have been sent on the 22nd of March. Could it have taken two weeks to arrive? It was possible.

Which could mean that everything was taken on one day. Probably the 7th as that would tie in with the sentence – *Thank you for your letter, received here on 7th April.*

But it was still one hell of a coincidence. One fortuitous trip to our letter box, one haul of letters – which just happened to contain a cancellation form and a valuation.

Unless they knew it was coming. Which brought Elaine Varley back into the frame.

Perhaps it was worth another phone call to Andy? Question him again, perhaps push him a bit harder as to why he was so certain that Elaine Varley was guiltless?

And I could tell him about the missing letter from Eastleigh and Howard.

So I punched in the now familiar numbers and waited for the explanation. Why couldn't it have been an inside job masterminded by Elaine Varley?

"Because it couldn't," came the reply, "she's the one who tipped us off."

The Screaming Detective of Castlenau

"What do you mean, tipped you off?"

There was a long silence. I could tell he wasn't entirely happy with the conversation or where it was heading.

"She alerted us to a ... to a possible situation."

"What kind of situation?"

"She was suspicious about your wife's signature."

What? But that must have been back in April? I ... I was lost for words. Why hadn't anyone contacted us if they thought there was a fraud underway?

There was a further embarrassed silence.

"Er ... we thought we were dealing with a ... a different crime."

What kind of a different crime?

And then it hit me. They were only suspicious of Shelagh's signature.

They thought it was me!

Husband forges wife's signature and tries to move all their money from a joint account into his own bank account. Is that why they didn't try to contact us at our original address – because they thought I'd intercept any letter to Shelagh?

I dragged a few more facts out of the conversation. They were suspicious but lacking proof. They wanted to wait and see how the situation developed. Ensure the money was destined for a joint account with Shelagh's name on it. They delayed the process as much as they could but couldn't act without firm evidence. And were afraid of breaching new financial legislation concerning our right to cancel and receive payment within designated timescales.

I couldn't help thinking – if that account in Spain had been in joint names or if I'd had the originals of the bond – the money would have been paid over in June.

And they would have had three months to make good their escape before we found out.

Amidst all our bad luck we'd had one huge slice of good.

But what about the time I phoned Elaine Varley? Why hadn't she questioned me about the letter I'd said she'd sent?

"I have the notes here, taken after your call. *Talked to Chris Dolley today. Not the same one as before.*"

Which explained why she hadn't said anything about not sending the letter I'd quoted – she'd been playing me along.

But why hadn't anyone reacted to the fact that there were now apparently two of me?

"We didn't know what it meant."

I left the phone, re-entering the now familiar state of mild shock. I'd been a suspect ... *the* suspect ... in a budding international financial scandal. There was probably a file on me. If not two – one for each Chris Dolley.

I conveyed my amazing news from the lounge doorway.

Silence.

I fell back onto the lounge sofa, still waiting for the chorus of support and general incredulity.

Silence.

"Imagine anyone thinking it was me!"

More silence, a sideways glance from Nan and the hum of five brains recalling past incidents in which I'd featured.

At least you can always count on the unconditional devotion of your puppy in times of stress. Gypsy stretched her giant legs into a standing position and walked towards me. I reached out to stroke her ... and she ducked down, picked up the dog chew lying by my foot and carried it carefully back to the safety of her bean bag. Life savings were one thing but a chew was personal.

The next day came with an assertion by Nan that the only possible 'non-dead day' itinerary was a trip to Castlenau. Even the threat of indigenous toiletnappers couldn't persuade her otherwise.

Gypsy cast her vote likewise. Staying in the house was a 'dead day' for dogs as well. Only Shelagh voted to stay at home but I wasn't having any of that. If Nan and Gypsy were going then so was she.

A frank exchange of views ensued. She's *your* mother. She's *your* dog. No, she isn't. Yes, she is.

Ten minutes later, the Great Detective, two willing passengers and one very unwilling one, set off for the Great Stakeout of Castlenau.

And twenty minutes after that, the Great Detective veered towards the ranks of the unwilling. He was hot, uncomfortable and having to drive with all the windows up. Not through choice, but because his dog had just told his mother-in-law that she didn't want the windows down.

It was like driving with Sooty[12] and Harry Corbett in the back seat.

"What's that, Sooty? You feel a draught?"

Needless to say, no such exchange of views had taken place – Gypsy couldn't care less whether the windows were up or down.

But Nan did. And being Nan, anything so direct as, "do you mind closing the window, I can feel a draught," was totally out of the question.

Hence the invocation of the beast from Hell.

Well, two could play at that game.

I craned my neck back. "What's that, Gypsy? You've changed your mind? You're hot and want the window down?"

An elbow caught me in the ribs. Quickly followed by a hissed "Stop it!"

I drove for miles with my clothes sticking to the seat.

Summer in the *Sud* did not stop for October.

The car, however, never failed to stop for tight bladders.

"What do you mean, you need to go!" A pretty meaningless question even for a rhetorical one, but I was a hot, sticky driver on his way to meet Moriarty.

"I can't help it," replied Shelagh. "It's something to do with the early mornings."

And drinking two cups of coffee with breakfast.

"Why didn't you go before we left?"

"I did!"

There's not a lot else you can say after that. But a driver will always try. All drivers having an intrinsic urge to complete their journeys with the minimum number of stops.

"Can't you hang on? We're nearly there. It's only another ten minutes to Castlenau."

"Ooh you don't want to go there. They don't have proper toilets."

Thank you, Nan. Only a hole in the ground or a bush tucked behind the end tables, I'd heard.

"Can't we sit in a car for five minutes these days without the word 'toilet' cropping up?"

"Gypsy probably needs to go as well."

"Oh well, that makes everything all right then. Gypsy wants the windows up, Gypsy wants to stop, Gypsy wants a bottle of sherry!"

I snapped.

I was hot, my shirt was welded to the back of my seat, my imagination projecting images of imminent confrontations with an army of enraged David Jarvis ninja clones and all anyone could talk about were dogs and toilets!

It had to stop!

I declared the car a toilet-free zone. We would stop – this once – and then that was it. No further discussion to be brooked. No bushes located, no bladders allowed to tighten.

End of discussion. The driver had spoken.

~

The journey continued in silence, my mind alive with every permutation imaginable and some beyond even that. Where was the best place to take a picture from? Where should I park? What if David Jarvis's car had photon torpedoes?

His office was on the side of one of the town squares. Other than market day, the square was a car park. Should I park there? Wasn't that how they did it in films? Wind the window down and snap away as the suspect climbed out of his car?

Except with my luck the car in the next bay would pull out just as David Jarvis arrived. He'd park next to me. I'd fall over backwards onto the passenger seat in a desperate attempt not to be seen and shoot off twelve perfect close-ups of his right ear lobe.

So I decided against the town square and voted in favour of our usual car park.

First problem solved, next one located.

Our camera.

It was old. Almost as old as me. Not one of those modern point and click affairs but one of East Germany's finest from the early Cold War era. I had to select the shutter speed, select the aperture, focus with the aperture fully open, stop it back down again, click and wind on. It took brilliant pictures. Of landscapes, nuclear missile silos and all things stationary. But a moving target?

I'd tried it several times with the cats. By the time I had a tail in focus, the whisker end had disappeared between my legs.

Best to keep the target at a long distance, I decided. At least twenty yards to make the focussing easier and hope he stood still long enough for me to get a few pictures off.

I tried a few practice focussing attempts on Nan's back as she shot off towards the town centre. It's amazing the speed an eighty year-old can clock up once the smell of the shops hits the nostrils. Shelagh set off in pursuit, leaving me alone with Gypsy who, now that Nan had left, had surprisingly little to say.

I left Gypsy in the car and slowly walked up the hill towards the old market square. Part of me excited, part of me wishing I was somewhere else. Perhaps he wouldn't be there, perhaps he'd take the day off or be away visiting clients?

Or maybe he'd be lying in wait?

Imagination had given up writing reports. Glossy brochures had been ditched in favour of shouted warnings – get the hell out, come back tomorrow!

A few steps later, I entered the square. It was a typical old Gascon market square: lines of shops set back beneath protruding first floors supported by huge stone pillars, creating a protected walkway against sun and rain. The square in the middle – sometimes a car park, sometimes a sea of stalls and striped canvas.

Today, it was a car park. And very busy.

I positioned myself behind a pillar within sight of David's office. And waited.

If I'd been a tourist looking for a close-up picture of a church tower or an artist searching out subjects for a portrait, I'd have been fine. But I wasn't. I was a private detective waiting to take clandestine snaps of a suspect and felt as though everyone knew it. I might as well have had a sandwich board with 'Detective on Stakeout' writ large upon it.

And it was dangerous, wasn't it?

People were killed these days for less than a pound. And if that was the going rate what would someone do for our nest egg – wipe out Eastbourne in a fit of pique?

I was trying to work out the population of Castlenau, when I saw his car.

Anticipation, fear, excitement. My heart may not have been in my mouth but it was close to my tonsils.

I watched him climb out of his car, only twenty yards away. I raised the camera, focussed, waited for him to turn his head ... and ... and...

He didn't.

Not once.

It was back of the head all the way to his office door. Not even a look to his right as he crossed the road. Did this man not know his Highway Code?

What do I do now? Plan B – wait for twelve o'clock and lunch?

Or Plan C – scream so loud that he'd be forced to leave his office to see what all the noise was about?

A plan I had not been considering but an unexpected hand on the shoulder and a nose in the crotch can work wonders. The hand belonged to Nan and the nose to Gypsy. The result couldn't have been more spectacular had the ownerships been reversed.

To say I screamed would do an injustice to the superb acoustics of the Castlenau covered walkways.

Unfortunately, even that wasn't enough to tempt an estate agent from his lair.

Though easily enough to tempt Gypsy into a frenzied bout of high-pitched yipping.

I couldn't have been more conspicuous if I'd spent the last ten years in constant preparation.

Why me?

I was on stakeout. Gypsy was supposed to be safely locked away in the car and Nan in the throws of a shopping frenzy. What had happened?

"Gypsy wanted a walk," came the reply.

I could think of something else Gypsy wanted. But I'd drawn enough attention for one morning.

Luckily Nan caught sight of set of tea towels in a shop opposite and they both left.

Leaving me alone with my nerves. I could hardly keep the camera still.

I tried calming thoughts. I am not a suspicious character, I am invisible, at one with the pillar, no one can see me.

"Aaaarrrgggghhh!"

Deja vu minus the nose in the crotch. Was my shoulder magnetised? Couldn't anyone walk by without feeling impelled to grab it?

"How's it going?" asked Shelagh.

"Great," I replied. "Every five minutes I scream and all of Castlenau comes to a halt. Another half hour and I'll become a tourist attraction – the screaming detective of Castlenau, you can set your watch by him!"

"You haven't seen Nan, have you?"

"She's with Gypsy."

"Back in the car?"

"No, she's taking Gypsy for a walk."

It was Shelagh's turn to scream.

"She's what!"

Nan wasn't that steady on her feet and Gypsy had a tendency to uproot anyone foolish enough to grab the other end of her lead. A rumour of a bare leg sighted in the neighbouring village or a pigeon flapping its wings three fields away – and she'd be off.

And now so was Shelagh.

I watched, powerless, as three figures moved between the pillars on the far side of the square: Nan, determined to prove she was still young and fit; Shelagh, determined to save her mother from being dragged across the town square and Gypsy, the most determined of the three, in search of a pack of giant Martian bunnies.

There's something about imminent disaster that affects the space-time continuum. Everything slows down. You can watch it unfold but can't do a thing about it. Time stretches into slow-motion action replay mode.

And memory captures it all.

As Gypsy approached a narrow alley off the market square her canine nose detected that which canine noses regard above all others.

Ah, the sweet smell of urine.

And brought to mind that old European proverb: a urinating Frenchman is worth two Martian bunnies any day.

Gypsy was away, dragging Nan into an unexpected and swift left-hand turn down the alley.

The man caught the movement out of the corner of his eye and immediately recognised the warning signs: large dog approaching, teeth bared, old lady in tow.

Large Dog lunged forward, Old Lady screamed, Urinating Frenchman screamed.

Shelagh arrived.

Unfortunately, I couldn't see much of what happened next. It was a only a small alley and easily filled by three people and a large dog.

I tried my telephoto lens.

Pointed ... and saw a familiar face cross my field of vision. It was David Jarvis. He must have left his office while I was distracted. Click, I had him. But had he seen Shelagh? I turned the lens back towards the alley. Unlikely. The current view of Shelagh was not one that normally adorned passports.

I turned the camera back to David, tracked him to his car, all the shots so far were in profile, if only he'd turn this way ... click. I had him, just as he turned to open his car door.

I stepped back behind the pillar and spent the next five minutes hoping he'd driven past and it was safe to come out. And wondering what was happening in a certain alley on the other side of the square.

Something, unfortunately, I'd never adequately ascertain.

A tight-lipped mother and daughter arrived back at the pillar. Shelagh firmly in control of Gypsy, the only one of the three who wanted to talk about the affair but lacking her usual band of telepathic channelers.

But I had a hunch there was at least one Frenchman who'd never use that particular alley again in a hurry.

I sighed. And assessed our morning's work.

Again we had terrorised Castlenau. But the investigation had advanced. We had photographs.

And a thorough knowledge of all the best places to pee in Castlenau.

Driving back, my bladder was tightening by the minute. But I daren't say anything after my earlier pronouncement. The car had been declared a toilet-free zone and a toilet-free zone it must remain.

So, I pushed the car faster. Swinging into bends and sending my rear seat passengers sliding into friendly piles against one window then the other.

"I don't think Gypsy likes this," said Nan.

I wasn't too happy either.

Why do they design seat-belts to press on full bladders? I tried adjusting the tension, pulling some slack through and holding it there with my hand.

That didn't work for long. I tried leaning forward, I squirmed, shuffled and hit the accelerator again.

"What's the matter?"

"Nothing."

I'd had lessons from the master; no one was going to prise the word 'toilet' from my lips.

"What are you doing?"

More agitation in Shelagh's voice this time. Has my husband been taken over? Is some alien creature about to explode from his chest cavity?

And why has he just unbuckled his seat-belt?

"Gypsy told me to."

I tried changing the subject – pointing at anything strange that flashed past the windscreen. I tried to block all thoughts of bladders, tried a few bars of a song.

Nearly there, a few tyre-screeching turns, a quick acceleration and ... hit the brakes, open the car door and run.

I was into the house and running down the hallway before anyone else could move. Thank God for a house with five toilets.

Three Slim Blond Men

Less than an hour later we were all back in the car again, bladders empty and a film to process.

Unfortunately, I couldn't remember how many pictures I'd taken in Castlenau, how many I'd taken before or what size of film I'd loaded. East Germany were not hot on such topics in the early sixties and although the camera had a picture counter, it never worked the way you'd expect – like adding one every time you took a picture.

Instead, it randomly rotated and reset itself at unexpected moments. I often wondered if I was missing a code book.

But we were well used to its idiosyncrasies and finished the film off with assorted pictures of the house, pets and Nan.

And then off we went to the *Leclerc* supermarket and hopefully one of those one hour development services.

Developing pictures is always a surprise in our family. Sometimes there can be as many as three years separating the first and last frames – strange pictures of people we'd almost forgotten, houses we'd stayed at, animals we'd known and hair I used to have.

One hour and a bit later, we ripped open the packet and there he was – a perfect rendition of David Jarvis. East Germany may not have been hot on user friendliness but they certainly knew how to build cameras.

Now, I'd seen my fair share of crime movies, and knew that detective don't just hand over a single picture of the suspect and ask – is it him? They produce a selection – three or four people of similar appearance – and ask the witness to pick the perp.

We'd do the same.

Or at least that was the idea. Unfortunately a detailed perusal of our collection of photos did not produce many David Jarvis/Peter Kennedy look-alikes. In fact it didn't produce many human look-alikes. Most of my pictures tended to be from office parties, where people were either in fancy dress or the final stages of inebriation – usually both. And Shelagh's were almost entirely of animals. If David Jarvis had been a rare-breed sheep or a red-eyed Tina Turner impersonator, we would have had a wealth of matches. Unfortunately he wasn't, so we didn't.

So I rang my sister and asked for a selection of slim, blond men.

"Aha."

"It's for an identity parade."

"Of course."

We drove over to Jan's late that afternoon and swapped Nan for two slim blond men. I think hunting for toilets all day was veering towards a 'dead day' classification.

So, armed with our mobile identity parade, we set off towards Boulogne and its infamous hotel. Would we be able to find it?

I was confident. We may not have had a street map of Boulogne but what did that matter to a Great Detective? Boulogne couldn't be that big. We'd drive around a bit, and if that failed, we'd ask someone. *Ou est l'Hôtel du Midi* didn't even rate a script. We'd ad lib, what could go wrong?

Amazingly nothing.

We drove all the way to Boulogne without being stopped by a single *gendarme* or a faulty warp coil.

And once in Boulogne we quartered the town, driving slowly through its major thoroughfares.

No *Hôtel du Midi*.

We tried the less major thoroughfares.

Still no *Hôtel du Midi*.

Had it been stolen? Was it camouflaged?

We tried even smaller tracks, skirting the built-up areas and extending our search into the surrounding *campagne*.

And then we saw it.

The *Hôtel du Midi*.

I recognised it.

I'd been there before.

I could not believe it – and I am a person who has worn out those particular keys on my typewriter. But there I was, staring at the infamous address that had haunted our last fortnight and it was a place I'd visited only a matter of weeks previously!

I'd played football in the stadium opposite. It was a friendly against Boulogne and, as was the custom, after the match both teams had repaired to the home side's local for free drinks.

This was Boulogne's local.

I walked in half expecting to be greeted by, "hello, Mr. Dolley, usual table?"

Not to mention a handful of faxes and forwarded letters.

But no, not even a, "what about that goal you missed last month."

We ordered our two drinks, found a table, sat down and ... waited for inspiration. Perhaps this wasn't going to be as easy as we'd thought. Do we just place the photographs on the counter and ask the bar staff if they recognised anyone? Or do we have to hide dollar bills under the pictures?

And shouldn't we have prepared a script?

We hastily cobbled one together. Perhaps if we started with something about the *gendarmes* visit last week? Or would that make everyone clam up? Would an uneasy silence descend broken only by the sound of fleeing customers diving through windows?

Maybe we should forget the *gendarmes* and ask if they knew a friend of ours who stayed here in May? Or would that just confuse matters. And label us as accomplices?

I decided upon a bold plan.

"Je suis le vrai Monsieur Dolley," I said, advancing on the barman and clutching my open passport like a crucifix before me. *"C'est moi."*

I think he was impressed, if not a little startled. It may not have been a genuine Pergonini but it did look official.

Shelagh, aka the true Mrs. Dolley, quickly chimed in with a sentence freely laced with *gendarmes* and visits.

Ah! He remembered.

But he didn't remember any faces. We showed him our trio of slim blond men and he didn't recognise a single one. Neither David Jarvis or any of my slim blond cousins. It could have been any of them, he said.

My eyes narrowed. I wondered where my cousins were last May.

A waitress was called over to have a look but she hadn't actually seen the man and neither had the receptionist. Nobody had, just the barman.

Which I thought strange for someone staying at a hotel. Where did he have his meals?

Not at the hotel, we discovered. In fact, he hadn't actually stayed at the hotel. He'd walked into the bar sometime back in May and struck up a conversation with the barman. He'd told him how he'd just moved to the area and was looking for work, could he use the hotel as a *poste restante*?

So, no hotel register to fill in, no address to leave or even a sample of handwriting. Just an occasional visit to check for mail.

We left the *Hôtel du Midi* slightly disappointed. After such a good description we thought someone was bound to recognise David Jarvis.

Could it be that it wasn't him after all? Was it the mysterious Peter Kennedy all along?

Luckily we still had the bank manager.

And the *notaire*.

Shelagh looked at her watch – nearly seven, darkness approaching – what were the chances of a *notaire* being open this late?

None, I thought. And we still weren't sure if the *notaire* was a witness or an accomplice.

So we drove back to pick up Nan and let our thoughts drift towards tomorrow and our trip to Les.

And speculate when Bank Managers' Day would be.

We set off mid-morning, slightly later than last time to give everyone's bladder a good chance of a stop-free run to Spain. We left to the usual howled lament from a puppy's head protruding from the cat-flap. I think she was howling last minute advice to Nan and Shelagh – I want the windows closed for the first ten miles and a stop at that nice lay-by with the waste bins.

I was more concerned with counselling the car through its daily panic attack. It's all right, boy, you can do it. Words of encouragement, hand on choke, ears listening for the slightest drop in revs.

Four minutes later, and with the car's confidence building steadily, our trip to Spain came to an unexpected and dramatic halt.

We'd turned into an unmarked roadwork.

Shelagh and Nan couldn't believe it. I, however, had reached the point where unbelievable was just another name for commonplace. I wound down the window to check. Yes, I thought so; we were parked on wet, steaming tarmac.

But that's life when you annoy Fate. One minute you're on a single track road not far from the middle of nowhere, you turn left at a T junction and suddenly you're surrounded by giant road-laying vehicles, fresh tarmac spewing out their rears and not a 'Road Closed' sign in sight.

God knows what this had done to the car's confidence!

Clouds of steam rose from the vehicles in front of us. The air was filled with the smell of tar and noxious gases, the incessant thump and clunk of moving parts on metal. The noise was deafening. It was like being on the Tartarus turnpike, tar and sulphur belching out all around us.

I threw the car into reverse. It didn't like it. Was it stuck or just terrified? We were drawing puzzled looks from the workmen. Who were we? Where the hell had we come from – the road was supposed to be closed!

The car stalled, fired, stuttered, slued for a bit and then shot backwards.

And kept on going.

I was concentrating so hard on avoiding ditches and keeping momentum that I aimed for the first spot I could see devoid of big yellow trucks.

And reversed straight past our junction and on for another thirty yards until I found a section of solid, unsteaming road surface.

Thank God for that!

If I'd been American, I'd probably have sued everyone in sight. If I'd been French, I'd have been grinding spittle for a week. But I was English, and I just wanted to leave.

Quickly.

A wish shared by my passengers.

"Go that way! Go that way!" screamed Shelagh. "It looks clear."

So I swung the car around into a quick three point turn and headed off away from the over-powering smell and noise.

But not all the noise.

A clang, tick, scrape and a grate came along with us.

I stopped the car, got out ... and saw that our tyres were caked in thick tar and stone chippings. They looked like my Wellington boots after an hour gardening in cloying heavy clay. There was so much tar that the wheels couldn't turn without hitting the wheel arch. Lumps of tar and stone chippings were being scraped off with every turn.

I looked back down the road to where the huge machines were still chugging and steaming. Still no 'Road Closed' sign in evidence.

Which was unusual in France. Even the smallest spot of hedge trimming usually rated an *'Attention! Fauchage!'* sign. And often a couple of men with flags and a van with flashing lights.

"It'll be fine," I said as I climbed back into the car. The driver's prime directive being 'Always keep the confidence of your passengers.'

And, in my case, the car's as well.

The passengers were of mixed opinions. Shelagh wanted to go home – she could recognise an omen when it spewed tarmac in front of her. Nan wanted to continue – missing out on day trips had been a 'dead day' chart-topper for years.

I decided to press on. I didn't fancy driving back over thirty yards of hot tar to reach our turning.

A minute later we turned a bend and ... saw another patch of embryonic highway.

No road laying vehicles this time – they must have finished this stretch thirty minutes earlier – but how many others were there?

I weighed up the options. Thirty yards of hot, wet tarmac behind us. God knows how many yards of not so hot tarmac ahead of us.

To go on or to turn back, that indeed was the question.

But only for the driver. Democracies can't handle a second swathe of wet tarmac.

And passengers should realise that what drivers really need in moments of stress is not advice but people to blame. *I told you we should have set off earlier. No, you didn't. Yes, I did.*

We ploughed on, through swathe after swathe of alternating new and old road. And eventually past an impressive 'Road Closed' sign complete with startled man with flag.

As we later found out they'd closed both ends of the road they were patching but forgot about a little-used single track road that intersected with it – our little road from the middle of nowhere.

Having survived the ordeal of the tar pits, we now had another one. Where were we?

This was a section of road we'd never travelled before and didn't seem to accord with any on our map. Nor did it favour the use of road signs.

Not surprising really, the first rule about driving in France is to forget the idea that road signs are there to help you. They're not. They're more of a confirmation that you made the right choice at the last junction. It's fairly normal in France to arrive at a busy junction with two lanes to choose from and find no clue as to which one you should take; the road sign cleverly placed on the far side of the lights – only readable after you've committed yourself to the wrong lane.

So, with no map and no road signs, what should we do?

Some people would keep going until they found a major road. But I wasn't some people. I was a person with a sense of direction.

The most dangerous sense known to motoring.

And I could see a left turn.

We took it.

"Why are we going this way?"

"Short-cut," I said. The most feared word a passenger can hear in a car, other than "Aaaarrrggghhh!" It's part of the drivers' creed – that however well-researched a route may be, there's always a short-cut for the determined motorist to find.

And I'd found mine.

We'd cut across over the foothills, boldly searching out other left turns until we found something I recognised.

Like that water tower on the top of the hill.

Wasn't that the one we could see from the top of our road?

I thought it was, Shelagh thought it wasn't and Nan was looking out the wrong window.

We turned left again, up towards the water tower and hopefully to swing back around to the main road and Spain. After all, I surmised, all we had to do was head for the mountains.

Unfortunately all mountains were currently obscured by foothills. Large, rolling, heavily wooded ones. And we were heading into the thick of them.

At least we'd have a good view when we reached the top.

Whenever that would be. Thick wood was closing in from all sides, the road winding and narrowing, potholes increasing.

"Is this the right way?" asked Nan. Never a good question to ask a driver when he's lost.

I explained calmly about the water tower.

"The wrong water tower," added Shelagh.

No, it wasn't. Yes, it was. No, it wasn't.

"What water tower?" asked Nan.

"That..." I stopped. A good question. Where'd it go? We were deep in trees, the road bending at every opportunity. Which direction was the water tower? All I could see was rolling forest. The road continued to rise, fall and wind its way through tree-infested hummocks. All major roads, mountains and left turns shrank from sight.

But there were plenty of bushes.

And if the car broke down we had a handy trail of black tar to follow all the way home.

We chugged along for miles. Above us, Fate danced and moved water towers, tempted us with shiny right turns and made the road bend and turn back on itself.

"Let's turn back." I heard Shelagh say more than once.

A few days earlier I might have been tempted. But I'd had enough of being Fate's whipping boy. I was going to Spain, with or without Fate's consent.

The nematode had turned.

And a few minutes later so did the car.

As we crested a rise, suddenly, there they were.

The Pyrenees!

A huge cheer greeted their appearance, all three hundred miles of them stretched out across the horizon. And, unless we'd found the Alps by mistake, we'd soon be back on the main road and en route for Spain.

The rest of the journey settled back into normality; no more unexpected road-layers blocked our route and no freak tornadoes diverted us from our path. Towns and villages flew by as we raced along the wide flat valley floor; the fields golden in their late summer splendour.

And then we were turning, arcing left towards the mountains, tracing the Garonne's descent from the mountains; the valley sides gradually closing in, tree-covered spurs appearing to our left and right as the valley started its slow waltz up the mountains.

We saw hamlets and farms high above us on the far valley side; houses that clung to the mountainside, houses with gardens that verged on the vertical, a sheer drop only a small field away. How could anyone live there? So high, so isolated. A single access road snaked up from the valley floor below. A road that would surely become impassable with the first breath of frost. Did they have to walk to the shops in winter? Did they have to carry their shopping all the way home?

Other valleys came and went, the fields and trees gradually giving way to towering cliffs of brown-streaked rock.

And then we were there.

Les.

Our destination.

It was with a growing sense of anticipation that we entered the Banca Zaragoza. In a few seconds everything might be over – the case solved and the mastermind exposed. I took a deep breath and pushed open the door.

Miguel's face brightened as soon as he saw us – it must have been as exciting for him as it was for us – to be the star witness in an international horse-laundering scam.

We shook hands and spread out our three slim blond men along his counter.

"*C'est lui!*" he said without hesitation.

And pointed straight at David Jarvis.

I almost floated back to Nan and the car. A great weight had been lifted from my shoulders. I'd solved a crime. I'd locked grey cells with the Great Pergonini and emerged victorious.

Shelagh was jubilant too. Life could return to normal; no more financial worries, no more suspicion.

Nan was less excited.

"I knew it was him from the start," she said. "It was obvious."

You can never be a prophet in your own back yard.

A Switch of Fate

Back home, I was still occupying the penthouse flat of Cloud Nine; nothing could tarnish my achievement – not even Nan.

I quickly set up camp beside the phone and proceeded to call just about everyone involved in the case. I called Andy and Simon and Jan and John. The number of road-laying vehicles increased with each telling, by the time I talked to Jan, I was leaning out of the driver's window balancing the car on two wheels as I drove at high speed between flaming walls of tar.

I was then hit by a swift bout of anti-climax. The case was over. That was it. No more detecting.

And what about the dénouement?

I'd forgotten all about that. Great Detectives don't end their cases in faraway banks with only three witnesses present. They invite all the interested parties to their consulting rooms. They expound, they accuse, they point.

And then, while everyone is reeling from one startling revelation after another, the door opens and ... in walks Miguel, the bank manager; the surprise witness, who turns and points directly at David Jarvis.

"That's him!" shouts Miguel.

The audience gasps. It can't be! Not him. He's too obvious.

"You'll never take me alive!" screams Jarvis, his face contorted by guilt, his suave sophistication skewered on the still quivering outstretched finger of the diminutive bank manager.

"Not so fast, Jarvis," I say, nonchalantly inspecting my finger nails. "You don't think I invited you here without taking certain precautions, do you?"

"What do you mean?"

I look towards the door.

A dozen eyes follow.

A shadow stretches into the room. It's enormous, it's black, it's hairy, it's straight from Grimpen Mire.

And in walks Gypsy, the Great Detective's faithful puppy.

"Go ahead, punk," she woofs, her eyes burrowing deep into the guilty and tormented soul of the evil purveyor of real estate, "make my day."

Gypsy woofed approval. That's how it should have ended. Dénouements were for dogs.

I wondered if there was still time to arrange it. But decided against it, the moment had gone but – paraphrasing *Casablanca* – I'd always have Les. As I contemplated that last sentence, I cursed Fate for not placing the Banca Zaragoza in a more romantically named setting.

Still, if I couldn't have a dénouement, I'd make sure I had a good *rapport* for the gendarmes. I'd give Jean-Pierre free rein; all the cold Anglo-Saxonisms would be banished, we'd embrace the poetry of the French language and write a report that flowed, that rhymed and could run for twenty six weeks on London's West End.

I rang Jean-Pierre to arrange a rendezvous.

And tell him how I'd been ambushed by an entire fleet of fully armed road-laying rocket ships.

As I replaced the receiver, the phone rang. I picked it up and my right ear immediately drowned in a torrent of indecipherable French.

I had no idea who it was.

Which wasn't that surprising, receiving a French phone call is a constant source of confusion in our household. It's one thing to walk into a shop without a script but at least you have an inkling of what the subject might be. But a phone call out of the blue? It could be about anything, and you can't fall back on sign language or ask anyone to write anything down.

I listened to the excited stream of words coming through the ear-piece – not a recognisable keyword amongst them.

I strained. I waited for a gap in the words. I strained again.

Was that something about a *rapport?*

Perhaps it was the gendarmes ringing up to congratulate me? Or maybe the *Sûreté?* Did they still have the *Sûreté* in Paris? Was Inspector Maigret still working there?

I was still wondering if the legendary sleuth had moved on from the French equivalent of Scotland Yard, when I recognised the words, "can you play tonight?"

For the *Sûreté?* Had the Jackal escaped? Were they asking for help from the world's greatest consulting detective? Were they in need of a dénouement?

No, it was Remy … from the football team. As he slowed down his speech and repeated every sentence several times, I managed to translate his message. He was desperate. Racing Club were desperate. Could I play tonight? It was an important cup match against Sepx and everyone else had flu.

I think my ego could have done without the translation of the last phrase. But my inability to refuse a drink is only exceeded by inability to pass up a game of football. After all, what a day it had been, and what better way to end it than with a pleasant kick about followed by a meal?

And there'd be a chance to regale the entire team with my exploits – if not the referee as well. Who could pass up on that?

Shelagh, for one.

"I thought you'd given up football?"

"No, I hadn't." I'd just taken a break, that was all. I didn't feel much like training the day we'd discovered the theft. And the week after that we were in the throes of changing all the locks to the house.

"Why don't you come and watch?"

I could tell by the glazed expression passing over Shelagh's face that watching her husband play football had suddenly entered her 'dead day' chart.

At a very lofty position.

Nan, however, disagreed. Watching her son-in-law make a fool of himself was never 'dead day' material. Especially when accompanied by a car trip.

Gypsy woofed approval. If she couldn't sink her teeth into a criminal, she could at least have a go at the opposition goalkeeper.

And so off we set later that afternoon, carefully avoiding all unexpectedly sticky road surfaces. At Cassagne, we joined the team convoy and plunged into another swathe of uncharted *campagne*.

We were soon at the back of the convoy. Car drivers in France treat country roads as unmarked rally sections. Maybe they all knew the route, maybe the lead driver's ESP told him that no oncoming traffic or stray cow would threaten his progress.

I greatly doubted it.

We flew along the straight sections. We swung into bends. We swung out of them again.

"Gypsy doesn't like this," said Nan.

I was not too enthused either. Only the car seemed to be enjoying himself – gone was all the nervous stuttering and stalling. Perhaps this is what he needed all along – company – to be part of a pack of wild boy racers.

We climbed, we descended, we passed fields, we passed woods.

Gypsy passed gas.

It was one of those journeys.

But we made it. We followed the convoy into the small town of Sepx; a place I could barely pronounce, let alone find my way back from.

The stadium at Sepx was superb. Like so many of the small grounds in the *Sud,* it was cut into the side of a gently sloping hill; giving magnificent views over the surrounding countryside, stretched out below, and a gently shelving bank above from which to watch the match.

Breathtaking. Miles and miles of undulating countryside in late summer greens and fading yellow browns; the tower of a distant church, the sky edged red by the slowly setting sun.

I soon discovered that Racing Club was not quite as desperate as I'd been led to believe. There were twelve of us getting changed. And, unless the laws of football had been altered in the last fortnight, one of us would have to be substitute. Surrounded by so much youth and fitness, the balding detective did not have to overstrain his little grey cells to solve that one.

The game started with the Great Detective watching from the grassy bank.

"Why isn't he playing?" I heard Nan ask Shelagh.

"He's too old," whispered Shelagh, "they're afraid he'll keel over and they can't afford the insurance."

I could now see why Great Detectives did not include playing football as part of their post-dénouement revelries – too much scope for detective-baiting. The tension of the chase over, the sidekicks turn on their master and exact revenge on the monstrous intellect at bay.

Five minutes later, Gypsy started singing. I wasn't sure if it was a verse from some well known canine football chant or a plea to the Racing Club manager to bring on the 'old guy'.

"Gypsy's cold," decided Nan. "Look at her, she's shivering."

"No, she's not," I said. "She's shaking with anticipation. She can't wait to see her master grace the hallowed turf."

Six pairs of eyes looked away from me – and the little bubble of dreamworld I inhabited.

"Are you cold, mum? Do you want to go back to the car?"

"I think Gypsy might."

Which, being as close to a 'yes' as anyone could extract without recourse to electrodes, was taken as an affirmative. I was abandoned. My entourage leaving for warmer climes. I suppose it was early October. And it was getting dark. The floodlights had just come on and added a cooling silver tint to the surroundings.

Half time came and went. The game flowed back and forth with neither team gaining an advantage, a goal for us, a goal for them. The crowd swelled as more and more people came home from work.

"When are you going to play?" asked Shelagh, on a flying visit from the car.

I didn't know. Every time I broached the subject with the manager, I received a Gallic shrug.

"I expect they're saving you for later."

When sidekicks give up baiting in favour of sympathy, you know you're in a bad way.

But I didn't need sympathy – I was the Great Detective! The Great Detective on his Greatest Day! Nothing could diminish that. Surely it was only a matter of time?

Indeed it was. With thirty minutes remaining and the score tied at one goal apiece, the call arrived.

It's tempting to suggest that playing me on the left wing brought a much-needed balance to the side; that the introduction of a fresh pair of legs and extra pace cut their defence apart.

But that wouldn't be entirely accurate.

Once or twice in every player's life, you play in a game where suddenly everything goes right. It's hard to explain, there's no reason behind it and it's something that can never be coached. But every once in a while, one team can do no wrong and one team can do no right.

This was one of those days.

Every attack we made seemed to result in a goal. And if one of our players didn't score, a Sepx player would step in and score for us. It was bizarre.

With the final whistle fast approaching, we were 6-1 up. Amazing. We weren't five goals better than Sepx – just five goals luckier.

The game moved into injury time. We were awarded a corner on the right hand side. I took up position on the left side of the penalty area. As I stood there, I looked up at the sky. Somewhere, high above the floodlights, Fate was laughing. Who else could have wrought such havoc on a game of football? And would it be so bad to let some of that luck fall my way? Just a little goal. Just one. Was that so much to ask? Something so that I could say that I played in a French cup-tie at the age of forty-one and was still good enough to score a goal. Surely that wasn't too much to ask?

Silence.

The corner came in hard and fast towards the near post. A gaggle of players leapt to meet it and the keeper punched the ball clear. It ballooned over my head, I turned and ran after it – I'd been the quickest to react. Time slowed around me as I set off in pursuit, keeping pace with ball. It was going to land about ten yards outside the penalty area. There was only one other player with a chance of getting there before me – a Sepx player running back towards the goal. Just the two of us, running towards each other, the ball dropping in between. Who would get there first? And what should I do?

Shouldn't I take advantage of Fate's switch of sides? Wasn't this the chance of a lifetime? For thirty minutes everything we'd tried had come off, hadn't I been handed a *carte blanche* to try anything I desired?

My mind flew back twenty-five years. What would I do if I was sixteen again? My back to the goal, ball dropping outside the penalty area, crowded goal mouth?

The looping overhead kick!

There could be no other choice!

I heard a scream from my forty-one year-old imagination. *Are you mad? The overhead kick? You have to leap into the air, hang horizontal, nearly five feet off the ground, waiting for the ball to come into position. Then wham! Not the sound of the boot meeting ball, but head meeting ground as you plummet five feet onto solid earth.*

You'll never walk again!

But it's the overhead kick! I've always wanted to score from an overhead kick in a big match and this has got be my best chance.

Best chance of being hospitalised! Not to mention the effect that flying feet first at the head of an approaching player would have on said player.

But...

I forwent the full overhead kick in favour of a sawn-off version, a stretch and a lunge, with my left foot firmly planted on terra firma. The Sepx player stretched and lunged too. Two legs arcing out to reach the ball first.

He got there first.

By a fraction of an inch.

And quickly wished he hadn't.

The ball flew off his boot, over my head and looped back towards the goal. Despairing defenders tried to get their heads to it ... and failed. The keeper lunged and flapped at the ball with a hand. He failed too.

In a scene reminiscent from the Great Goal, the ball looped over a crowded goal mouth and found the smallest of gaps between the keeper's hand and the angle between the far post and the cross-bar. The net bulged and a cheer rang out.

And a large overhead snicker from Fate.

I was mobbed. An overhead lob from thirty yards? Never had such unerring accuracy been seen in the *Ligue du Comminges*. I tried to explain what really happened and pointed to the Sepx player, who quickly denied all knowledge of the goal – it hadn't been him, he'd never touched it.

We had no trouble keeping up with the convoy for the trip back to Cassagne – I was too excited to be left behind. I may not have scored but I'd still been responsible, hadn't I? Hadn't Fate intervened the moment my feet hit the pitch? Turned a one all draw into a 7-1 massacre? What further proof did anyone need? Fate had forgiven me – more than forgiven me – Fate was now actively on my side!

Gypsy woofed in agreement.

She knew which side her bread was buttered.

We pulled into the old square at Cassagne. Everything was in darkness. But not for long. Soon one, then two overhead floodlights flickered into life and the old square came alive – the church, the *Mairie,* the old stone buildings. Soon the square was bustling with people and voices, the clink of glasses and the smell of food cooking over an open fire.

It didn't take long for Gypsy's nose to sniff out the latter. As we sorted through our change to find the 120 francs necessary to purchase three places at the meal, she turned her big brown eyes towards Shelagh and woofed a plaintive "four?"

Shelagh looked at me and I looked at Gypsy. It *was* a day of celebration ... and she hadn't eaten yet. But...

"They wouldn't allow dogs, would they?" Shelagh asked.

From my experience of the after-match football meals, there wasn't much they wouldn't allow.

Gypsy nodded agreement.

And it wasn't as though she'd eat much...

An angel would have been hard-pressed to match the expression of righteous probity that beamed up at us. Me? Eat much. Why, I'm practically a vegetarian.

"We'll ask Remy," I said.

Who we found tending the barbecue, a glass of *Ricard* in one hand and a spatula in the other, and a large apron covering his ample middle.

We pointed at Gypsy and asked if it was all right to bring her to the meal?

"We'll pay," I added.

But Remy would hear none of it.

"Pay? Bah! Look at her tiny stomach," he said – or words to that effect – reaching down and giving Gypsy's wasp-like waist a squeeze.

We froze, waiting for the crocodile jaws of our hell-hound to turn and fasten on Remy's arm.

The crocodile jaws cracked into a smile, a tongue popped out and rakishly draped itself over a set of teeth. A tail wagged.

Someone must have switched dogs on us!

We both eyed Gypsy suspiciously.

Remy patted her head.

We both flinched – expecting the worst – and I could see Shelagh's eyes counting Remy's fingers as he withdrew his hand.

Definitely a different dog.

Although, come to think of it, it wasn't out of character at all;

we'd become so used to Gypsy's demoniacal behaviour at home, we'd forgotten what a paragon she was with strangers.

Only my ankles and a yellow squeaky dinosaur named Kevin knew the real Gypsy.

Nan tugged at Shelagh's sleeve. "Do they have any chicken?" she whispered.

Shelagh looked at the large tray of steaks and chops.

Remy caught Shelagh's glance. "Meat for victory!" he said, beaming as he pushed steaks around the barbecue grill.

I wasn't sure if this was some ancient blood-curdling oath or Racing Club's win bonus. I wasn't too sure how Nan's request for white meat, *sans* sauce, *sans* spice would go down either. It had a distinctly defeatist tone about it to me – red meat for victory, white unseasoned meat for unmitigated defeat. But I had to mention it to Remy or Gypsy would be asking all evening – where's the chicken?

Remy couldn't have been more helpful. His huge arms enveloped me, the scorer of goal number seven. Never had he seen such a goal. Chicken was a small price to pay to witness such a spectacle.

Remy was not alone in thinking I'd scored. So did everyone else. I tried to disabuse them, explaining how it'd been the defender. But nobody believed me. Typical English reserve, I think they thought – lobs a packed penalty area from thirty yards and blames a defender!

After my fourth *Ricard*, I agreed with them. And wasn't it nearer forty yards?

The drink flowed and the meat sizzled. The square rang with laughter and accounts of derring-do. I tried a few lines from the Great Detective's exploits but found it impossible to translate. By the time I'd explained what a mutual fund was, why ours was in Dublin and yet we were English and the bank was in Spain, I'd lost myself as well as the audience.

So I fell back on sign language, improvisation and – quite unexpectedly – a Giant Elk. People liked the road-layer story best; they'd never heard of a killer mutant road-laying Deathstar before, but they liked the elk. Which just goes to show that after six *Ricards*, any story with a Giant Elk in it is a sure-fire winner.

Nan was in her element – surrounded by people and deep in conversation. The fact that no one understood a word she said was irrelevant. They were just quiet, she said. Like many English people of a certain age, Nan was convinced that all people were born with an innate knowledge of the English language. They might not know it, but if they heard enough of it, and it was spoken loudly, they'd remember.

Gypsy was in her element too, surrounded by food and people feeding her. Why hadn't someone introduced her to football earlier?

"It has been worth it, hasn't it?" I asked Shelagh as the last of the food made its final round.

"If every day was like this one."

"Including the road-layers?"

She smiled. "I think I could have done without the road-layers ... and David Jarvis."

"And the wasps."

"And the *insert*."

"And the move."

"And the plumbing."

"But wouldn't it have been boring? A year ago we rarely left our farm. Now we have lunch in the mountains and steak by starlight. All in one day."

Above us, a family of owls flitted back and forth from a nest in the church tower. We watched, enthralled, as they perched on a high ledge, their white faces picked out by the swathe of light. And then one would launch itself into the night, its huge wings outstretched embracing the cool night air. And then it would be gone, swallowed up by the blackness. Back and forth they flew, hunting and feeding, silent and magnificent.

Magical.

I wanted that night to last forever.

And it has.

A Plausible Epilogue

David Jarvis was interviewed by the *gendarmes* the following week, admitted responsibility for the crime but fell back on the 'something snapped' defence.

He claimed that not long after our purchase, he received a package of mail to forward to us. It came in a large Post Office envelope and was partly open – so partly open that he couldn't help but look inside. The first page he saw was the invitation to surrender an insurance policy and the next was a breakdown of what it was worth. He was in dire financial straits, a client's cheque had recently bounced...

And naturally something snapped: an honest man tempted into crime by cruel circumstance and entrapment by the postal services.

Unfortunately for him, the Great Detective had yet to hang up his deer-stalker. As I explained to the *gendarmes*, why would the Post Office – be they French, British or Irish – hand over mail to someone who does not appear in any of the correspondence, is unknown to the sender and lives twenty miles away from the destination address?

Not to mention the fact that we'd been receiving mail *sans problème* since the day we arrived in France.

And there was other evidence.

Like the extra deposit he'd asked us to pay on our house. As soon as we established the fact that David Jarvis was not to be trusted, we naturally started to look at our house purchase – had he cheated us on that, as well?

We'd thought it strange at the time but, like many buyers in the throes of moving, we didn't want to lose our house. David had given us a very plausible story, telling us that the major creditor was a bank that had had problems before with overseas buyers pulling out at the last minute. The bank was now insisting we paid a higher deposit of 16% to prove we were serious.

He'd said he was phoning from a meeting with them and a decision was needed immediately. If we agreed, he could pay the money over for us and we could reimburse him. If we didn't, they were likely to press for the house to be sold by auction instead.

With hindsight this was classic con-artistry – we were put on the spot, no time to think, house purchase at risk – and he made it look as though he was doing us a favour.

But had it been fraud?

All the money had been accounted for at the completion of the sale. We'd sent a cheque over for the full house price minus the deposit. So what would he have gained other than the use of our deposit for a few months?

Perhaps that was all he needed? The classic fall from prosperity into fraud. I just need a few thousand to tide me over until next month – and then next month arrives and you need a bit more and before you know it you're up to your armpits in clients' money.

And we weren't the only clients.

An English couple were having their holiday home renovated by him. They sat at home in England writing cheque after cheque as David regaled them with stories of unexpected problems – planning delays, architect's fees, consultant's expenses. David cashed the cheques and, needless to say, nothing was done to the house.

Estate agents didn't fare any better. While I was checking up on the legality of our house purchase, I phoned the agency in England who'd introduced us to David Jarvis and had shared the commission.

Not as big a share as they'd expected.

"Of course, the dispute over the wood didn't help," they told me.

"What?"

"The wood. That's why the payment was delayed, wasn't it?"

Our house sale had apparently been delayed by a mythical wood dispute. A dispute that became so entangled that the value of the property plummeted as the months dragged on.

Builders were not immune either. He had several working on renovation projects that lasted longer than his cheque book. They complained, he talked, they believed. This was a very plausible individual.

Even when a creditors meeting was called, an assessor appointed, iron mask beckoning in the corner ... he walked out on stage, took a file from his briefcase and ... oh dear, silly me, I've brought the wrong file. Creditors meeting adjourned. Everyone goes home, much arm-flapping and grinding of spittle.

As for the mysterious female accomplice, the police never found one. David Jarvis said he did it all himself. Which, in hindsight, makes sense – if he'd had a female accomplice he would have taken her to the bank as soon as Mutual Friendly insisted on the account being in joint names. Which was probably why he tried The Bankers Power of Attorney Ploy – to convince Mutual Friendly that Shelagh would have access to the money without having a woman go to the bank in person.

~

In July 1996, David's plausibility finally deserted him. He was convicted of fraud and escorted to Toulouse prison.

By now, he's probably governor.

Glossary

1. **Vera Lynn:** the forces' sweetheart from WWII whose most famous song was 'The White Cliffs of Dover'

2. **Meccano:** a model construction set. Also known as an erector set.

3. **Heath Robinson:** an English cartoonist famous for drawings of eccentric machines. Now used as a description of any unnecessarily complex and implausible contraption.

4. *Ricard:* an aniseed liqueur also known as *Pernod* or pastis.

5. **Euskadi:** the Basque language.

6. **Unsub:** FBI-speak for the 'unknown subject' they are searching for.

7. **MFI:** a British furniture retailer.

8. **B&Q:** a British DIY retailer.

9. **I-Spy Books:** Spotters' guides published for children. Each book covered a topic and awarded points for each object spotted.

10. **Snowpake:** a white correction fluid used to cover typing mistakes.

11. **Deed Poll:** the process used in the UK to change a person's name.

12. **Sooty:** a glove puppet bear who had his own TV show. He could only communicate by whispering into the ear of his operator.

About Book View Cafe

Book View Café (BVC) is an author-owned cooperative of over forty professional writers, publishing in a variety of genres including fantasy, romance, mystery, and science fiction.

Our authors include *New York Times* and *USA Today* bestsellers; Nebula, Hugo, and Philip K. Dick Award winners; World Fantasy and Rita Award nominees; and winners and nominees of many other publishing awards.

BVC returns 95% of the profit on each book directly to the author.

Made in the USA
Columbia, SC
18 March 2018